S0-ARM-325

Other TAB books by the author:

No. 1349   *How to Build a Lie Detector, Brain Wave Monitor & Other Secret Parapsychological Electronics Projects*

DRAW YOUR OWN HOUSE PLANS

BY MIKE & RUTH WOLVERTON

TAB **TAB BOOKS Inc.**
BLUE RIDGE SUMMIT, PA. 17214

FIRST EDITION

SIXTH PRINTING

Printed in the United States of America

Reproduction or publication of the content in any manner, without express
permission of the publisher, is prohibited. No liability is assumed with respect to
the use of the information herein.

Copyright © 1983 by TAB BOOKS Inc.

Library of Congress Cataloging in Publication Data

Wolverton, Mike.
Draw your own house plans.

Bibliography: p.
Includes index.
1. Dwellings—Designs and plans.   2. Structural
drawing.   3. Building.   I. Wolverton, Ruth.   II. Title.
TH4812.W64   1983   728.3′7′0222   82-19305
ISBN 0-8306-0381-6
ISBN 0-8306-1381-1 (pbk.)

Cover design copyrighted by the Reader's Digest Association, Inc. 1982. Used with permission.

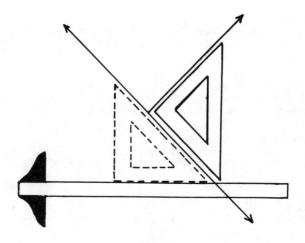

Contents

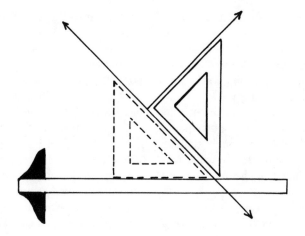

Introduction

ARCHITECTS SPEND MANY YEARS OF STUDY in their profession. They will immediately talk learnedly about the balance of masses, the importance of focus, the integrity of form. They will also strongly advise you to consider the three-dimensional geometric aspects of the project, agonize over the choice between preserving the consistency of period design or going eclectic. They will recommend an organic approach or that you opt for monolithic functional priority.

Then, and only then, will they casually ask you about the number of rooms, the site, and other such incidentals. After such an initial meeting, most architects disappear for extended periods. We have often wondered where they go because most of their clients seem to suffer this temporary desertion at the same time. When your architect does surface again he will bring along what he calls rough sketches (you won't believe the price). By that time you are ripe to agree with most anything. You've

been impressed by the show of expertise and you've been worn down by the time delay. Only monetary considerations will seriously hamper the architect in selling you his idea or design for your new house.

From here the projects gain momentum. Finished sketches are rendered, plans are drawn, and blueprints are made. At each step, you're assured that you can change anything you like. And you can (for a price) if you stand up to the, "Your architect knows best" argument.

We've heard many sad tales along those lines and experienced one or two ourselves. One dear friend, who in the excitement of renovating an old farm house into a showplace with the help of a renowned architect, somehow ended up without a bathtub on the entire second floor, not even in the master bath, although the lady was and is a tub addict. The only tub in the 10-room, 5000-odd square-foot abode was downstairs at the opposite end of the house from the master suite.

We've admired architects' innovative ideas and applauded their novel uses of space. We've been impressed by beauty of design and seriously coveted a few special intriguing conveniences. And while we might wonder if we really would like to have a swimming pool in *our* living room or have serious doubts about all those sleeping lofts opening up as balconies onto the living room, we appreciate efforts to find new ways to use interiors.

Those who like pools in living rooms should have them. But never should an innocent bystander end up with such a thing inadvertently while forfeiting something that had long been a desired comfort or necessity.

An architect is going to charge you a stiff fee. Basically, all that fee will cover is a plan—a floorplan and elevations—for your proposed house, addition, or remodeling project. If your suite is a difficult one, if you want far-out design concepts that no one has thought of yet, or if you simply wouldn't feel right about the whole thing without an architect, then by all means go ahead and employ one. You can still read this book and benefit from it. At the very least, you'll be able to understand the terms and easily read the plans.

If you want to save the money, you can buy a set of predrawn houseplans and go from there. There are books and more books of houseplans of all kinds (although they do tend to favor the five-bedroom-solarium-six-bath-and-two-cabana type), and you should browse through as many of them as you can. The trouble with these ready-made plans is that they were designed with no one in particular in mind.

It's much the same as when one buys a dress-making pattern that is designed and cut to a size—a norm—that fits very few individuals. Luckily in dress-making patterns there's always a page that shows in detail how to make adjustments and where to do what to correct at least the most commonly encountered problems. Not so with your house patterns. Oh, they might indicate that you have the option of finishing the upstairs or leaving off a bedroom wing, but that is the extent of it. The rest you'll have to figure out yourself if you want the house to suit you. And even for that you'll need to know how to draw and read house plans.

When it comes to building an addition or remodeling, you can still use ready-made patterns, but you'll have to do a lot of adapting and customizing. That requires house-plan drawing know-how.

Are you dissatisfied with the inconvenience, space wasting, energy inefficiency, and general blahness of tract houses? Do you yearn for something special? You can come up with exactly what you want if you use this book and some research on whatever type of building you select: A-frame, split level, or dome. You can use a number of features from different predrawn plans or you can use a good helping of your own inventiveness.

Drawing house plans is easy and fun once you've mastered the few necessary fundamentals. The more house plans you draw the more readily you'll reach for your pencil and paper for any alteration or addition. It is absolutely truth (although one of us denies it vehemently) that, when asked to help move the living room furniture in preparation for a major rug shampoo job, he reached for paper and pen to make a plan first.

It is so much simpler to wield an eraser than a crow bar or to change a line instead of changing a room full of furniture. To begin drawing your house plans, lay in a good supply of graph paper, several drawing pencils, and a few of the other accoutrements mentioned in the following chapters. Then clear a space for yourself on a table, a desk, or a counter and you're in business.

Please go through all the steps we describe before you embark on a major project. We heartily recommend that you start out with very simple plans for something very simple—such as rearranging your furniture. Draw your plans exactly and precisely. Then shift the furniture according to the plans. See how you like it. Make changes on the plan. Change the arrangement to match. This allows you to experiment with changes without your having to install or tear out anything. At the same time, it gives you practice in translating from reality to plan and back again, and makes it easier for you to read plans. It also helps you learn basic plan-drawing skills.

Before you know it you'll be showing your friends through your remodeled, added-on-to, or brand new home. So let's get to work.

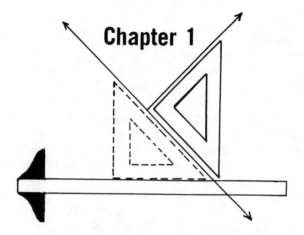

Chapter 1

Preliminaries

BEFORE YOU CAN BEGIN DRAWING HOUSE plans you have to have a design. The word design strikes stark terror in the hearts of the uninitiated. They feel they'll be called upon to come up with some artistic creation or other that they don't even know the proper words for much less the basics of execution. Relax. Design is only another way of specifying what you want.

DESIGN GOALS

Before you tackle any job, you must know what you want to accomplish. For example, when you rake your yard your intention is to get the leaves up off the lawn and either on the compost pile or in leaf bags to be taken away by the garbage collectors. So you'll have to have, in addition to your rake, a compost pile or leaf bags. Otherwise, even with the best of raking, your lawn will be covered with the same leaves when the winds begin to blow. The same type of thing holds true for designing a re-modeling job, an addition to your house, or an entire structure. You have to know what you want to accomplish, identify the necessary ingredients, and work out ways to include them in your projects.

There are six headings that comprise the larger category of design goals. These are:

- ☐ Intended use and special features.
- ☐ Special needs.
- ☐ Comfort and convenience.
- ☐ Light and ventilation.
- ☐ Noise control.
- ☐ Aesthetic considerations.

Under the intended use and special features heading, you will be dealing with such questions as, what use are you going to make of the proposed alteration or new building? What is the general life style of your family? How many people? What activities? What are you trying to accomplish with the remodeling or building? What have you always wished you had? How can you include it? How about the other people in your family? What is their input? How can you get it all together?

When it comes to special needs you might be dealing with special occupational requirements or uses for the proposed area. If you're going to use the space for an artist's studio, for instance, your requirements are going to be different than if the intended use will be a playroom for the kids, a sewing room, an indoor gardener's workshop, or a master bedroom. In addition, you might want to consider special needs for wider doorways and ramps for a mobility-impaired person or extra-high doorways and ceilings for that 6-foot-4-inch person in your midst. Other considerations include higher counters or work surfaces and lowered surfaces and cabinets to put everything in reach of the shorter-than-average person who has gotten tired of stepstools and step ladders. You might also consider the person who is broader than usual, the short-reached person and accommodations for your pets.

The comfort and convenience heading is the one you should explore most thoroughly. We have been brainwashed to think that comfort and conveniences are extras. This is far from the truth. While we can put up with a lot of discomfort, irritation, and inconvenience, there'll be a price to pay for it. Plan for comfort and convenience even if it costs a little extra in time and money? It'll be cheaper than the doctor bills.

Comfort and convenience can be subdivided into the following:

☐ Privacy.
☐ Traffic patterns.
☐ Activity areas.
☐ Storage.
☐ Step and time savers.

In order to identify these one by one requires two distinct operations. First analyze all the irritants in the present living quarters. Second, you'll have to come up with solutions.

If the lack of privacy heads the list of problems with stressfully designed living quarters, then misdirected traffic patterns that abound in stock plans for homes the housing developers use runs a close second. We feel particularly abused in this instance. Probably more so because we should have seen the trap when we bought our present house. But we liked everything else and thought we could easily find a way to get around the particular problem. Five years later, we are still exposed to people being mainstreamed through our small kitchen on their way to the family room, the offices, or the laundry. No relief is in sight. We are the victims of brick exterior walls juxtaposed with walls that carry the brunt of plumbing and electric wiring. Any alteration would take lots of time and money. So we make do.

Kitchens, living rooms, family rooms, and master bedrooms tend to suffer the most from fouled-up traffic patterns. Furniture arrangement can help, but noise problems and drafts from opening exterior doors are not so easily circumvented. In the design stage, figuring out a good traffic pattern is simple and inexpensive. What it takes is thought and a thorough knowledge of how the family goes about the daily business of living.

A 13-year-old will always bring his or her friends in the front door and through the kitchen unless a more direct route can be engineered. This sort of thing doesn't only apply to people. Pets, groceries and the laundry must be considered.

Traffic patterns through entertainment areas are also important. Let's say you have the latest in home video games, a giant-screen TV, a piano, and huge library of slides and movies from your various trips. Logically, these would all be arranged in the entertainment area. Wouldn't they? You can use only one of these modes of entertainment at a time. Right? Not unless you live alone. If there's a family, inevitably someone will want to watch a show or listen to a tape when someone else has to practice the piano or wants to show slides. Therefore, it's much better to banish the piano to the entry way where it might get an occasional draft of cool air but where the child can practice in peace (yours that is). Set up the video equipment elsewhere.

The same holds true with other activities. How would you like to be engaged in your favorite hobby of sewing while someone else is using the power saw inches away from you and your precious ultrasuede that cost $35 a yard on sale? How would you feel about working with your photographic equipment while someone else is happily messing about with clay and the clay dust is seeping everywhere?

Other things to keep in mind for activity areas are such things as being near a source for water if you will be needing it for clay work, photography or gardening, having ample electric outlets for your power tools if you go in for wood working (also make sure you have adequate circuits), installing the proper kind of wall and floor covering to make cleaning easy, and installing sufficient noise insulation.

Storage areas are very important. It isn't just the amount of storage your house or apartment provides that counts, it is the kind of storage, the location of the storage, and the accessibility of the storage that makes the difference. Adequate, accessible storage is another one of those things that can be easily included in a plan, but takes time and trouble to include after the remodeling or building is "finished."

Some of us are more aware of noise than others and some of us suffer more acutely from excessive or abrasive extraneous sound. But all of us, whether we are aware of it or not, are stressed by excessive and unrelated noise. Noise cuts down on efficiency and causes irritability.

It is relatively simple and inexpensive to keep extraneous sound to a minimum. Noise control begins outside your house. If you live in an area with heavy automobile traffic, consider the solution now used extensively along city expressways in Texas. Seven-foot high wooden fences are erected to act as baffles. They can be painted with sound-deadening materials on one side. They provide a tremendous reduction in traffic noise. If you plant a thick hedge on the inside of your wooden board fence, you will cut the noise even further.

If your doors and windows fit tightly and if you use either thermopanes or double windows, you're several steps ahead in keeping the outside noise where it belongs—outside. There are all kinds of accoustical materials available that will cut down on noise. Accoustical ceilings have been improved in recent years and they are now rather attractive. The same material can be used on walls to cut down on noise. If you set electrical outlets directly back to back they will act as sound conductors. Offset your outlets unless you're eager to transfer sound from one room to the other.

When you plan to remodel or build a new structure you can make use of storage areas to cut down on noise. Closets and other storage, such as book shelves, can act as buffer zones between rooms that have a high decibel range and those that you want to keep quiet. If you want to be extra quiet, you can cover the closet walls with soundproofing, inside and out.

Another consideration in noise control is your floor covering. Hard covering carries noise, but soft covering buries noise. Draperies will also act as sound baffles and so will cushions and upholstered furniture. As a rule of thumb, the more soft things you have in a room—rugs, draperies and curtains, hangings, and furniture—the less noise you will have. If you're a plant lover you're in luck. Large plants will also contribute to sound absorption.

If you're remodeling and changing the exterior to some extent, as in cutting new doors or windows, you will want to make sure that the new windows won't look as if someone in a hurry had thrown them at the structure. It is best to use new windows and

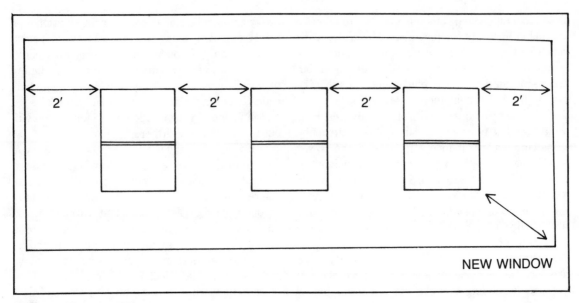

Fig. 1-1. Adding new windows.

doors that are as close as possible in style and size to the ones already in the building. Another thing to watch is the placement of the windows. Make sure that the spacing between openings remains even. Don't end up with several windows scrounged together. See Figs. 1-1 through 1-6.

On the indoor side of the wall; woodwork, doors, windows, and wall coverings within a room or rooms should match in design, height, and width and be compatible with other doors and windows in adjoining rooms. That doesn't mean that you can't have a cute little window in a small alcove or a low door in a corner, but avoid such things unless they have a special purpose or are set off by an architectual oddity.

When it comes to building additions to houses (Figs. 1-7 through 1-10), you have to be concerned with the site as well as the neighbors. If your lot is long and narrow, you're naturally going to put your addition out back rather than on the side. By the same token, if the land falls off sharply in the back but is flat beside the garage it would be more

economical to extend sideways. Unless, of course, your house has a basement that could open out onto the drop off in the back and you could extend there.

Other considerations when you are placing an addition are the existing landscaping, the proximity to streets and neighbors, and the direction the addition will face. You must also consider personal preference, fashion, and economics. Yes there are fashions in architecture. Behold the long, low ranch house that has been with us as a status symbol in spite of its inefficient use of space, time-wasting attributes, and energy wasting. All you have to do is walk along some older neighborhoods and you will, after a while, be able to tell what decade the buildings were erected. There was the time of the bungalow, the time of two-story box, the revival of the ersatz Southern mansion, the pseudo-Cape Cod, and so on and so forth.

Right now the fashion is to look to alternate building solutions to solve some of the problems we have had with the more traditional methods. Not only are these alternate solutions fresh and excit-

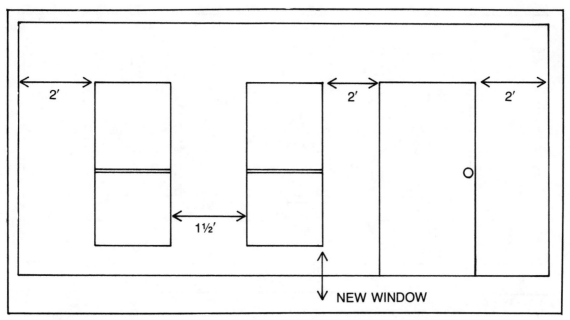

Fig. 1-2. Adding new windows.

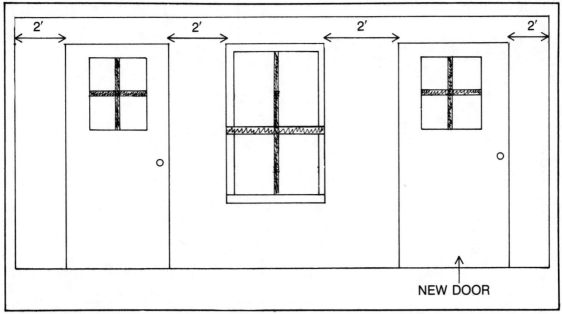

Fig. 1-3. Adding a new door.

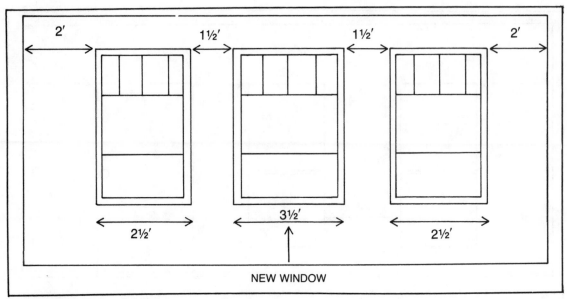

Fig. 1-4. Adding a new window.

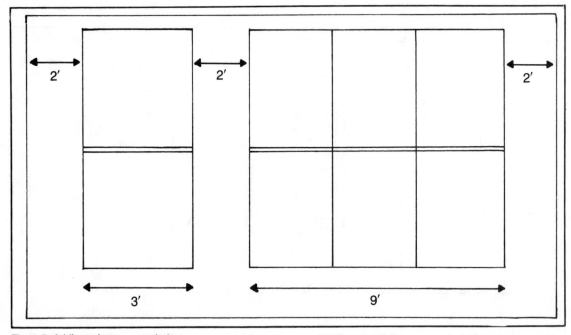

Fig. 1-5. Adding a large, new window.

6

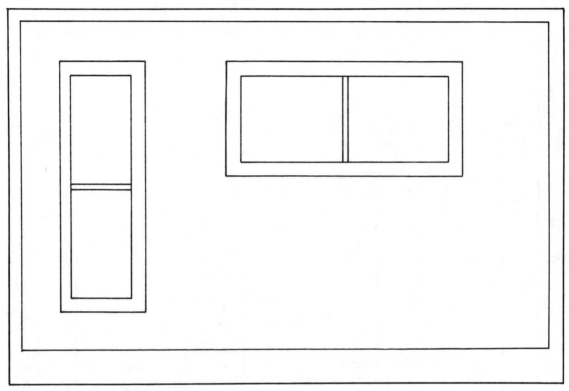

Fig. 1-6. Adding an odd-shaped window.

ing, they usually offer a considerable saving per square foot of building cost. Before you decide to put up that A-frame on your suburban street or build a dome on the vacant lot in the older section in town, look over the neighborhood and try to visualize how your A-frame or dome would look among the fake Georgian and neoantebellum. That doesn't mean that you have to give up the idea of alternate building or trade that option for city conveniences, but it takes a bit of research as to the feasibility.

First of all you'll have to check to see if such an alternative structure would pass the zoning ordinances. If there is no serious problem along those lines you might consult with the prospective neighbors and see how they feel. A little tact at this point will make for a pleasant relationship later. Be sure to stress that you're going to do all you can to keep the character of the street intact. This might mean planting a tall hedge, conforming to a type of fencing or nonfencing, etc.

PREFERENCES

As far as we are concerned, personal preference is the most important single item when it comes to deciding on design options. After all, you have to live in the house after it is built and you are an individual with strong personal likes and dislikes.

Before you decide on any alternate home design, spend some more time in a similar home. If you can, go on different days, in various kinds of weather, and at odd times of day. When you get there, don't just wander about. Sit down. Lie down.

7

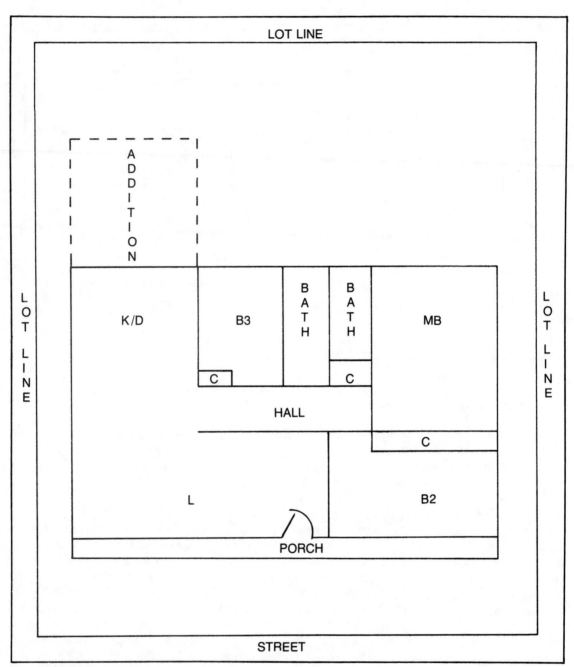

Fig. 1-7. Building an addition on a narrow lot.

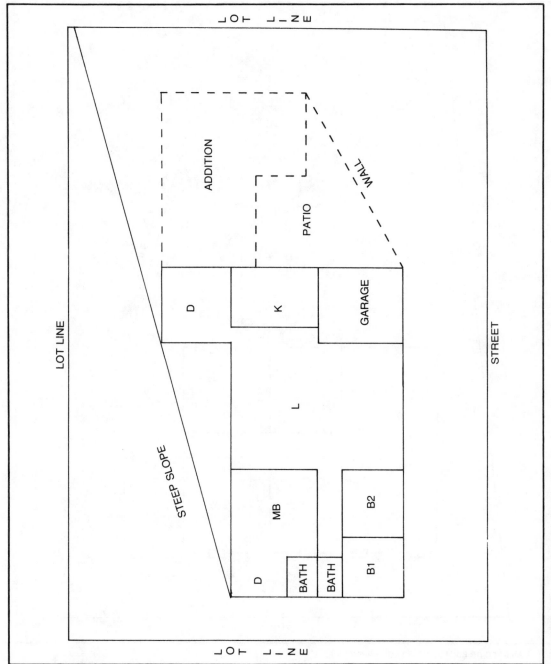

Fig. 1-8. Building an addition on a sloping lot.

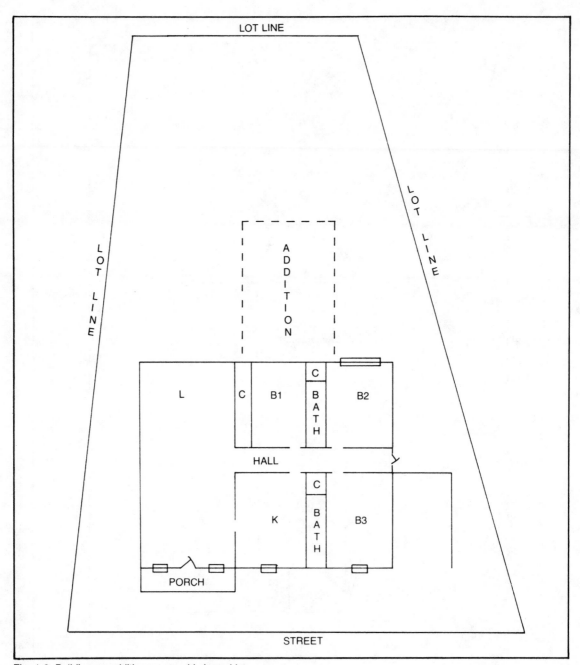

Fig. 1-9. Building an addition on an odd-shaped lot.

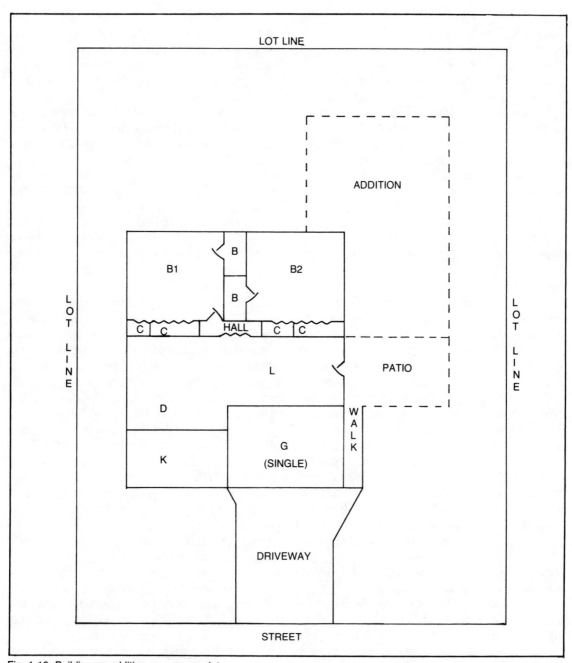

Fig. 1-10. Building an addition on a narrow lot.

Pretend to do hobby activities. If you can't carry all this out or if you feel embarrassed, sit or walk and do these things in your mind. Watch your reaction when you leave. Are you more irritable than when you came? Do you feel relaxed, happy, or edgy?

Keep a record of these feelings, noting also down how you felt before you got to the place. If there's something that either appeals to you strongly or upsets you it will show up in your notes quite consistently. Actually, the way you feel about a dwelling can affect your relationship with the people who live there.

Quite a few years ago, an interesting couple—Jess was a budding executive and Martin an industrial designer—built there own house. The house-warming was to be a gala affair, but the party didn't quite jell. There was a good deal of tension, bickering, and teasing.

Nobody thought too much about it until the next gathering of the clan, again at Jess' and Martin's, when we experienced a repeat of the tension. "I feel as if I'd been impaled on one sharp rock after another," one highly verbal member of the group announced at a postmortem of the occasion. Instantly, other people expressed similar feelings. "Why it's that . . . triangular design," someone exclaimed at last. "Wherever you look you see nothing but angles and sharp corners."

The mystery was solved. Martin, impressed by the structural strength of the triangular design, had built his entire house as a triangle: triangular foundation, rooms, windows, and roof line. The house was as structurally sound as it possibly could be, but it had a distinctly adverse effect on quite a few people. Including, unfortunately, Jess who professed to love the place she had helped build from the ground up with her own hands.

Martin, once he became aware the threat the design posed to their relationship, modified the inside of the house considerably. This helped a lot but the house never became anyone's favorite place. Design should follow function.

Consider how you react to more conventional design options. There is, for instance, the choice between the open plan and the enclosed or divided one. Both have pros and cons; neither plan is intrinsically superior to the other. It is mostly a question of personal preference.

The *open plan* has been in fashion quite a while. It was said to reflect changes in life-style, the openness to new experience, and the breaking of ties with the past. The open plan originated with the mass production of tract houses. When those tacky little boxes first marched up and down the hillsides, in the late '40s and early 50s, each equally boxy and tiny interior was claustrophobic. Some bright person realized that, by removing walls that divided the living room from the dining areas and kitchen, they could counteract the enclosed feeling without adding a square inch of space.

Once the building industry caught on to the idea, it was only a matter of getting with Madison Avenue and soon everybody who was anybody had a house built on the open plan. There were some houses in which only the bathrooms had doors and, it is rumored, one or two where even those traditional bastions of privacy fell to the glories of the open plan. Then came the energy crunch and a growing awareness that the sprawling ranch house plan is the most costly in energy consumption.

What are the pros and cons? Let's take the open plan first. If you have a house of average square footage and you open up your living area into one large, single room, the areas will seem larger and give a feeling of spaciousness. It will make entertaining easier because there will be more room for people to move about. It will make it possible to carry on conversations, while you are engaged in cooking or other such tasks, with people who are otherwise occupied in other parts of the living area. Ventilation is usually good and adequate, natural light is easy to come by.

While the open plan works rather well when the house is occupied by two working adults, it confers a lot of strain when it's tried by a family with children. Children and the open plan don't mix too well. They emphasize the lack of privacy and contribute mightily to the noise that resounds through the wide-open spaces.

There is also the matter of energy. While it is true that it is more economical to duct an open area for heating and cooling, and it is also true that it is less expensive to heat or cool one large open room than three smaller, separate ones, it leaves you no other option but to heat or cool the entire area at any one time.

When it comes to the *enclosed plans* the pros include the advantages of privacy for family members, specified places for special activities, (this keeps down clutter and mess and makes housekeeping easier) and the possibility of efficient noise control through buffering. While the overall energy saving of the open plan is stressed by every architect we know, with an enclosed plan you have the option to heat certain areas or not as you choose.

For instance, if you have upstairs bedrooms, you might decide to turn the heat (or the cooling) off to the second story during the day and only use it for a brief time at night. If your proposed house is a large one, you could shut off the living and dining room during the cold weather except when you have company.

The cons for the enclosed plan are small cluttered rooms that engender feelings of claustrophobia, a tendency for smaller rooms to be dark and poorly ventilated, and the difficulty of working on large projects in limited space.

Before you throw up your hands in dispair, consider the great possibilities of compromise. A combination of the open and enclosed plan works very well. If you leave the sitting/lounging/eating/cooking areas as open space and make provisions to closs off less often-used space such as a separate living or dining room or extra bedrooms, you can have the best of two design worlds.

Make sure that these separate areas will truly function as such. In other words, if you reserve the living room for music and company, see to it that any noise from the open area doesn't carry into the room. Music from the living room shouldn't interfere with the TV or other activities that might be carried out simultaneously by the kids or other adults in the open area. We favor folding doors that allow you to throw open a large area and also close it off quickly.

When you plan and design it is a good thing to keep in mind the numbers 4 and 8. Most material that is available in panels—plywood, particle board, Masonite and plasterboard—all come in 4-foot widths. The usual size for these panels is 4×8 feet. You can find 4-×-9 foot panels and even 4-×10 foot panels that you might need in a remodeling job. Prepare to pay quite a bit extra for the taller panels. Because 4 and 8 seem to be the magic numbers, it follows that if you design in multiples of 4 you will save a lot of time and material. You won't have to make many cuts and you won't have many leftovers.

Another factor is that studs in walls are often 16 inches on center. There will be an upright, a 2×4 most likely, every 16 inches (the center of the 2×4 will be on the 16 inch mark). Doors and windows come in many sizes, but they too are engineered to be compatible with the magic 4 and 8 routine. Floorcoverings are often available in 8-foot roles (or in 12- or 16-foot ones). Ceiling materials follow the same pattern.

Another crucial bit of knowledge concerns what lumber people call a certain piece of lumber: the 2×4. Now any reasonable person would assume that such a piece of lumber would have the dimensions of 2 inches by 4 inches. But it doesn't! When you measure it after you've brought it home, your 2×4 will actually measure 1½ inches by 3½ inches. There is an explanation for this madness. The 2×4 that now measures only 1½×3½ was at one time an actual 2-inch by 4-inch piece of wood. That was way back when they first cut it out of the log and it was what they call *green wood*. After the wood dried out,

Table 1-1. Lumber Sizes.

Table 1-1. Lumber Sizes.

Nominal and Dressed Sizes of Boards and Lumber		Nominal	Actual (Dry)
Boards	(Up to 12″ Wide)	1″	¾″
		1¼″	1″
		1½″	1¼″
Lumber	(Thickness: 2″, 3″, 4″ Width Up to 12″ And Over)	2	1½
		3	2½
		4	3½
		6	5½
		8	7¼
		10	9¼
		12	11¼
		Over 12	Subtract ¾″

however, it shrank and became your present 1½×3½ piece. As a matter of tradition we still refer to it as a 2×4.

In order to make things simpler for you, we have compiled Tables 1-1 and 1-2. They will make it easy for you to find out the actual size of a piece of lumber.

One time that you really have to watch these lumber abbreviations is when you plan your walls. We usually go with 4½-inch walls for the interior and 6-inch walls for the exterior. The 4½-inch wall consists of a sandwich of a 3½-inch 2×4 and 2½-inch thick panels of plywood or plasterboard on either side. The exterior wall still has its 3½-inch, 2-×-4 core, but it is faced with some interior finishing material, and exterior siding is added to that. Be sure and keep Tables 1-1 and 1-2 handy.

PRELIMINARY ESTIMATES

You can't begin too early to make estimates of what it will cost to build what you have in mind. If you

Table 1-2. Computing Board Feet.

Number dimension	Lineal Feet								
	8	10	12	14	16	18	20	22	24
1×2	Sold by lineal foot								
1×3	Sold by lineal foot								
1×4	2⅔	3⅓	4	4⅔	5⅓	6	6⅔	7⅓	8
1×6	4	5	6	7	8	9	10	11	12
1×8	5⅓	6⅔	8	9⅓	10⅔	12	13⅓	14⅔	16
1×10	6⅔	8⅓	10	11⅔	13⅓	15	16⅔	18⅓	20
1×12	8	10	12	14	16	18	20	22	24
2×2	Sold by lineal foot								
2×3	Sold by lineal foot								
2×4	5⅓	6⅔	8	9⅓	10⅔	12	13⅓	14⅔	16
2×6	8	10	12	14	16	18	20	22	24
2×8	10⅔	13⅓	16	18⅔	21⅓	24	26⅔	29⅓	32
2×10	13⅓	16⅔	20	23⅓	26⅔	30	33⅓	36⅔	40
2×12	16	20	24	28	32	36	40	44	48
3×6	12	15	18	21	24	27	30	33	36
4×4	10⅔	13⅓	16	18⅔	21⅓	24	26⅔	29⅓	32

Board feet = thickness (inches) × width (feet) × length (feet)

wait until you have all your design work done and your plans completed, you will most likely be in for an unpleasant surprise. Building of any kind costs big money and the costs are rising constantly. You can trim costs considerably without sacrificing what you really want. The trick is to know where and what to cut to make the design fit the cost you can afford.

There are many methods you can use to make an estimate. For your most cursory estimate, the one you can do practically off the top off your head, you need only the dimensions of the proposed space (addition or new structure). Take out your trusty calculator and a pen. Then simply multiply the dimensions to arrive at the square footage of your proposed project.

If you are planning a conventional structure, multiply this by the current local building costs (about $50 per square foot). You can check with your local building trade association for approximate figures in your locality. Once you get that cost, enter it in your calculator and multiply. A 20-×-20 foot addition will come in at $20,000. To be on the safe side, add on a 15-percent contingency figure (another $3,000).

If you're planning on using alternative construction methods, you will still get your dimensions first, but you will multiply them with a different cost per square foot. At the moment, the going rate for dome square footage is $35. Other alternate methods range from a $35 minimum up to conventional building costs of $50.00 per square foot. These costs are variable and will rise right along with the cost of conventional building. Domes will usually be about one-third less expensive per square foot and that the other alternate methods will go on up from there. Consult with your local building trade association.

Before you decide to chuck the whole idea of planning an addition or a structure because the costs seem so exorbitant, remember that these are not fixed figures. You can bring down the costs considerably by several means. Your variables are the materials you use and your labor costs.

To bring down your material costs you have to first know exactly what you need to build the structure. This applies to remodeling as well as new construction. The best way to do this is to use a chart (Fig. 1-11). On it enter the number of 2×4s you'll need. You get that number by adding up your studs (remember they go 16 inch on center and are doubled at corners and doorways), your sole plates (the two lengths of the structure plus the two widths), and the top plates (the number of 2×4s needed for the sole plates doubled, you use two 2×4s for each top plate).

Next add your wall covering or sheathing. Each panel is 4×8 feet and each wall has two sides (so double the amount you get). Divide the dimensions by 4 feet. For any length less than 4 feet still figure on a panel because you might not be able to use the left-over piece anywhere else.

If you need a foundation, call up local companies, get estimates for your size structure. Price the doors and windows you want to install and enter that number also. If you need a roof you'll have to arrive at the number of needed joists, trusses if any, rafters, and the amount of plywood needed for the decking and shingles. Also you will need nails, siding, door and window facings, baseboards, ceiling materials, and flooring materials.

The next thing to do is to find out the current prices for each item in your town. You'll be surprised how the "current" prices differ from lumberyard to lumberyard day by day. You can usually save a bundle on building materials if you take advantage of sales. This also holds true for finishing materials such as paint, floor coverings, and wallpaper. Another way to save might be to use second-hand lumber. At least you'll know that it is not green and won't distort. Doors and windows often can be bought at a reduced price if you take the time to snoop around building supply places and lumberyards.

MATERIALS		PLANT CENTER	BOOK SHELVES	STORAGE WALL	NEW WALL INTERIOR	NEW WALL EXTERIOR	PAINTING	FLOOR	FINISHING
PLYWOOD ¼″									
PLYWOOD ½″									
PLYWOOD ¾″									
HARDBOARD									
DRY WALL									
LUMBER	1×2s								
	2×2s								
	2×4s								
	1×4s								
	2×10s								
	2×12s								
MOLDING									
BASEBOARD									
NAILS									
	2d								
	4d								
	6d								
	8d								
	10d								
	16d								
LAG SCREWS									
CARRAGE BOLTS									
SCREWS									
	WOOD								
	METAL								
PAINT									
	INTERIOR								
	EXTERIOR								
PARTICLE BOARD									
TILES									
	CARPET								
	CERAMIC								
MASTIC									
SEALER									
WINDOWS									
DOORS									
BRICKS									
MORTAR MIX									
SPECIALTY HARDWARE									
MISC. HARDWARE									
OTHER									

Fig. 1-11. Material checklist.

Once you have the prices you are willing to pay in hand, arrive at the total costs of your building materials. You might have reduced your cost per square foot significantly already. The next variable item is labor.

The least expensive way to go is often the do-it-yourself route. We have found that hiring a builder/carpenter for the things we can't do ourselves and acting as helpers has cut building costs a great deal. In addition our experiences working with a craftsmen have been great for learning the secrets of the trades. If your time is limited, you probably can do best by hiring you a craftsman and one helper for small jobs and two or more helpers for big jobs. Remember, however, that there is a limit to the number of people who can work efficiently at one job site.

Our preferred way of saving on building costs is to do the labor we feel confident we can do ourselves and let the experts do the rest. On the whole, the interior finishing work, which is usually the most time consuming, is the easiest for the amateur to do.

Brick laying, if you can do it, is another job that will save you a bundle. You can also make your own forms for concrete work and nail siding and shingles under the supervision of one who knows how.

The time it will take to get the job done, by yourself or by the people you hire or both is a tremendous cost factor. Unfortunately it is also one of the greatest variables. It is extremely difficult to say how much a person can do in a given eight-hour period. Are you thinking about framing in a wall with precut lumber or are you thinking in terms of installing windows and doors? The framing will go much faster than the fitting of doors and windows particularily if, for some reason or other, the openings aren't quite plumb.

In many instances like this you'll get a great variation of the time it takes to get work accomplished. There is also the rate at which people work. Some people rush around on hot wheels while others tread to a different drummer. Often it is best to get a time estimate for a job and then contract for a flat rate rather than an hourly one. That keeps you and the people who work for you happier.

Other factors can interfere in your time estimate. Weather is high on that list. It might be simply too hot or too cold for shingling a roof or painting an exterior wall. The ground might be frozen too hard to put in footings. The temperature might be too low to pour concrete. Another time loss might occur if your workmen have to provide their own hardware—the nails, screws, bolts and so forth. It's amazing how often the men will run out of something or the other that necessitates a trip to the nearest (or favorite which might be not so near) hardware emporium. On your time, naturally. It's much better to offer your assistance as an errand person from the start and see to it that a good stock of all those necessary items is kept on the premises.

It is good practice to have all the needed lumber, doors, windows, and hardware ready for your workmen. Go and fetch the stuff if the building supply store doesn't deliver. Don't send your workmen unless you want the hourly rate of their work added to the cost of your supplies.

At best, estimating is guess work. That is the reason for the 15-percent contingency figure. If you have $40,000 to spend for a house, you'll know that, with conventional construction (even if you do part of the work yourself and trim corners here and there), you won't get much over 900 square feet. You won't design a 2400-square foot rambler. But you could think seriously about a two-story box that might give you a bit more room for the same money.

If a lot of room is your main concern, you could design the space in such a fashion that part could remain unfinished for awhile. If you like none of the above solutions, you could scrap your conventional building ideas and try a dome that would allow 1114 square feet. You could probably get around 1500 square feet if you cut corners and help yourself.

If domes are too far out, you might figure out the comparative costs of an A-frame or an underground home. It's up to you. You can design exactly what you want and what you can afford.

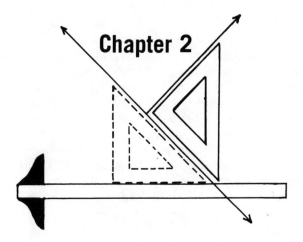

Chapter 2

Remodeling Projects

W HAT WE CALL REMODELING IS BASICALLY the alteration of an existing structure to conform to new criteria. This might involve the removal of walls, the erection of partitions, the cutting of new windows and doors, or the shutting off of existing windows and doorways. It might be a matter of adding storage closets and cupboards, of removing a ceiling and exposing rafters, of installing a skylight, or recovering the walls, ceiling, and floor. Remodeling is also the modification of space for a different use and function.

For example, if you have a double garage that you want to use as a family room, you would be changing its use and function. If you want to turn an enormous, drafty sleeping porch into two bedrooms for your kids, that would be a matter of building partitions and closing up windows. Converting your kitchen, breakfast room, and back hall into a large kitchen would necessitate the removal of walls, the closing up of some openings, and the cutting of other openings.

People who catch the remodeling bug are usually those who need more space and feel they already have that space under their roof in a different form. Conversion of a garage is usually the most popular option because it's probably the most inexpensive way to add anywhere from 120 to 240 or more square feet of living space to your home.

Next in popularity is remodeling the basement. This lags behind garages because about a third of the houses in the United States are built without basements. A remodeled basement adds an enormous amount of square footage without investing in foundations, roofs, or siding.

Attic conversions are next in line. They are not as popular because the construction requirements are usually greater. Such things as cutting and constructing dormer windows, working with slanting walls, and adding heavy insulation are required.

Taking in screened or open porches is also popular. The foundation and roof and usually two walls are already there. The other walls are relatively simple to erect. In this case. You would have to add insulation and exterior finishes.

The need for extra space, usable space, or space for a specific purpose is the motivation for changing the interior of an existing house. It might be that you are stuck with a cut-up, older bungalow and you yearn for open, flowing living space. You might squeeze nightly into a cramped kitchen and equally cramped dinette area or bump your shins every morning as you try to dress in a corner between a tiny closet and a cavernous hallway.

When you start making plans for your remodeling job, you have to know what you want, what you need, and what you are willing to exchange for it. There is always an exchange when it comes to remodeling. So making an office/TV room from an attic will only add to your living space. The story is slightly different when it comes to remodeling a garage. Your car and your lawn mower and other gardening paraphernalia will be without a home unless you provide storage sheds and tool sheds.

If you intend to incorporate your porch into your home, you face still another possible loss that you better consider before you go ahead. By enclosing the porch, you very probably will cut down on the natural light that comes into whatever room the porch adjoins. Now that might not be all bad. It might help if you have too much western exposure. You could offset a loss of windows by installing skylights.

You must think about what changes to the existing structure will do to what's left. Most of the time, a little planning will make it possible to avoid some of the pitfalls that often go unrecognized until the job is finished. Some friends of ours were remodeling the rear room in their large, old house. They had in mind to divide the space of what had been, in its first incarnation, a huge backporch and later on a large room without any particular purpose.

They decided to make a plant room out of part of it. The rest of the space would be used for a couple of large closets, additional room in the bath, and a back passage way. While the extra divided space served nicely for the purposes for which it was planned, it left the dining room window, one of those oversized jobs, looking out onto the closet. True, light from the plant room came in from one side, but still, when you looked out of the dining room window, all you saw straight on was a closet door or two. Not the most spectacular of vistas.

That disaster could have been easily avoided by planning to put the plant room in the middle, rather than at one end, and forfeiting some of the extra storage area. Of course, our friends might like their solution better. Judge for yourself. See Figs. 2-1 and 2-2.

WANT LISTS

Give each member of your family a pencil and piece of paper. Tell them to write their name across the top and then list what they hope to gain from proposed new or converted space. For those not yet mature enough or capable of the above task, perform the chore yourself. That goes for your four-legged friends and those members of your entourage who cannot speak for themselves (your fish, plants and rocks).

Maybe we better define what we mean by gain. For example, if you suddenly have room for a large table that will allow you to have a proper sit-down dinner for 10 where you could not even seat four comfortably before, that's a gain. Gains are a new closet for your hobby needs, a room for your exercise equipment, or a hallway so you don't have to trek through your living room every time you go from the kitchen to the bedroom. A gain can also mean the removal or alleviation of a discomfort without anything extra being added. Such a case is the removal of a wall between the kitchen and breakfast nook that will keep you from bumping into walls, scrounging in your seat at meals, and bumping your shins when you move too fast.

After everyone has listed all the new things

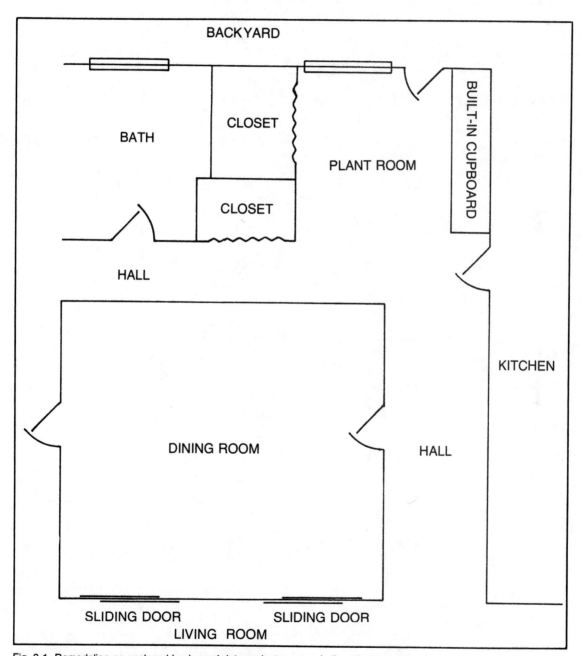

Fig. 2-1. Remodeling an enclosed back porch into a plant room, a hall, and storage space.

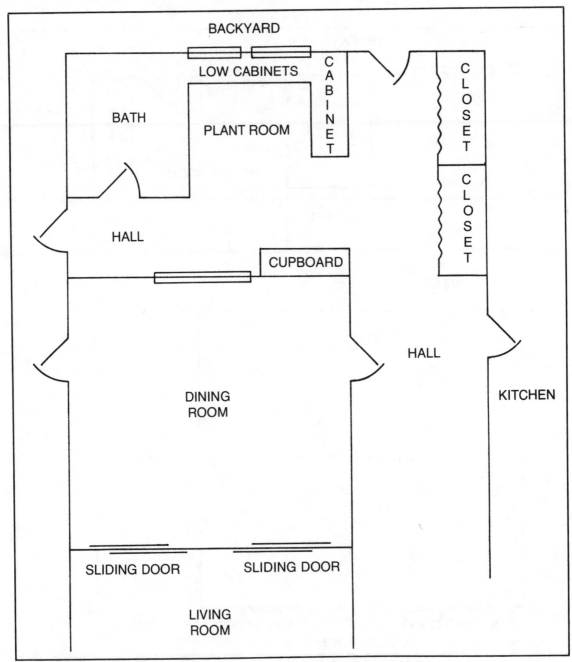

Fig. 2-2. Remodeling the enclosed back porch into a plant room, storage space, and hall.

they hope to gain from the extra space, it might be wise to list on separate sheets of paper, also headed with names, all the gripes about the present living conditions. It might be that some of these can be rectified by incorporating solutions to them into the proposed remodeling plans. Once you total up the needs and desires on the one hand and the complaints on the other, you might end up revising your original plan or even scraping it and starting with a different concept of how the new space could be used for the greatest benefit to all.

One house we lived in had a rather conventional plan. We felt, at first sight, we could live there provided we took in the garage to serve as a family room. The house was a three-bedroom, two-bath, roomy structure (Fig. 2-3). After living in it a few months, we were ready to start on our garage-conversion project. We found out that the solution was somewhat different from what we had first envisioned. Our want lists after those first few months read like this.

Alyson (6 years old):
A place to play with clay.
A place to make a mess.
A place to paint.
A playhouse.
Room for all my dolls.
David (9 years old):
Room to play.
A place to watch TV while other people listen to records and tapes.
A place to paint.
A place to play with clay.
A place to build models.
Melissa (16 years old):
A room of my own.
A room of my own.
A room of my own.
A room of my own.
A room of my own.
P.S. I'm tired of sharing a room.

Ruth
Peace.
Quiet.
A living room to entertain in without kids dragging through. Not having to drag the laundry all the way through the house. A place for the kids to play that is *not* the kitchen or dining room. A place to work, please, please.

Mike
A place to sleep late on weekends.
A place to sit in peace and think.
A place to write.
A living room that isn't a traffic circle.
A more gracious entry.

As you can see we were thoroughly disenchanted with the life-style that the house seemed to impose on us. Putting a family room in the garage required more than the usual construction (Fig. 2-4) without solving most of the problems. The children still had to come through the living room into the family room. Everybody seemed to be passing through the living room constantly. The concourse at the local airport seemed quiet by comparison. And truly, Melissa needed a room of her own.

So we went back to our want lists. Obviously a room for Melissa and a playroom for the children would help a lot. If, at the same time we could reroute the traffic around the living room and set ourselves up in a bed/sitting room arrangement which could double as Ruth's office most of our gripes would be eliminated.

Looking at it from this new perspective we first tried to locate a space for Melissa's room. The garage was the obvious solution once more. It also offered plenty of space for a playroom (Fig. 2-5). But to get to the playroom the kids had to trek through the living room from their bedrooms. Each trip to the bathroom entailed a similar voyage. The very idea that pots of clay and pans of paint were going to be transported to and fro through the living room caused Ruth to veto the plan in a hurry.

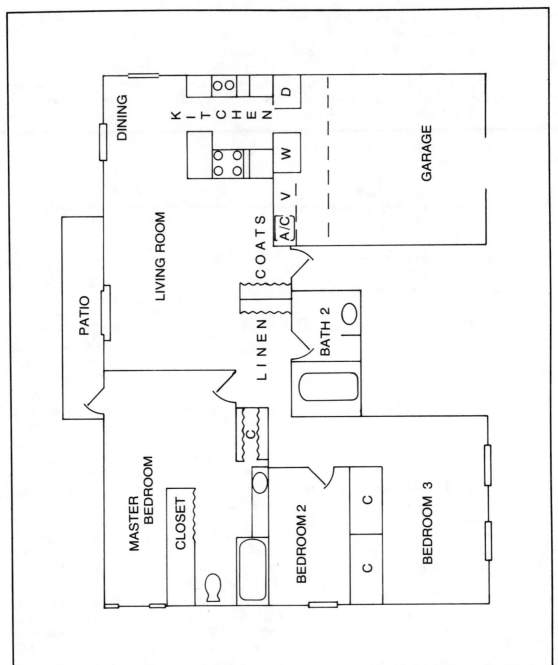

Fig. 2-3. A house plan.

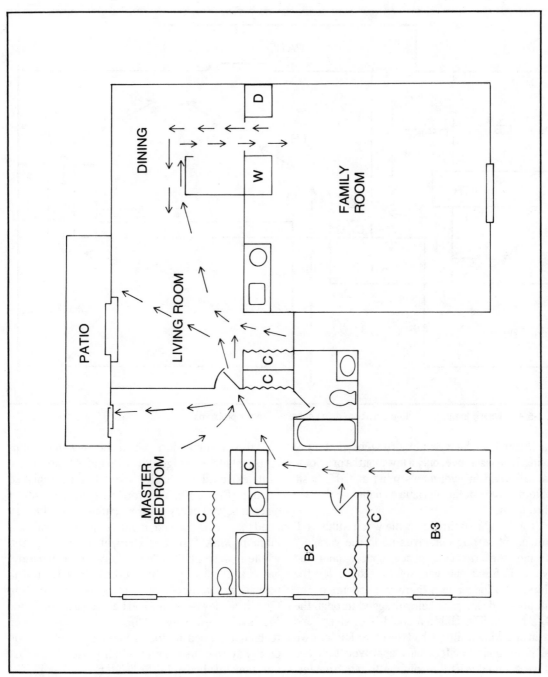

Fig. 2-4. Trying to put a family room into the garage did not begin to solve the traffic problem.

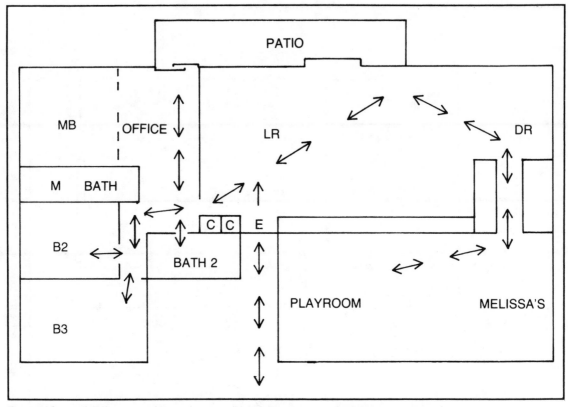

Fig. 2-5. Converting the garage into a playroom didn't solve any major problems.

Gloom hung heavy and there were mutters of moving. The last move, only a few months previous, was still vivid in everyone's mind and the basic problem of remodeling became a challenge that we had to meet.

The first breakthrough came when Mike said, "How about setting ourselves up in the garage?" This met the criteria of peace, space, quiet and privacy. It freed one wing of the house for the children! No longer was there the specter of the paint pots and clay pans being dragged through the whole house. The children could live, sleep, and play in one wing while we had the other for our own use. Everybody vociferously approved the idea and we adopted it as the solution to our troubles.

It took some more pencil chewing and innumerable sketches (Figs. 2-6 through 2-9 are a few samples) until we finally arrived at the finished version (Fig. 2-10). We were all delighted with it since it solved every gripe and fulfilled most every need that we had voiced. It did, admittedly, call for a bit more work than we had bargained for, but on the whole it wasn't all that much because, fortunately, we could leave the bathrooms; intact. It was primarily a matter of tearing out closets and putting them in somewhere else and building a partition for Melissa's new room. Our divide-and-conquor technique gained us four rooms and a glamorous entryway that also sheltered all those plants that overflow our house in the winter.

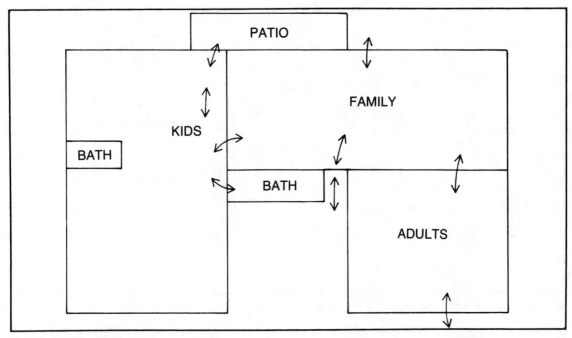

Fig. 2-6. A schematic of zones.

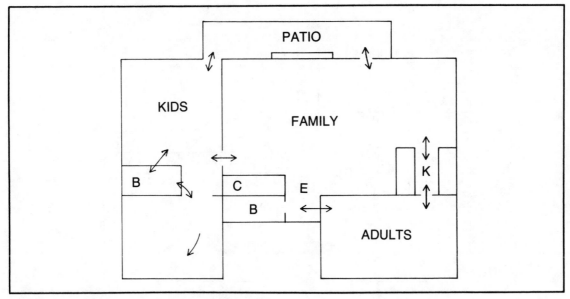

Fig. 2-7. A schematic showing access to the bathrooms.

27

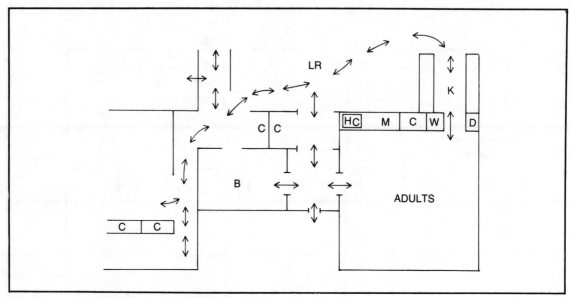

Fig. 2-8. A rough sketch to chart traffic flow if we took in the porch.

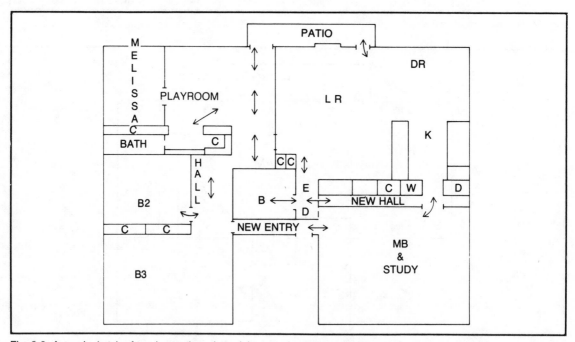

Fig. 2-9. A rough sketch of two innovations that might save the day: a new entry and a new service hall.

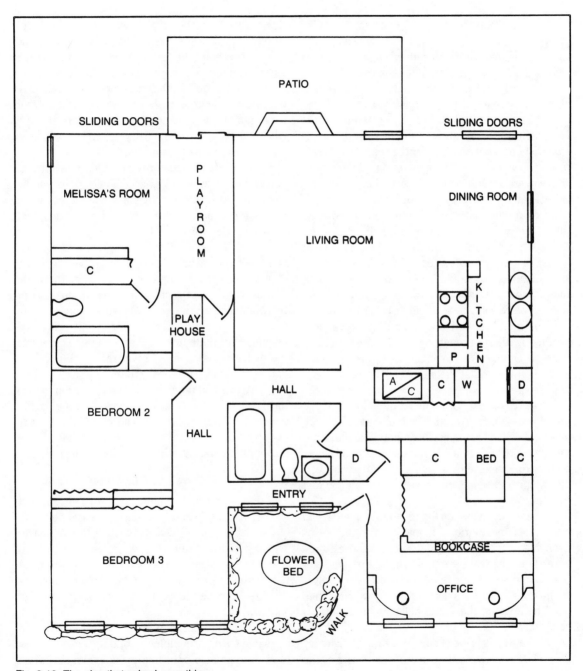

Fig. 2-10. The plan that solved everything.

You probably won't have to go through that many stages to arrive at a satisfactory remodeling solution. If your first plan doesn't work, by all means tear it up and try again. It is ever so much easier to draw a new plan than to live with a remodeling job that isn't satisfactory.

It is a good idea to take the planning of the remodeling in easy stages. For instance, do the want list one weekend and, for the rest of the week, be on the alert. Observe how your family functions in the present surroundings. Are there any bottlenecks in the way the traffic flows? Do you have a room or rooms that seem to function as glorified hallways? How about your eating habits? Do you have adequate room to sit down comfortably at meal times? Is there room for guests? Do the kids seem to be underfoot constantly? Do they have adequate and suitable play space? How about storage? As long as you're going to be wielding that hammer and saw you might as well whip up a few shelves and closets. Is there enough space for dressing and makeup? Do the kids have somewhere to put their stuff when you yell at them to clean up their rooms (right away?)

You'll come up with more questions to ask. Write everything down that you observe. The following weekend bring up these points and discuss them with the other family members. It might well be that for some reason they were not aware of a discomfort or annoyance or that they felt it couldn't be changed.

Once you have finalized all the needs and wants, look for solutions. In many cases, the gripes even have priority over the wants. The attitude here should be that for every gripe there is a solution. Some solutions are perfect, some are simply adequate, some are just fair and only good enough to take the edge off the gripe, but they are solutions nonetheless.

Take Ruth's gripe of having to drag the laundry through the living room to the opposite end of the house every time she put in a load of wash. With three kids at home, that meant hauling laundry through the house at least twice a day, coming and going. The solutions could have ranged from the simple and inexpensive expedient of getting a laundry cart to streamline the transportation problem to the relocating of the washer and dryer in the former master bedroom closet (the most practical one). Alternately the washer and dryer could have found a home in the center bathroom.

The children needed an area that was not carpeted, where water was accessible for clean-up, close to a bathroom, particularly when there were playmates about, and plenty of floor space that wasn't needed for other traffic.

While a playroom in the garage would have met some of the criteria—lots of floor space, proximity to water (in the kitchen which brought the little darlings underfoot again), bathroom trips meant traveling through the kitchen and the living room. In addition, the children were used to storing and playing with their toys in their rooms. There was the distinct possibility of toys trailing all over the house on the way from here to there or back again.

In a pinch, it might have been a solution to turn the living room into a playroom and convert the garage into a living room. The choices are many once you open your thinking up to include all the possibilities and rate them in order of desirability.

MULTIPLE USE OF SPACE

The real secret of designing a great room, suite of rooms, or even an entire house is to learn the tricks of overlapping and making multiple use of space. While there is often a lot of lip service paid to multiple-use areas in modern homes, usually what is actually there is a counter or a row of cabinets that are supposed to be used for cooking, laundry, and sewing.

True multi-purpose space allows you to use the same space or equipment for different activities at various times. For example, open floor space can be used by the kids to run their race tracks, roll their doll buggies, practice acrobatics, or for a slumber party. A multiple-use bedroom serves as as a sitting room, an adult oasis, an away-from-the-office office, and a sewing room.

Rooms that are shared by a number of people, such as living rooms, family rooms, dens or playrooms, should also be designed so that they can function in a multiple-use manner. The first step is to make a list of all the equipment needed for each of the wants on your lists. Next make a list of space requirements needed to find solutions for your gripes. Make sure that space, such as in "three extra feet to set up an ironing board next to the dryer" is also included either as a want or a solution to a gripe.

While all this list making might seem tedious, it is much better to waste a bit of time with pencil and paper than to find out much later that you left something vital out of your plan. You might or might not be able to fit it in even with a lot of adjusting and extra work.

Let's go to our revised sample want and gripe lists for our remodeling job. We'll begin fulfilling the wants.

Alyson

An area that was easy to clean for painting and clay work.

A sink and cabinets for clean up and storage of craft supplies.

A 3-×-4 foot area (minimum) for a playhouse.

Some low shelving for dolls.

David

An easy-clean area for painting and clay work.

A sink and cabinets for storing craft supplies.

A table or counter for model building, plus shelves for drying.

Floor space.

TV.

Melissa

Floor space of about 90 square feet (minimum)

A closet.

A partition for privacy.

A door with a lock.

Ruth

A playroom for the children.

Space for a desk, a table, and shelving for storage of writing materials.

Mike

Space for a desk, a table, and storage for writing materials.

Space to think in peace.

The next step is to list possible solutions for the needed space and equipment. The first two requests on Ruth's list were for peace and quiet; utmost on her priority list was a place to work. Mike's list echoed the desire for a quiet work area. Both also felt that the children should have a room to play and watch TV in while the adults and their company had the living room to themselves.

Ruth/Mike

Playroom for the children.

Den/office or bedroom/office.

That still left the laundry and traffic problem, but we felt we had at least determined what it was that we needed. The next step was to find out exactly what we had in the way of space that could be made to fulfill our needs.

ROUGH SKETCHES AND SCHEMATICS

The time had arrived for rough sketches. When we refer to rough sketches that's exactly what we mean. Figure 2-12, 2-13, and 2-14 are our first rough sketches for possible ways to remodel the garage to meet our needs. As you can see, rough as they are, the bottlenecks show up bright and clear. The next series of rough sketches show possible solutions to the traffic problem. See Figs. 2-4, 2-5, and 2-8. Figure 2-9 was the magic key that not only unsnarled the traffic, but gave us the basic idea of how we could have every single thing on our list without buying a new home or even adding on to the present structure.

Rough sketches, because they leave out most detail, are ideal for analyzing structures and finding

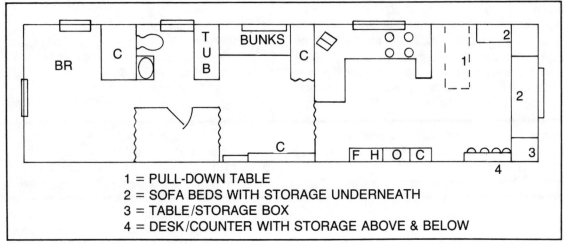

1 = PULL-DOWN TABLE
2 = SOFA BEDS WITH STORAGE UNDERNEATH
3 = TABLE/STORAGE BOX
4 = DESK/COUNTER WITH STORAGE ABOVE & BELOW

Fig. 2-11. A mobile home.

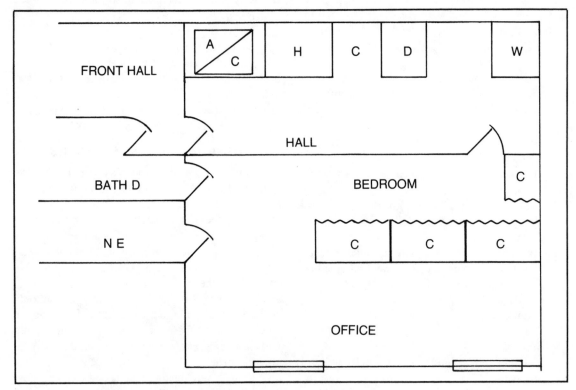

Fig. 2-12. A rough sketch of our proposed bedroom/office in the garage space.

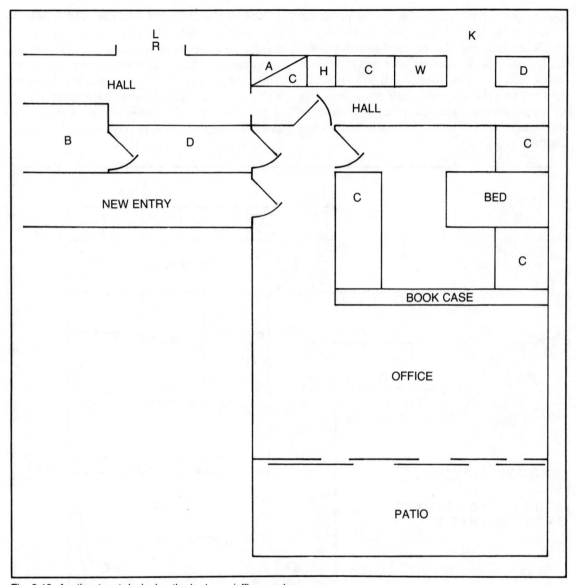

Fig. 2-13. Another try at designing the bedroom/office combo.

solutions for problems. A particular kind of rough sketch called the *schematic* is probably the most valuable because by its very nature it emphasizes the important aspects of planning: projected use and resulting or associated problems. Figures 2-6 and 2-7 are schematics for our projected remodeling job. They include our ideas on what would be most desirable. They show a wing for the children and another one for us, separating the living/dining areas from the family freeway, and so forth.

Schematics can also be used to indicate activities and special-use areas in multi-purpose rooms, to figure out distribution of light and ventilation, and to work out traffic patterns. Schematics are simple drawings and a quick way you can scribble out as many options as you can think of in a few minutes.

HOW TO MEASURE THE EXISTING STRUCTURE

After you've completed your schematics, it is time to make measurements so you can see which option or options are the most feasible. Measure accurately and record each and every size and distance. We've found that accurate measuring can save a lot of grief later. Even a couple of inches can make a vast difference in the size of a doorway and what you can or cannot get through it.

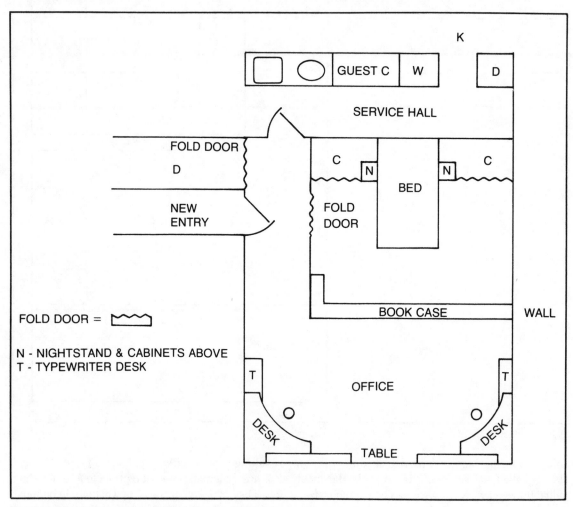

Fig. 2-14. The design of the bedroom/office we liked best.

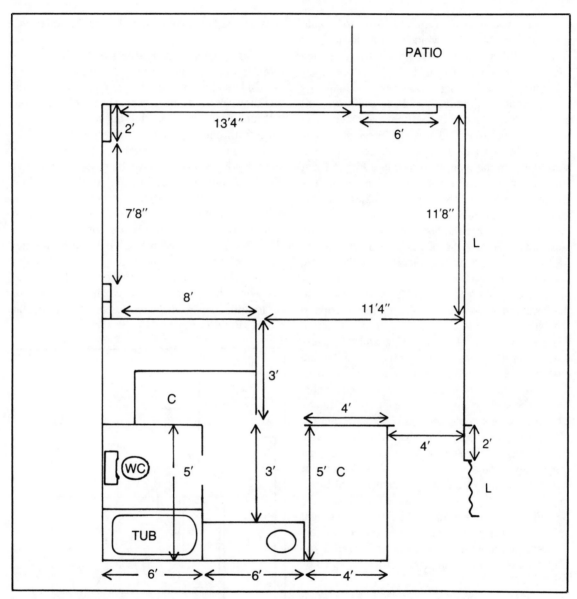

Fig. 2-15. The "before" plan of the master suite (with measurements).

We prefer to use a retractable metal measuring tape; one of us wields it while the other records the numbers on a sheet of paper on a clipboard. Incidentally, clipboard's are great for making rough sketches and schematics. And, of course, for keeping it all together.

When you measure a room, be sure to include the distances between windows, the location of doors (and their exact size) and any irregularities such as niches and protrusions. The latter might hide plumbing or heating ducts or even a chimney.

Back at the drawing board you can now compare your rough sketches and schematics with the real world out there. When we measured our existing master bedroom suite and entered the measurements on the plan, it looked like Fig. 2-15. A comparison with the schematic which specified a children's wing for sleeping and playing made us jump for premature joy.

It seemed that the good old master bedroom suite might be just the place for a playroom and Melissa's private quarters. It looked like the sliding doors that led onto the patio, a convenient shortcut for the kids on their way to and from their rooms to the backyard and also on equally numerous trips to the bathroom, would at last fulfill a proper function. The same was true of the immense walk-in closets that haughtily relegated our clothes to collecting dust, cobwebs or mildew, according to the season.

It was simple to see that one closet would give Melissa more than ample storage for all her things. The other closet could be readily converted into a playhouse, plus storage, for Alyson. So far so good.

A schematic and measurements confirmed that the garage would yield plenty of room for our office/bedroom, retreat. We discovered that locating the master bedroom in this area would add the benefit of easy access to the kitchen for midnight snacks and early morning cups of coffee. Nevertheless, the problem of a master bath as well as the traffic hassel in the living room still needed to be solved.

Figure 2-9, commonly referred to as the golden key, held the answer. It involved removal of two closets, the taking in of an open porch area into the house proper, the relocating of the main entry, and the creation of a back hall. It also seemed to solve the traffic problem admirably. There was noth-

ing that needed moving in the bathroom except the door.

Our neighbors across the street, whose bathroom layout was flipped to ours (Figs. 2-16A and 2-16B) but who were so intrigued with what we did that they wanted a similar plan, had to relocate their bathtub. That was affordable but not inexpensive. Their bathroom ended up as shown in Fig. 2-16C.

When your measurements and roughs just don't work out, you'll have to resort to what is termed *design modifications*. We would have liked to have opened up the living room to the back hallway adjacent the kitchen wall to use the bare minimum of floor space for access to the dining area (Fig. 2-17). The place we had designated for the door opening proved too narrow. To widen the opening would require moving the water heater and that would have been expensive and troublesome. In addition, we would have need for a new coat closet (Fig. 2-19).

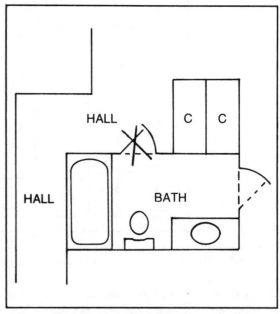

Fig. 2-16A. Remodeling our second bathroom into a master bath.

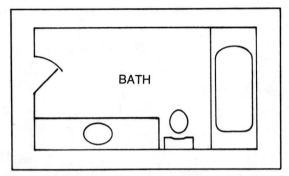

Fig. 2-16B. This is how our neighbor's bathroom was flipped compared to ours.

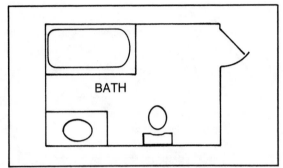

Fig. 2-16E. Another way to rearrange the bathroom.

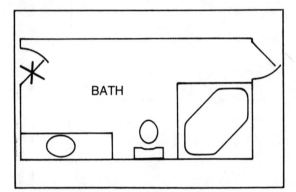

Fig. 2-16C. Remodeling the neighbor's bath into a master bathroom, similar to ours, using a small tub.

We decided to leave the main entry to the living room where it was and install heavy folding doors so we could completely isolate this area without any added expense except for the doors. The place we had picked for the door became an ample coat and storage closet.

We compromised in Melissa's new room by running the new wall so that it would start at the corner of the existing closet rather than a couple of feet over. That would have resulted in a larger room for her, but a mishapen, narrow playroom (Fig. 2-18).

When you have decided on the best plan or plans from your sketches, you might like to draw

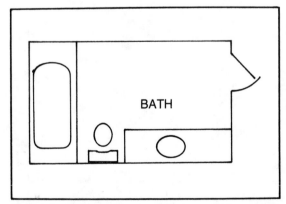

Fig. 2-16D. Another solution, moving the tub to the opposite wall, is a bit more costly.

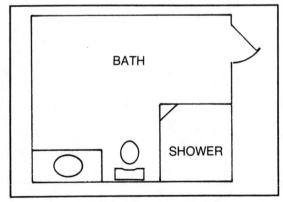

Fig. 2-16F. Installing a shower instead of the tub.

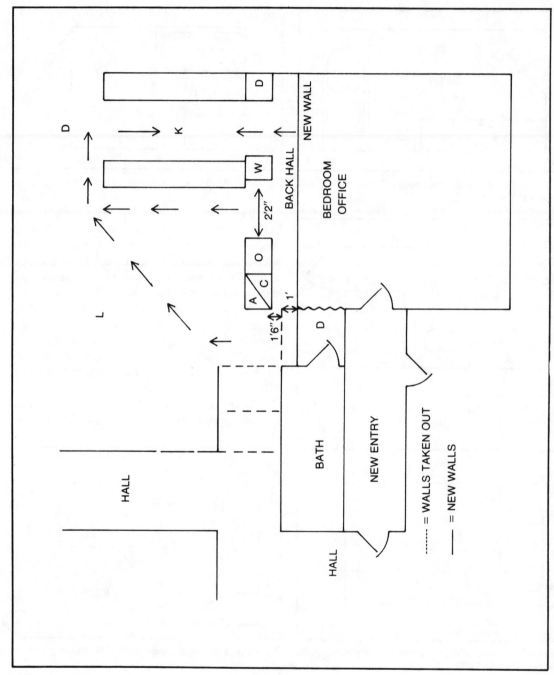

Fig. 2-17. Trying to locate a new living room door that will reroute traffic along the wall of the kitchen.

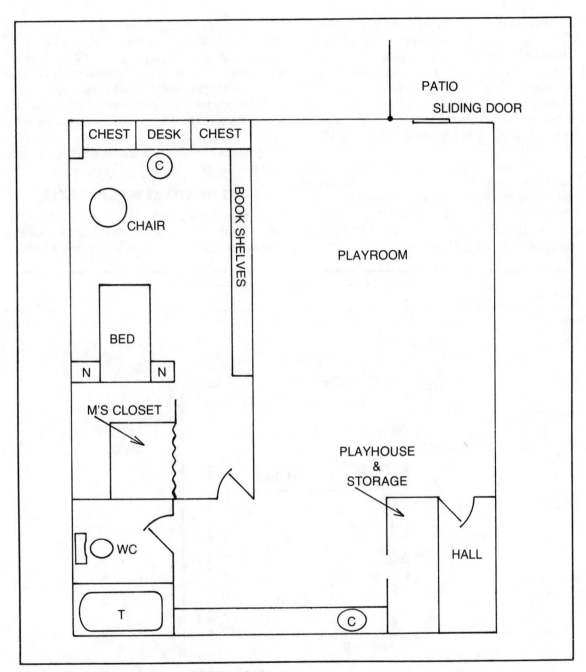

Fig. 2-18. The old master suite remodeled into a bedroom.

some rough sketches of new or remodeled walls. As with your other roughs, start simply by guess-timating and positioning the proposed doors or windows by eye. You might sketch out different solutions as we did in Figs. 2-12 and 2-13. Figure 2-14 shows the new wall that divided the bedroom/office from the back hall and the ones that showed various ways of enclosing the new entry. See Figs. 2-19 and Fig. 2-20.

Don't worry at this point about exactness, you are strictly after ideas. All of your constructing and tearing down is done on paper so you can be as wild as you want without hurting anything. It will help you generate ideas and give you a feel for what the finished remodeling job will be like.

If your remodeling involves outside walls, in-clude elevations of the exterior to make sure your windows will be in the proper places. Consider also any plantings that might affect your exterior eleva-tion. Large shrubs might have to come out, trees might be only a few feet from doors, and other such considerations. These rough elevations will remind you of things that you have become so familiar with that you don't notice them anymore until you trip over them after the fact.

TRICKS FOR STAYING WITHIN A BUDGET

Remodeling costs money. There's no way around that, but plans can save you money. Plans will show up added cost factors that can be avoided. As with

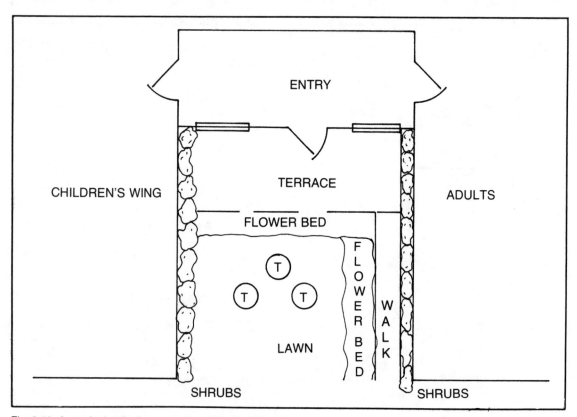

Fig. 2-19. A rough sketch of a new entry and landscaping idea.

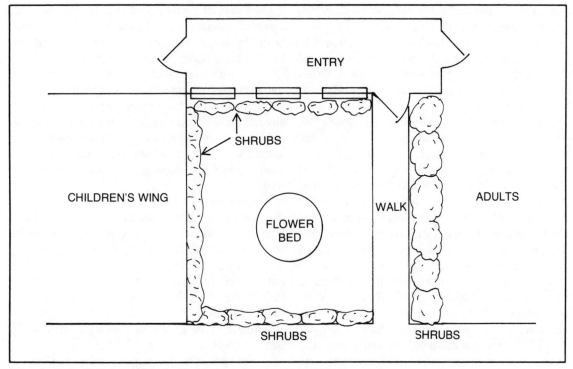

Fig. 2-20. A rough sketch of another idea for a new entry and landscaping.

the roughs for the new entry conversion, the floor plan of the second bathroom was a distinct added cost factor. This added quite a bit of additional cost for our neighbors (Figs. 2-16C through 2-16F).

If you can avoid moving plumbing, doing major electrical reworking or breaking through masonary walls, do so if you want to save. Another, less obvious, fact of remodeling is that it costs less to close off or divide than it does to open or throw together. On the surface, this seems contradictory because anybody with any sense can see that when you build a new wall or partition you will have to pay for 2×4s, wallboard, paint, nails, door framing, doors, and so forth while when you pull out a wall you end up with a nice little stock of said 2×4s, wallboard, trim, and whatever.

True enough. But you also end up with a ceiling that shows an all too obvious scar, a floor that does the same and, if there's carpeting it will not match. Even your hardwood floors stop short at the wall. You will have anywhere from 4 to 6 inches of sub-floor or slab.

As you can readily imagine, this is hard to cover up without resorting to new wall-to-wall something. Your ceiling can usually be patched, but it will require a complete repaint job. So will the walls. Cutting doorways, however, is not as bad because you can cover the gap in the floor with a threshold of some kind.

This doesn't mean that you should forget about removing walls. It simply stands to remind you of the costs you might not have thought of straight away. Also, removing a closet does not fall into this category if the closet has folding doors. Putting in planter boxes, low cupboards, or bookcases can also cover a bare strip in a larger area.

A more unconventional, but effective way is to bring in some contrast and cover the gap with it and then use the same contrast in different places on the floor to show people that you really planned it that way all along.

If you are in for an extensive remodeling job, you can often plan to use what you take out in one area to close off in another. Because your doors, windows, and often even your wall panels will be of the same size, this makes also for speedy work. Another way is to go to your favorite lumberyard or building supply store and find out if there are any *overs* available (materials a contractor ordered and had cut to size, doors and windows in particular, and later found he had too many of). These can often be had at a mere fraction of their original cost (folding doors as cheap as $3.00 a panel). If you know the size ahead of time, you can plan and design with them in mind and save yourself a bundle.

Using less expensive and unusual materials is not only easy on the budget, but it often allows quite interesting results. To a certain extent, this also applies to the erection of partitions. After all, you do not have to use A-1 2×4s if you build in a new closet or partition off a corner of the family room for a dark room. Neither do you need the best grade of plywood, unless you plan to have it show prominently.

We've found that two ideas we discovered, more or less accidentally, work beautifully in old homes and they can be adapted for newer ones as well. The first idea is great because it doesn't cost you anything except some varnish and your sweat equity. It applies to homes built prior to World War II and below the Mason-Dixon line. Prior to the manufacture of plasterboard or gypsum board, interior walls were made out of wooden boards, shiplapped. Over these boards, cheesecloth or very thin muslin was stretched and wallpaper was applied over the whole shebang. Usually several layers of wallpaper could be applied to that original layer of muslin and only every 20 years or so did one have to think about remuslining the walls.

When we were helping our relatives strip away the wallpaper of a turn-of-the-century frame house we were struck with the beauty of the walls without any further adornment. Luckily the room belonged to our adventurous nephew who pitched right in and helped with the tack pulling (that's the worst) the sanding, and the staining and varnishing of the walls.

The room is a beautiful cross between super modern use of plank paneling and the mellow warmth of antique wood. If you have a house in which you can use that trick by all means try it. One of our friends liked the idea so much that he went out and bought some second-hand boards that he nailed to his walls and finished as described. Because the boards where beautifully weathered, it only required some clear varnish for a "driftwood" paneled room.

The second idea is simpler and it can be used anywhere in the country. The trick here is to stretch muslin over your poor pitted and bumpy walls and then cover same with wall paper. This works particularly well if you have a partial wall that has been redone. Examples are a door or window cut or a closet removed. Whatever accidental dents might have appeared will be nicely covered up and you will be spared the time and expense of repainting or refinishing the entire room.

A third way to take advantage of the same idea is to cover the walls with fabric. This is considerably less expensive than plywood but not much if any less expensive than particle board. You can staple the fabric directly to the wall if the wall is in good condition and your fabric fairly heavy. You could stretch fabric over strips of wood much like the furring strips you use for paneling if you want to hide bumps or cracks.

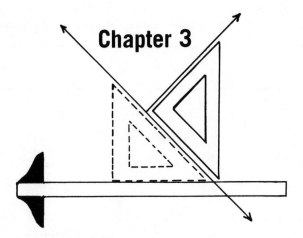

Drawing Plans for Additions

I N MANY CASES, THE MOST CREATIVE AND IN-
ventive thinking can't get around the fact that
there is simply not enough room in a house. You can
take out walls, divide rooms, do all sorts of interesting things, but if the original square footage is
too small then all you can do is build an addition onto
your home.

Many people are scared silly at the mere men-
tion of building an addition. They seem to think
there's some magic, esoteric knowledge necessary
to build something that doesn't yet exist. There are
others who will point at a corner of the backyard and
say, with authority, this is where the new bedroom
is going to be. They won't give it a second thought
or even a few lines on paper.

While building an addition presents some new
challenges it is not all that different from doing a
remodeling job. It often is more time saving because you don't have to contend with corners that
are far out of plumb and floors that have settled so
much that you can demonstrate the pull of gravity

anywhere in the room with any handy marble or
pencil. While it will cost a bit more to add to your
existing house than it does to rearrange what you
have, you will get back those x number of dollars
per square foot not only in comfort, convenience,
and enjoyment for you and your family, but in the
real dollar value you have added to your property.

You must know what you're going to do before
you do it. Furthermore, you must see what it is you
plan, compare it with what you have, see if it inter-
feres with any of the present comforts and conveniences (such as light and ventilation), and whether it
will give you exactly what you want for your labor
and money. This is, of course where the plans come in.

Before you even pick up a pencil, take a walk
around your house and tentatively pick out a location for the new addition. In most cases, if you are
planning to add on ground level, this will be to the
back because zoning laws are strict about keeping
all houses lined up like proverbial tin soldiers so
they can salute the street in unison.

In towns and many suburbs, the majority of the lots are too narrow to add onto the side of the house and still leave the required number of feet between your dwelling and the neighbors. If you do have room, the side of the house might be a great place to use. Don't overlook any room between structures.

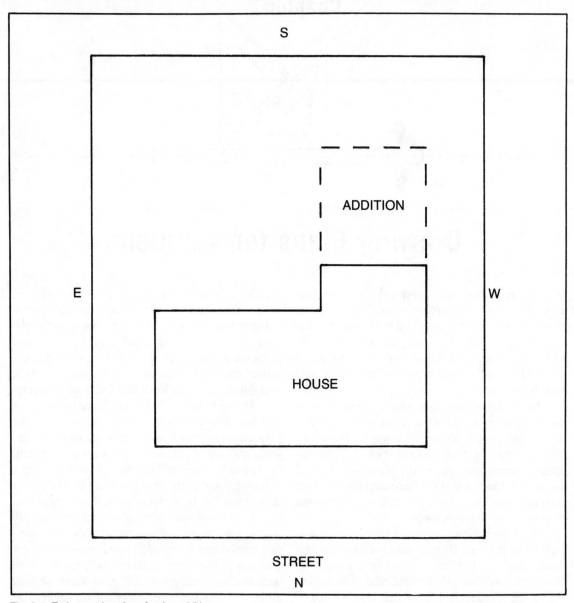

Fig. 3-1. Trying out locations for the addition.

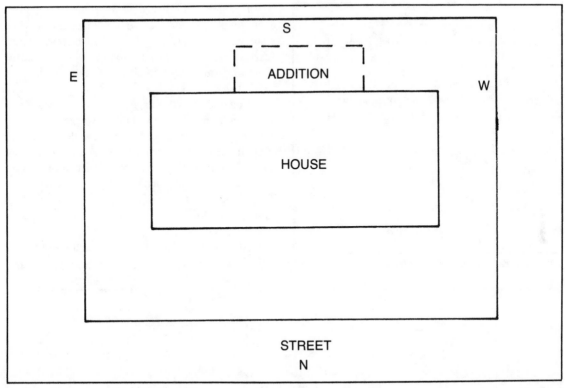

Fig. 3-2. Another way of adding an addition.

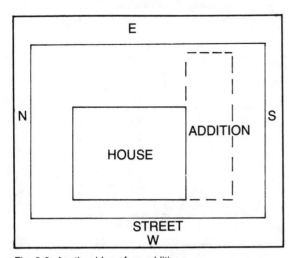

Fig. 3-3. Another idea of an addition.

A very good place might be between your free-standing garage and your house. You might want to enlarge the breezeway and go from there (Figs. 3-1 through Fig. 3-5).

While you are on your tour of the property be sure to look at the site in detail. Is the ground sloping away from your preferred place for the new addition? If it is, you might have to bring in some fill dirt and level it off before you pour a slab. Would you like a cantilever design modified, perhaps, to a super-pier-and-beam construction? That would be a lot less costly than filling in, but it would require special insulation. Do you have a septic tank? Please don't pour a slab over the access to it. This could present problems of a considerable magnitude.

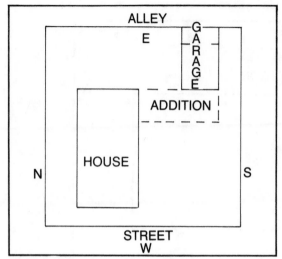

Fig. 3-4. Another way to add an addition.

Does your backyard have a hill? You might have to level the site before building. Next, look at your plants. Surely you don't want to uproot that Arizona ash that you have babied the last three years or do away with the lovely maple that is your wife's pride and joy?

Consider the drainage patterns of your yard. This might not be important if you're the lucky owner of a flat lot with sandy, loose soil several feet deep. It does matter if your house sits on heavy clay only a few inches above bedrock with your ground slanting toward the place for the proposed addition. If you ignore this kind of thing, you might find that your new addition will double as a swimming pool after a heavy rain.

Now go back inside for your paper and pencil and, taking all that we've discussed so far into

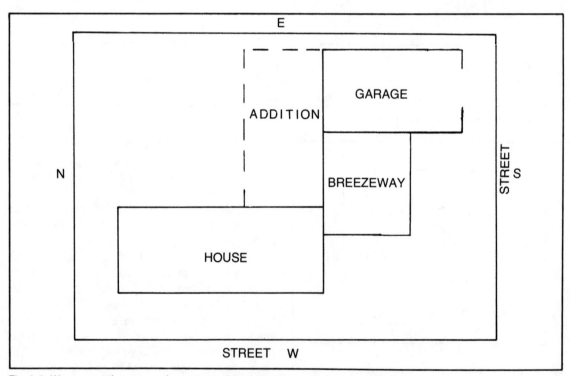

Fig. 3-5. We connect the garage, the nouse and the breezeway with a new addition.

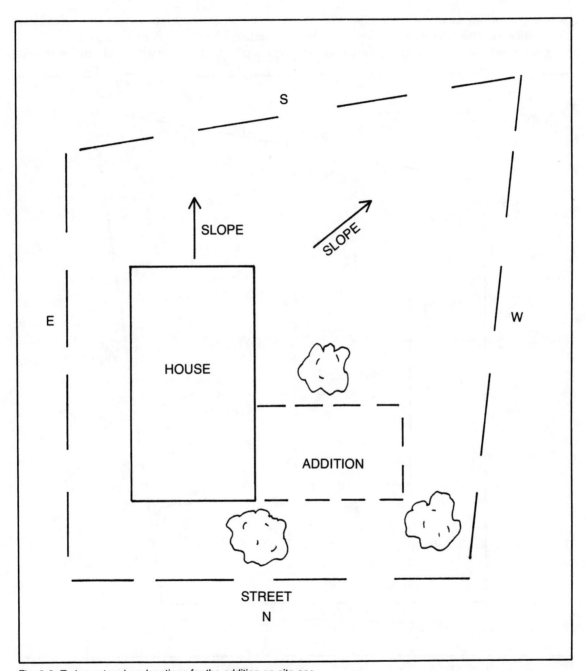

Fig. 3-6. Trying out various locations for the addition on site one.

consideration, draw some rough schematics of the possibilities you have come up with. There won't be many unless you own five or more acres of land and have an unlimited budget. Your schematics will look something like Figs. 3-6 through 3-10.

Study the drawings with an eye to the next set

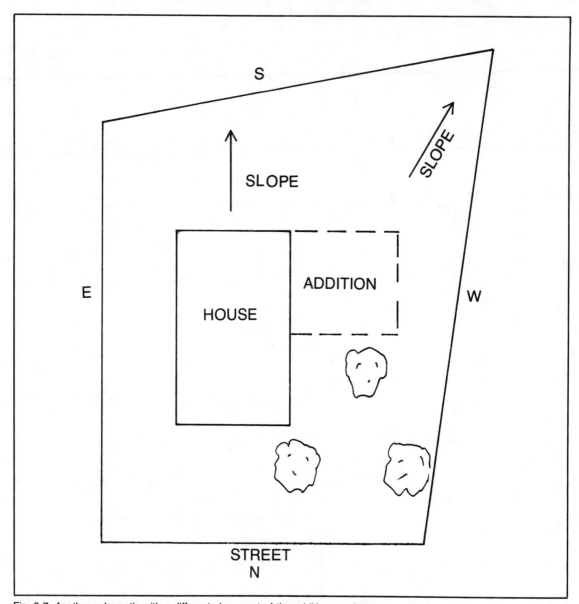

Fig. 3-7. Another schematic with a different placement of the addition on site one.

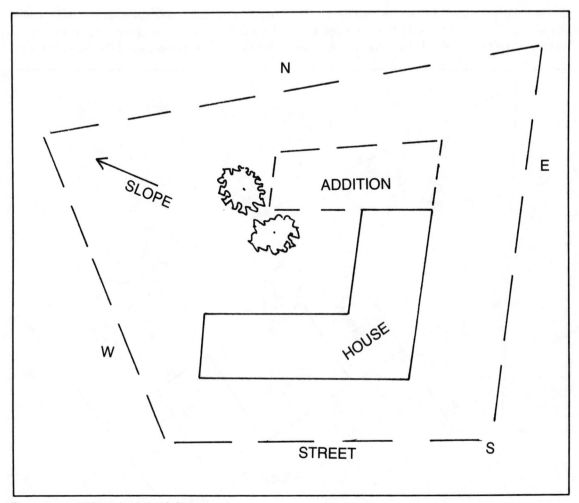

Fig. 3-8. An addition schematic of site two.

of important considerations: sunlight, privacy, proximity, view, and traffic patterns.

SUNLIGHT AND WEATHER CONSIDERATIONS

You will want sunlight in your new addition and, at the same time, you won't want to deprive your present house of any sunlight if you can help it. Sometimes that presents quite a problem. If you're persistent enough, you'll usually find a way.

The *exposure* of the addition is another important aspect of where to put the whole thing, in the first place, and how to orient the windows and doors. If you live in the North, you'll want a lot of sunlight to get in your house during winter for its passive solar heating effect. Therefore, you'll want to stick the addition on the south side if at all possible. If you live in the South, you'll try to have as little western exposure as you can to keep the cooling bills from equaling the national debt. The prevailing wind direction is another consideration to take into account. Take this into consideration as you plan the location of your addition and the windows and doors. A few schematics indicating the directions of the compass and the prevailing wind

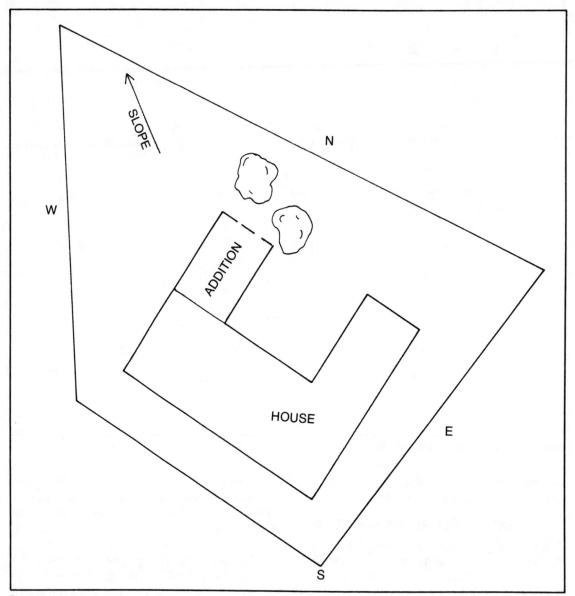

Fig. 3-9. A different version for site two.

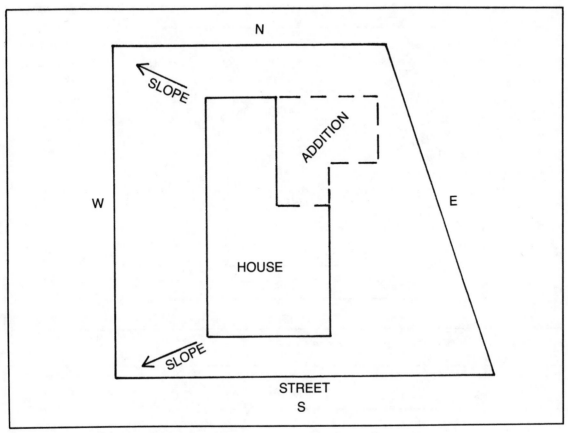

Fig. 3-10. A schematic for an addition on site three.

patterns will give you a clear picture of what to put where. See Fig. 3-11, 3-12, and 3-13.

PROXIMITY AND ACCESS

Go back to the drawing board for a very rough sketch of your present house. We are still referring to a one-story, ground-level addition. All you need is a sketch of what you presently have on the ground floor (Fig. 3-14). Next, roughly sketch in the new addition.

Unless you are fabulously lucky, you will discover one or a number of the following complications:

☐ The proposed addition covers up two or more windows in a room and makes that room a vault for practical purposes (Fig. 3-15).

☐ The proposed addition covers up only one window, but the only access to the addition will be through the garage (Fig. 3-16).

☐ The proposed addition does none of the above, but you'll have to break through a masonry wall that houses most of the plumbing for the second floor (Fig. 3-17).

☐ And so on and so forth.

The solution is to play put and take. Hook on that addition in different places and in different

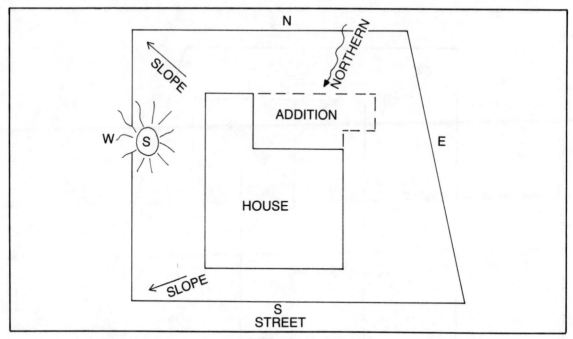

Fig. 3-11. A schematic for exposure considerations on site three.

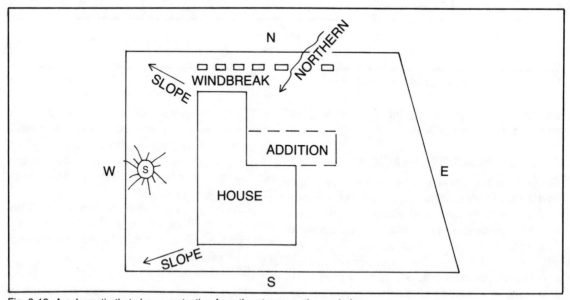

Fig. 3-12. A schematic that shows protection from the strong northern winds.

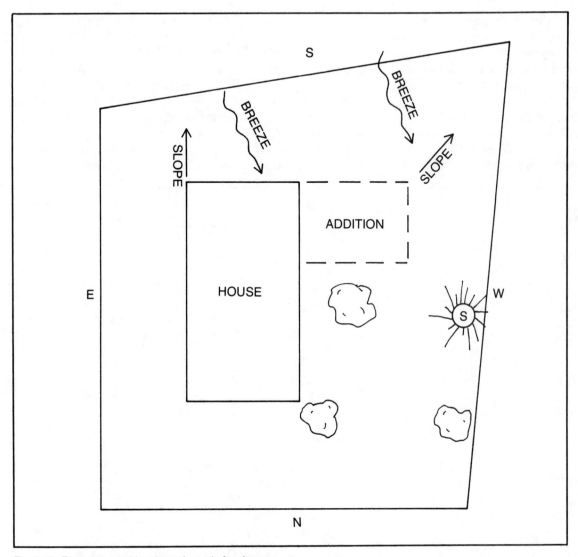

Fig. 3-13. Exposure consideration schematic for site one.

ways until you find what you want. It might be that you'll have to scrap your first idea of where to place the addition. You might even have to start again with a new tour of the premises.

You might discover that you'll need to do a bit of reshuffling in the existing structure to accommo-

date the added rooms. This is not as bad or as outrageous as you might think. Your house was built to a plan—a good plan, a so-so plan or a miserable plan, but a plan nonetheless. It was designed for certain functions and it carries out these functions, at least in a limited way. But adding new rooms shifts the basic concept of the plan and you'll have to incorporate this shift into the new design. You're doing more than adding a room or rooms: you are redesigning the basic traffic pattern of the house as well as some of the availability of light and ventilation.

When you look for access from the existing structure, don't just note any doors or windows opening in the general direction and let it go at that. You might end up with people traipsing through your bedroom on their way to theirs or leaping across the dining table with the groceries en route from the garage to the kitchen. Omit bedrooms as access unless:

☐ They are large enough to withstand amputation of a few feet for a hallway along one wall.

☐ The proposed addition will replace a bedroom and the former bedroom will be turned into a sitting room/den/study/what-have-you inhabited by the same occupant.

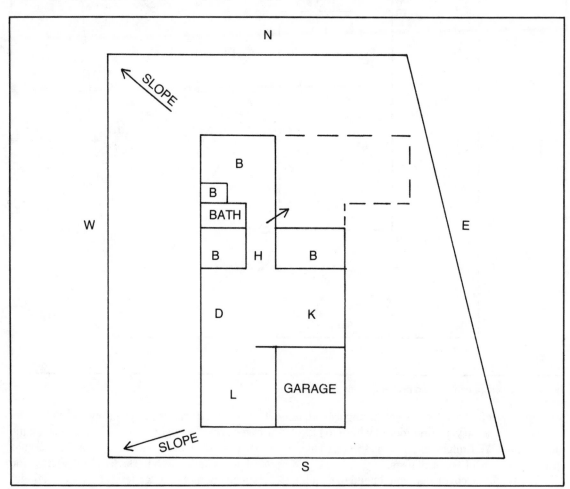

Fig. 3-14. Access schematic.

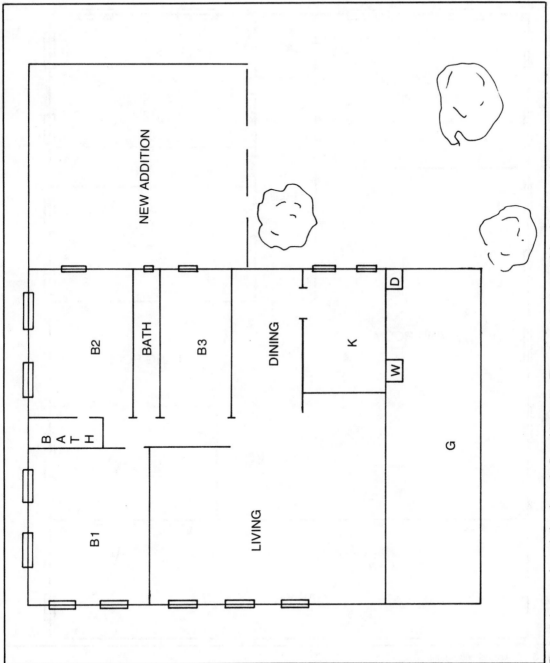

Fig. 3-15. Access schematic that shows the flaw of the design. There is a windowless vault for a bedroom and no ready access to the addition.

55

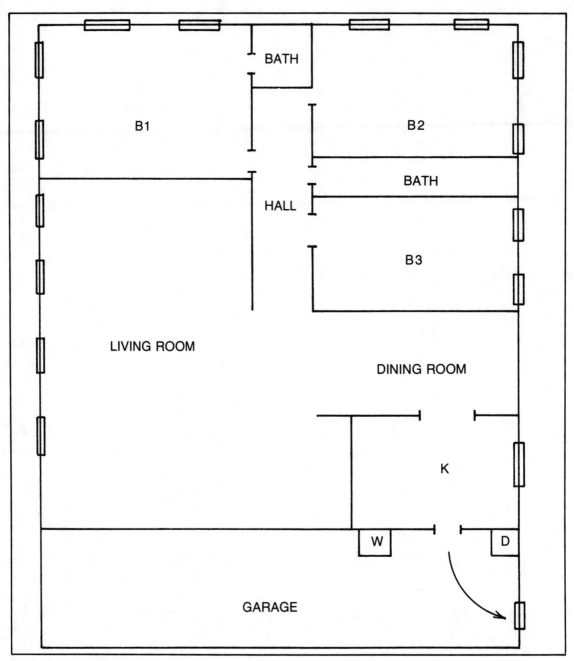

Fig. 3-16. Access schematic.

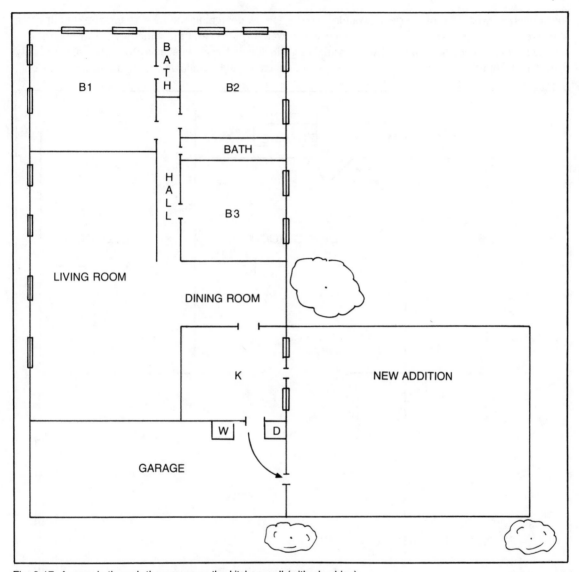

Fig. 3-17. Access is through the garage or the kitchen wall (with plumbing).

This leaves for your consideration the dining room, living room, family room, kitchen or (if you've lived right) any hall that dead ends at the appropriate wall. If you have a hall, cut a door and you're home free.

A dining room usually will provide a good access place. An exception is the house of some friends of ours. They not only had lovely, big sliding doors that made getting into the addition a cinch, they had a large concrete patio out those same doors plus an existing roof. Perfect, wouldn't you say? Well, not quite. While the dining room had been fairly dark to begin with, it got what available light it had from the porch.

In designing the new room, the dining room was forgotten and the windows are located at one short end, the farthest away from the door, and only narrow, high windows are in the other short end.

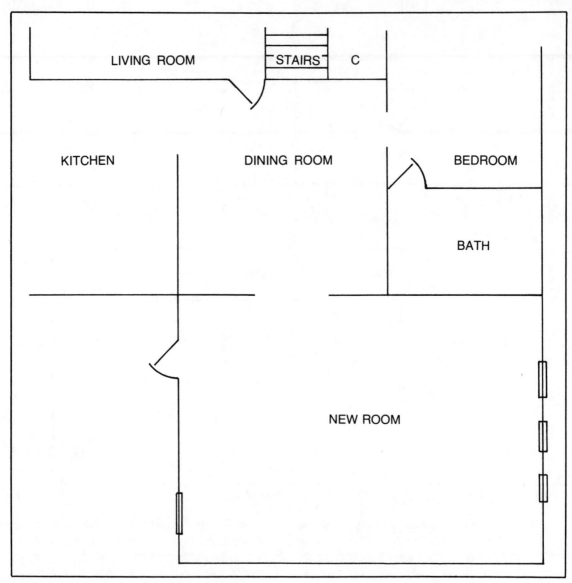

Fig. 3-18. A deep dark dungeon (our dining room).

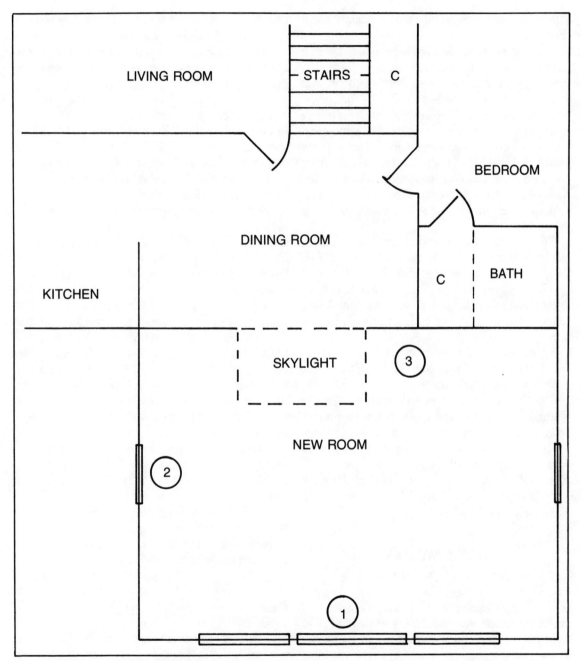

Fig. 3-19. What could have been done to help that poor dining room?

The result is a deep, dark dungeon dining room (Fig. 3-18).

This disaster could have been avoided with a little planning. If the windows had been located in the long wall, directly across from the door, that would have helped considerably (Fig. 3-19). In addition, a skylight could have been added to the dining room or just in front of the door in the new room and everything would have been lovely. Either of these solutions depended on the proposed use of the new room which, in this case, happened to be a studio. Had it been designed for a bedroom, the only real solution would have been adding a skylight in the dining area.

Living and family rooms lend themselves nicely to the task of providing access to an addition. They are usually fairly large and they usually have several windows. The only thing to watch for here is the location of the new door so that the living room or family room won't get a weird traffic pattern.

Kitchens are not desirable as access areas except in the case of a family room or dining room. But even those cases are dubious.

Bathrooms and bedrooms should be close to one another. Dining areas should be only a few feet away from the kitchen. A master bedroom can easily be located next to the living room party area because the people who sleep in the master bedroom will be cavorting at the parties. A family room/play room should be off the bedroom wing where the children sleep.

TRAFFIC PATTERNS

Traffic patterns are basically the way people and things move from one place to another in your home. The movement of things include getting in groceries, taking out trash, transporting laundry to and from the washer and dryer, and serving meals. These traffic problems are usually pretty obvious. When it comes to the movement of people we are often less aware of what causes the feeling of simmering annoyance or impatience.

Take the case of our walk-through kitchen. We like to have company when we are doing chores. By company, we mean one person in one place talking to us or giving a hand. The picture changes radically when that one stationary person becomes two or three people walking back and forth chasing cats and dogs, emptying and filling trays, or even just draped over every bit of our meager work space.

Sooner or later one of us will sweetly, or not so sweetly, depending on which of us is the chief cook at the time, yell for everyone except the helper to get out and stay out till dinner is ready. Notice the words *sooner* or *later* and *yell*. For quite a while we have gritted our teeth and hoped the traffic will stop snarling of its own accord. There is quite a bit of stress there.

The best way to identify and pin down potential traffic hurdles is by making some schematics of how the traffic is going to flow from the main house into the addition and out again. These can be quite crude (as in Figs. 3-20 through 3-21), but they will show you exactly what is going to happen. To make the patterns even more highly visible, use colored pens or crayons: red for people, blue for things, and green for pets.

Shifting a proposed door from a prominent center position to one side will often solve a lot of problems (Figs. 3-23 and 3-24). The creation of a small hallway is often very helpful (Figs. 3-22 and 3-25). In spite of what seems logical, too many outside doors can produce quite a traffic snarl. This is particularly true if there are children and the resulting traffic pattern is a circle.

Children adore these runarounds and they will ride their trucks and trikes on that course despite the most dire threats. They will also tear around on roller skates, run their racetrack through and, if all else fails, chase each other for hours. This is good entertainment for them if your nerves can take it. If at all possible, dead-end some room or rooms in the

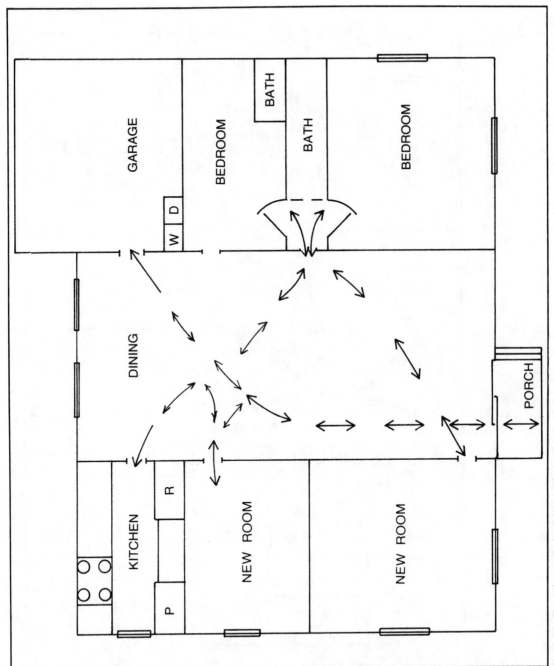

Fig. 3-20. The living room freeway number one.

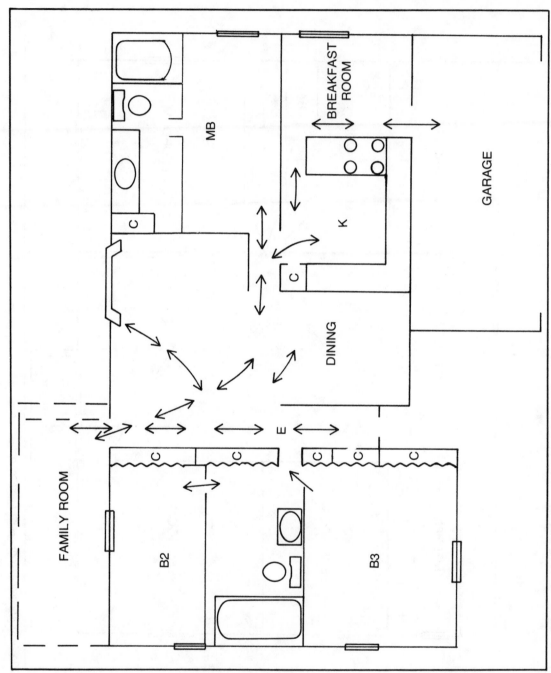

Fig. 3-21. Another version of a living room traffic snarl (number two).

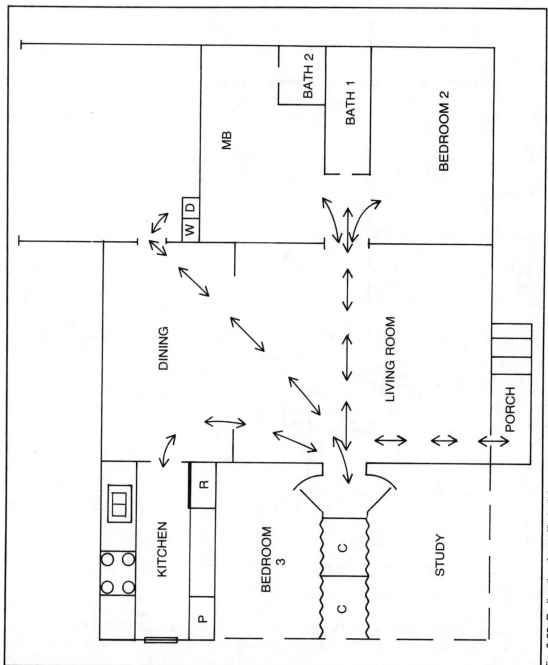

Fig. 3-22. Redirecting the traffic in living room number one.

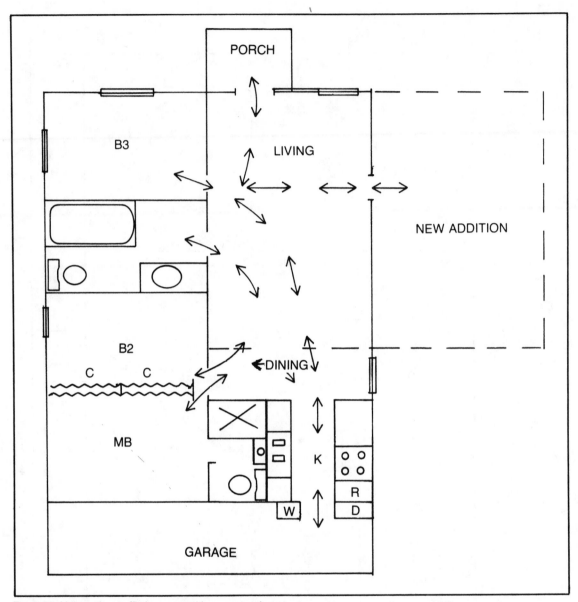

Fig. 3-23. Yet another traffic jam caused by a center door.

sitting/living area so you can talk, watch TV, entertain, or just relax without watching a constant parade go by.

UPSTAIRS/DOWNSTAIRS

As long as you are putting in an addition, you might as well consider a two-story one that will give you

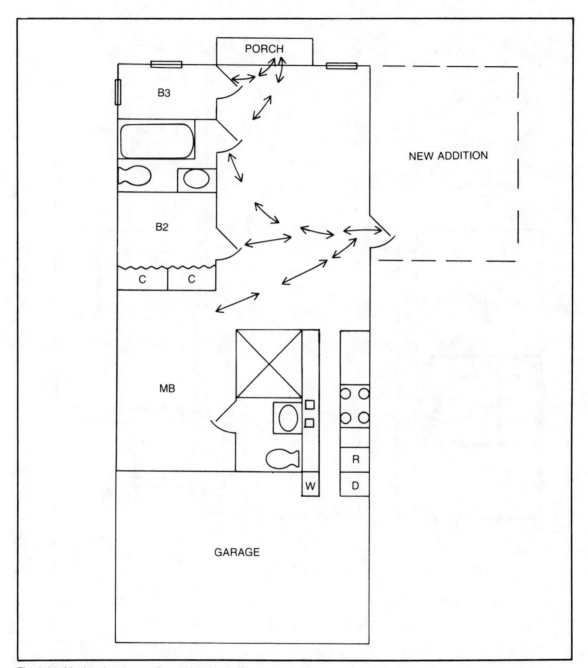

Fig. 3-24. Moving the door and rerouting the traffic.

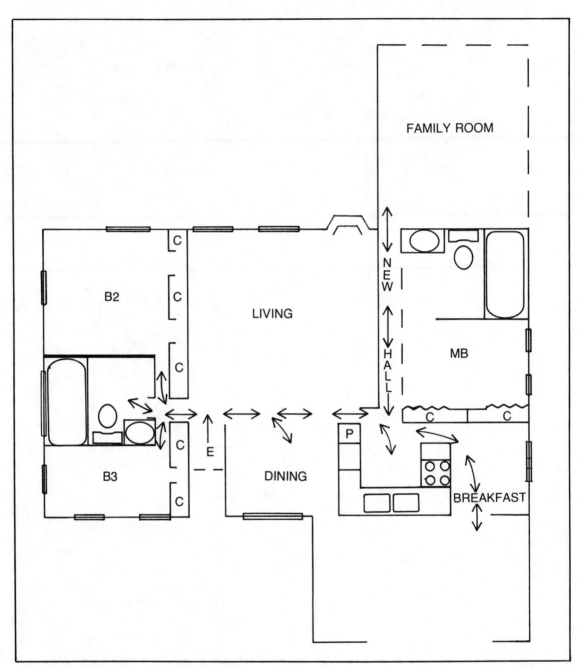

Fig. 3-25. How a new hallway reroutes the traffic.

double the space for approximately half again the cost. An even more radical step might be to think about adding a second story to your house. If you're less adventuresome, maybe you could raise the roof over your garage.

Another way of arriving at a two-story solution would be if your land sloped away from your house enough so that the addition's top floor would be level with your present structure and the extra space underneath. If you have a walk-out basement, you could add your room or rooms at that wall and again come up with a two-story addition.

When you add a second story you have to remember three very important things to keep the costs down and the traffic flowing:

☐ If you are going to have plumbing in the addition, plan to have it as close to the existing plumbing as possible. It is usually best to place it in the common wall between main house and the addition.

☐ The farther hot or cold air has to travel the more is wasted and the higher the cost.

☐ Allow enough space for a good-sized stairway and plan its location most carefully.

If you've never lived in a 2-story house, you'll be wise to pause and think about how things have to be moved up and down and down and up again. The steady movement of things from one floor to another can cause serious traffic blockage. Our stairway curves back on itself without a landing. Before you install such a stairway, think about the furnishings you want in that upper room. How are you going to get the stuff up there? In one house we lived in with just such a problem, we had to move the bed in through the window of the second story. That proved to be quite an adventure.

Plan your stairway so that you and your things and pets can use it in comfort and safety. If you don't have room for a landing at least make the stairway wide and not too steep.

The location of the stairway depends on how you plan to use the added space. Usually, having the stairway adjacent the main house makes access to the addition simpler and avoids using the new room as a glorified hallway to the new stairs.

A really nice thing to add, if you are going to have bedrooms upstairs, is a laundry chute. If you can, have it open either from the bedrooms or the bath. If it can end right above your washer, great, but even if it can't, and you have to terminate it in a closet somewhere on the main floor, it will still save a lot of trouble.

Another practical idea is a dumbwaiter. In case you are not familiar with the term, a dumbwaiter is a platform (in a shaft) that is pulled up or down. It's like a hand-propelled elevator that moves things, but not people. Dumbwaiters don't take up much room and they can be a real convenience.

DESIGN GOALS

It's time for your want lists. You have a pretty good idea of what you want, but as in the case of remodeling it is necessary to write down all you and your family hope to get in the new structure. Proceed exactly like you did before with each family member making lists. Consider possible alternatives to your most obvious solutions. It's amazing how many ways you can use a plain 18-×-12 addition or a 15-×-15 one, or a 24-×-12 foot marvel. Figures 3-26 through 3-32 will give you some ideas. These sketches are in rough, but you can hone them.

Make your own rough sketches. Make sure that you draw individual sketches for each room that you plan to add and for the room that is going to provide access to the addition as well. Compare, alter, combine, and shuffle the components until you've covered all the gripes and most of the wishes. Set it aside for a time, to simmer on the back burner of your mind, and pull it out after a week or so for further pursual. In the mean time, there's plenty to do looking for ways to design and tie the addition into the existing structure.

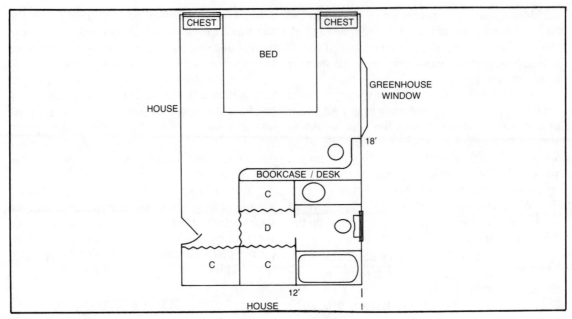

Fig. 3-26. An 18-×-12-foot addition (version number one, bedroom/bath).

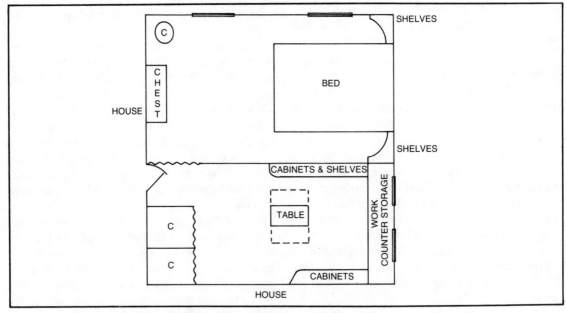

Fig. 3-27. An 18-×12-foot addition (version number two, bedroom/studio).

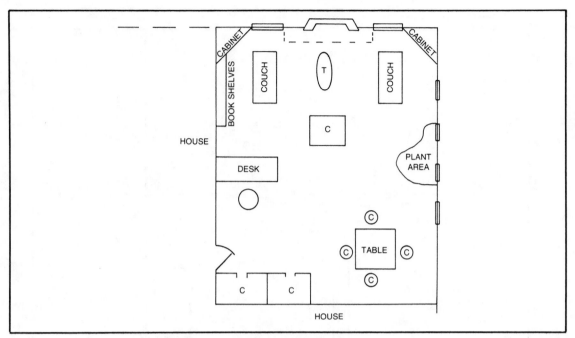

Fig. 3-28. An 18-×-12-foot addition (version number three, family room).

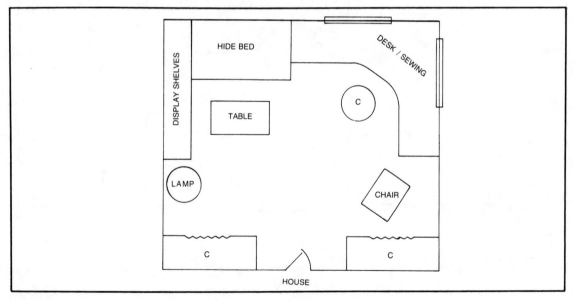

Fig. 3-29. A 15-×-15-foot addition (version number one, study/guest room).

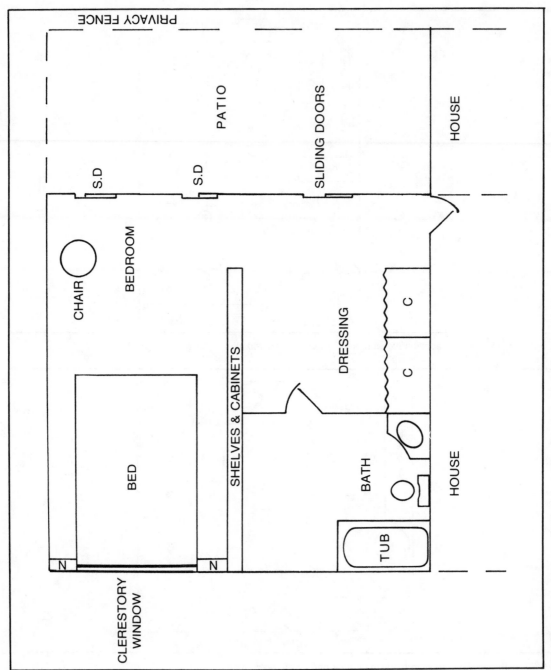

Fig. 3-30. A 15-×-15-foot addition (version number two, master suite).

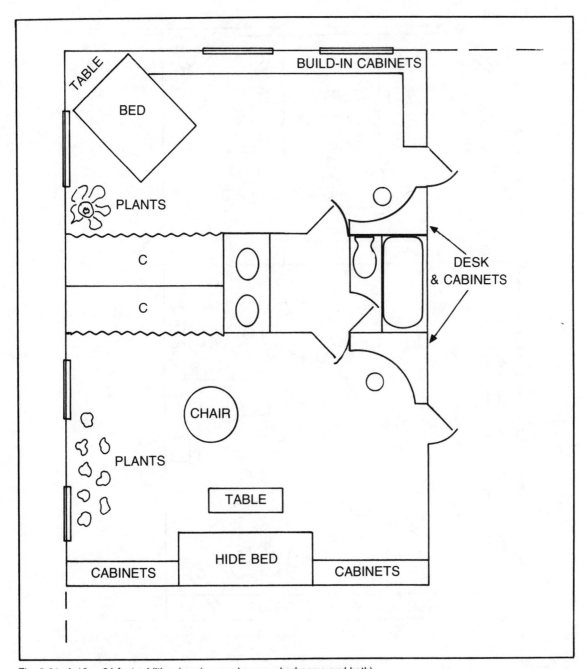

Fig. 3-31. A 12-×-24-foot addition (version number one, bedrooms and bath).

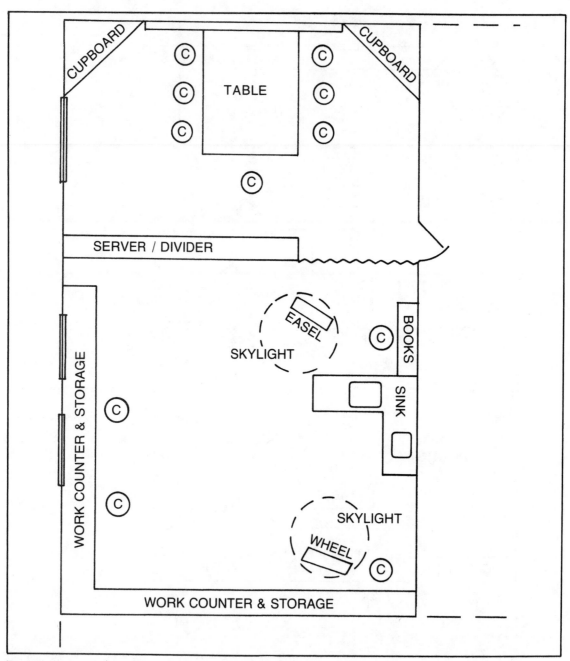

CUPBOARD

CUPBOARD

TABLE

Ⓒ Ⓒ Ⓒ Ⓒ Ⓒ Ⓒ Ⓒ

SERVER / DIVIDER

EASEL

SKYLIGHT

BOOKS

Ⓒ

SINK

WORK COUNTER & STORAGE

Ⓒ

Ⓒ

SKYLIGHT

WHEEL

Ⓒ

WORK COUNTER & STORAGE

Fig. 3-32. A 12-×-24-foot addition (version number two, dining room and studio combo).

TIEING INTO AN EXISTING STRUCTURE

Begin by considering the orientation of the new structure in relation to the original structure, the site, the sun, and the weather. You will need to make a drawing, accurate and to scale, showing the entire site under construction. Include the present building or buildings, all streets, alleyways, property lines, easements, location of utilities, and the location, size and type of all trees that can be saved. Contour lines will be needed unless the site is totally flat.

Once this information is in hand, look up all deed restrictions and local zoning ordinances at your city or town planning department and mark off on your drawing where your building must not intrude. With these limitations known, you are ready for the next most important element in orientation: the sun.

The most important orientation factor of any structure, original or add-on, is its relation to the sun. The effect of the sun on any building is determined by the latitude of the site and the time of year. You will find many references on file at your local library showing the horizontal and vertical angles of the sun at your latitude at different times of the year. In general, the vertical angle the sun makes with the ground is larger in summer than in winter and, in the Northern hemisphere, is larger in southern latitudes than in northern latitudes, at any given time of the year. The horizontal angle of the sun (between sunrise and sunset) is larger in summer than in winter, which is why summer is warmer than winter.

In order to work out the proper orientation of your add-on structure, you will want to work out the orientation of the add-on independent of the orientation of the present structure or any neighboring structures. For years builders have been orienting buildings "square" on their lots with no consideration at all to the sun, prevailing winds, etc. If a window wall turns up on the west exposed to the summer sun, so what? The electric company was always ready with another 2 tons of air conditioning to cool things down.

You can orient your tie-on structure so that it needs no additional air conditioning by drawing a view of the site and present building, a cross section of your add-on structure (drawn to scale), and the sun tables for your locality. You will need to establish three important aspects of your structure with these drawings and tables.

☐ The location and size of windows.

☐ The extent of the roof overhang above windows.

☐ The location of landscaping and/or sun screens to control the sun relative to your addition, the present structure, and any outdoor-living areas.

Use your drawings in conjunction with the sun tables as shown in Fig. 3-33. It is possible to determine the shadow line of the roof overhang at any time of day on any day of the year.

Here are some general facts to keep in mind while drawing plans for your additions. If windows face south and west, your addition will tolerate more of the sun's heat in northern latitudes than in southern latitudes. In southern latitudes, very little

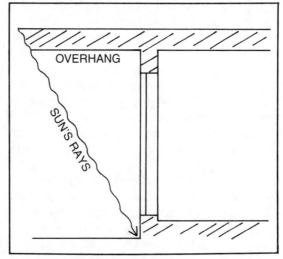

Fig. 3-33. Determining shadow line.

73

sunlight comes in from the north except in the early morning and late evening hours during the summertime. Because the sunlight in the morning is almost never objectionable, windows on the east side of your addition will probably be highly desirable. The western sun is almost always undesirable at any latitude in summer. Large windows facing west are almost never a good idea.

If there is a view to the west that just must be framed by a picture window, perhaps you can design an extensive overhang, use a sun screen, or plant some trees to shelter the window from too much glare.

Large windows on the south or an entire window wall on the south can give you the largest amount of heat energy from the sun in winter. By designing the south roof overhang properly, using your scale cross-section drawing and sun tables, it is possible to keep the sunlight entirely out in the summertime. You can even pick the date in the fall and spring you want to start and stop admission of the sun, and have it appear or disappear every year on that very date!

The landscaping around the building and proposed addition will have considerable effect on orientation. It can have a modifying effect on all of the above general rules. Large trees on a building lot allows tremendous versatility in orientation. Deciduous trees will admit winter sunlight and screen out summer sunlight.

Heat loss through window areas is an important consideration. Be wary of large windows on the north side if your area has strong north winds. If such windows are planned, you will need to specify double or triple glazing and plan to have the windows well draped.

Altitude and the proximity to large bodies of water should have a profound effect on your planning as far as orientation is concerned. This rule can be illustrated by considering the tale of three cities: San Francisco, Pueblo, and St. Louis: all are located at the same latitude (approximately 38°N). The sun angles will be the same for the three cities, but San Francisco, California has its weather moderated by the Pacific Ocean. As a result, the temperature range between winter and summer is small: there is negligible snowfall, average rainfall, and high humidity. Pueblo, Colorado is on a high plateau where the swing between winter and summer temperatures is very large; there is lots of snow, but little rain, and low humidity. St. Louis, Missouri, on the other hand, is in the wide Mississippi Valley where humidity is high and the yearly temperature variations is great; and they get frequent snowfalls. These differences in local weather conditions must be taken into account even though the latitude is a constant.

Other things must be considered when you are deciding on the orientation of your addition. You might like a lot of sunlight or none at all. Perhaps you like sunlight only in the morning or only in the afternoon. Perhaps you value privacy more than sunlight and a good view.

Other External Factors

Where heat loss through outside walls is of major concern in cold climates, the shape of the addition and its relation to grade level become important considerations. A square addition will have less wall space through which heat can be lost than a rectangular or rambling kind of addition. A geodesic dome addition will have the very least wall space for area enclosed. The dome provides the most efficient geometry for preventing excessive heat loss through walls. Another solution would be to build the lower half of the windward wall of your addition below grade. Berm, or so-called underground construction, can reduce the cost of summer air conditioning as well as winter heating bills.

Consider putting the entire addition below grade level. You do not necessarily need to excavate for this. You can bring your grade level up to the roof line with 5 to 10 feet of earth against your walls and accomplish the same savings.

Don't overlook such considerations as designing your roof to carry heavy loads if your area is noted for its heavy snowfalls. Include gutters, downspouts, insulation, and weather stripping.

Structural Principles

Once you have decided on the orientation of a new addition you will need to draw some plans showing how to tie into the existing structure. Some attention needs to be given to a few simple structural principles.

It is much more helpful to think of the structural components of any building as parts that work together to transfer loads down to the ground. They should not be considered only members that hold the building up. The structural integrity of any building is determined by the *continuity* of its load bearing members from roof to ground.

Any building, from a hut to a skyscraper, consists of four main parts: The load carrying continuity begins with the weight of the protective *roof.* The roof must carry down to the *vertical supports* that enclose the structure and carry the load downward to the *floor.* The weight of people, furniture, etc., is added and passed downward to the *foundation* where the total load is transmitted to the ground.

Building engineers define two supporting systems in a building: the *horizontal supporting system* (floors and nearly flat roofs) and the *vertical supporting system* (walls, columns, and foundations). The structural components of each of these systems has a different function in transferring its loads downward. It is important that the structure you are adding on has the same type of construction as the original building. You will find that your existing structure will be one of three kinds: framed with columns and beams, load-bearing walls supporting roof and floors, or so-called light-frame construction (a combination of the other two).

Most high-rise buildings and many smaller buildings are framed with steel columns and beams.

The loads of the structure are transferred through the steel frame downward. The floor loads are transferred through the columns to the foundations. The walls perform no supportive or load-bearing function. They are often referred to as *curtain walls.*

Many brick and masonry structures make use of the walls as load-bearing members instead of "curtains" for privacy or to retain the heat or air conditioning. In this type of structure, the walls and partitions transfer the weight of the roof and floors to the foundation all along the whole length of the wall. Obviously, the number and size of openings in these supporting walls is very limited. Large openings will mean that the builder must go to a post-and-beam type of construction around the opening so that the loads can be transferred across the beam to the columns supporting the beam and down to the point supports of the columns.

A building of light-frame construction using slim structural members, such as 2-×-4 studs spaced close together, is a combination of the post-and-beam and bearing-wall structure. By positioning the studs close together and nailing sheathing on to brace them, a "curtain" wall is converted into a load-bearing wall. If all the walls are constructed this way and openings are kept relatively small, the walls can transfer the roof and floor loads to the foundation very nicely.

Two light-framing methods are currently in use for most residential structures: the *balloon frame,* and the *western frame.* The balloon frame is used most often for two-story houses that are to be faced with brick or stucco. It uses 2-×-4 studs that run vertically from the foundation to the roof. The frame is not rigid (thus the name "balloon frame"). It must make use of diagonal bracing or plywood sheathing for its rigidity.

The western frame is actually the simplest method of construction and in wide use in the building trades today. In this type of construction, the entire subfloor is constructed first. Then the walls are fabricated horizontally on the floor. Next, they are tilted up, plumbed straight, and nailed to the subfloor.

ROOF EXTENSIONS

Roof extensions for additions, like all other aspects of extending an existing structure, need to be compatible with the existing structure and the climate. The load the roof must support and transfer involves the pressures of a driving rain, powerful wind forces, and the weight of snow. In most northern climates, the snow load is the most significant factor. Snow loads of 20 to 30 psf (pounds per square foot) are not uncommon in many areas of the northern United States. The load will, of course, depend on the pitch of the roof. If the roof slopes steeply, the snow will tend to slide off. Therefore, the design load for steeply pitched roofs is less than for those that slope more gently.

The pitch of a roof is a ratio between the *rise* and the *run* of the roof. If the run is a 10-foot rafter that rises 5 feet, then the slope is said to be 1 to 2. If expressed in inches, as is sometimes the case, it would be 6 to 12.

Check your local building code for the allowable load figures in relation to pitch. A flat roof will have a wide variation of design loads. Much depends on the climate and whether or not it is to carry the weight of human traffic or recreational or gardening activities.

Although there are many roof configurations in use in contemporary building today, the three most common shapes are the *gable roof,* with an attic underneath, the gable or *shed roof* without an attic, and the *flat roof.*

Whatever roof design you are contemplating, you will need a roof plan similar to the one illustrated in Fig. 3-34. We recommend that you sketch a plan and an elevation of the existing roof and the proposed new roof over the addition. Show how the two will tie together. Draw both at no smaller than ½″ scale. On the plan, be sure to show the double plates of the top floor that support load-bearing walls and partitions. You will then want to draw a section like the one represented in Fig. 3-35. You may want to modify the pitch of the roof so as to use your lumber most economically. Joist-rafter stock is sold in increments of 2 feet. Remember that the total length of your rafters will include the span plus the overhang.

WALL EXTENSIONS

Most wall frame construction you will be dealing with will consist of 2-×-4 studs, about 7½″ long running vertically between a horizontal 2-×-4, called a *sole plate,* on the subfloor and a pair of plates on the top.

Plywood sheething is usually used to brace the wall framed by 2-×-4 studs. Studs are traditionally spaced so that the center of one stud is exactly 16 inches from the center of the next stud (or 16-inch spacing "on center"). Although studs can be spaced 24 inches apart if the wall is to carry only its own weight—or 12 inches on center if it is to carry an exceptionally heavy load—most architects design their walls with 16″ on-center spacing. This works most efficiently in almost all cases.

The space between studs is usually filled with insulating material, which comes in a standard 4 inch thickness. Insulation comes in "blankets 15 inches wide so as to fit snugly between studs. Figure 3-36 shows typical standard wall design and construction.

FLOOR AND FOUNDATION EXTENSIONS

Floor extensions and designs have a lot in common with roof extensions and designs. Loads and the transfer of loads structural members are the most important considerations even though the loads on a floor are substantially heavier.

The use of concrete floors is fairly common for the first floor of a house without basements, but we do not recommend that you design an extension of one of these floors unless it is going to be poured by an experienced, professional builder. A wood plat-

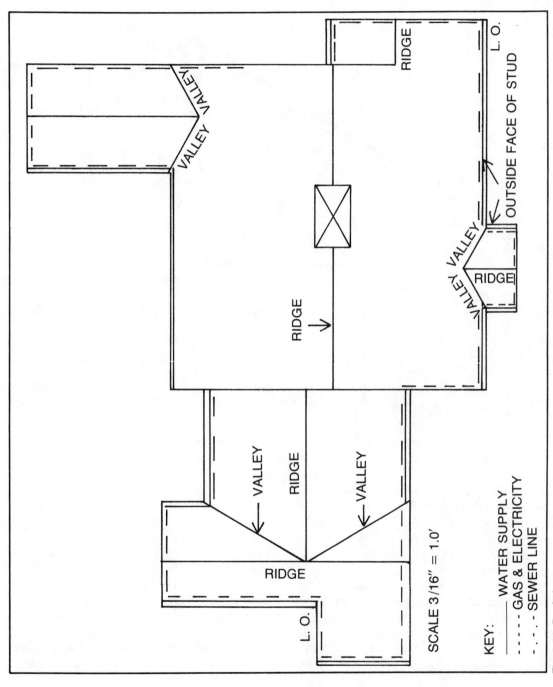

Fig. 3-34. Roof plan.

KEY:
— WATER SUPPLY
- - - - GAS & ELECTRICITY
- · - · - SEWER LINE

SCALE 3/16″ = 1.0′

RIDGE

VALLEY VALLEY

L. O.

OUTSIDE FACE OF STUD

VALLEY VALLEY VALLEY

RIDGE

RIDGE

VALLEY

RIDGE

VALLEY

RIDGE

L. O.

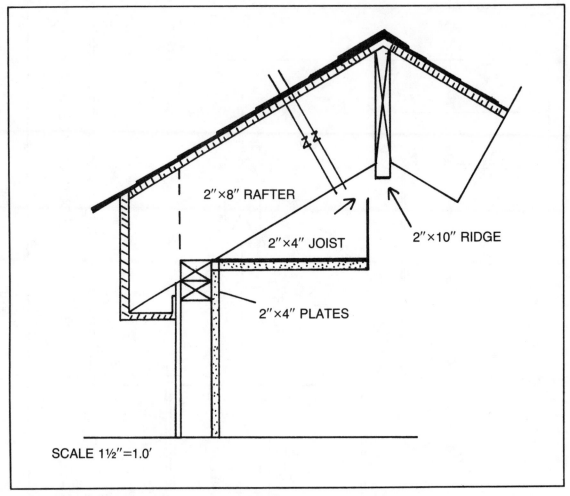

2″×8″ RAFTER

2″×4″ JOIST

2″×10″ RIDGE

2″×4″ PLATES

SCALE 1½″=1.0′

Fig. 3-35. Section through cornice.

form floor is simple to construct and easy to design and draw plans for. It can be used as an extension of a concrete floor very nicely.

In the design of a wood platform floor, keep in mind that each component of the floor works to transfer the weight placed on it to the ground through the foundation. The floorboards receive the weight and transfer it to the joists. The joists transfers the weight to the girders or beams which,

in turn, transfer the loads to the foundation. The foundation unloads on the footings that place the entire load on solid ground.

A platform floor should be a platform on which you can frame and erect walls and partitions. It will consist of a subfloor (the finished floor will be installed only after nearly all other construction is complete) usually made of sheets of plywood nailed to the floor joists. The joists are long, horizontal

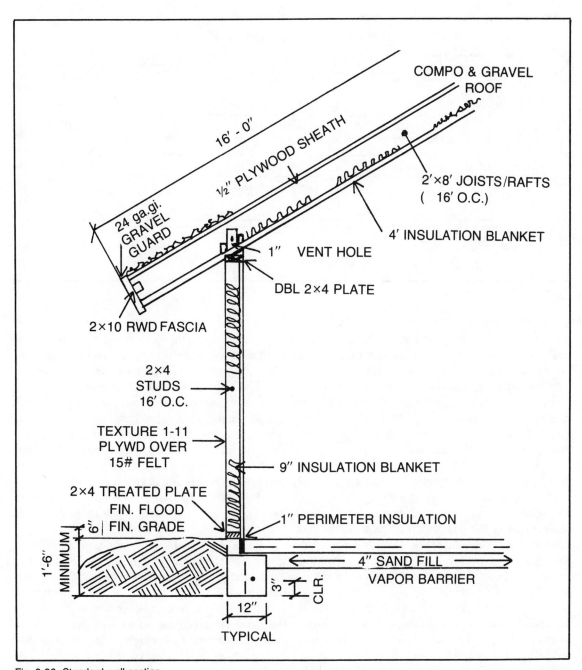

COMPO & GRAVEL ROOF

16' - 0"

1/2" PLYWOOD SHEATH

2'×8' JOISTS/RAFTS (16' O.C.)

24 ga.gl. GRAVEL GUARD

4' INSULATION BLANKET

1" VENT HOLE

DBL 2×4 PLATE

2×10 RWD FASCIA

2×4 STUDS 16' O.C.

TEXTURE 1-11 PLYWD OVER 15# FELT

9" INSULATION BLANKET

2×4 TREATED PLATE
FIN. FLOOD
FIN. GRADE

1" PERIMETER INSULATION

6"

1'-6" MINIMUM

4" SAND FILL

VAPOR BARRIER

3"

CLR.

12"

TYPICAL

Fig. 3-36. Standard wall section.

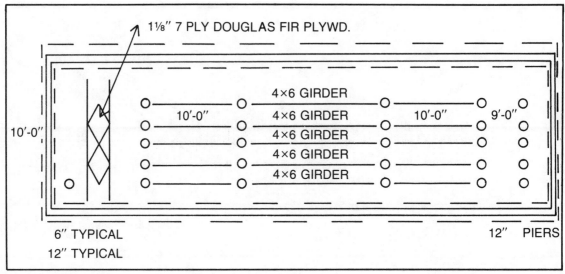

Fig. 3-37. Floor framing plan.

structural members spaced either 12, 16, or 24 inches apart on center, similar to the spacing for wall studs. As with wall studs, the spacing depends on the load to be carried (16″ on center is the most common spacing). Beams or girders, the heavy structural members on which the floor joists rest, are spaced as much as 8 to 10 feet apart. The spacing will determine the configuration of the foundation supporting them.

A rule of thumb used by architects says that 10 feet is the maximum practical length for a wood girder. The total width or length of an addition must be divided by some factor so that no girder is longer than 10 feet. A 14-foot addition, for example, should have two sections of girders, each 7 feet long. A floor framing plan (Fig. 3-37) will show where the foundation piers would go under such a floor.

Foundations can take many forms, but where you are extending a foundation it is usually best (and easiest) to use the foundation method employed under the building from which extensions are being made. In order for a structure to be firmly rooted in the ground, it will be necessary to transfer its loads

in two basic ways: either by *point loading* or by *uniform loading*. In contemporary construction, point loading is done from piles or piers and uniform loading is done from continuous foundation walls.

The foundation wall is the most durable. It rests on a footing that is a continuous base around the perimeter of the structure. The loads of the roof, walls, and floors are uniformly distributed along the foundation walls that transmit them to the earth. Continuous foundations can be either poured concrete or concrete blocks.

Piers are built on normal soils, either cast or laid in place, and transmit the loads to the ground at various points.

Piles are used mostly for construction in marshy land and in water. They are driven into the earth, and preferably down to bedrock. They are often made out of chemically treated tree trunks.

Now that we've worked our way down through the foundation, you should be on solid ground to start planning and designing an addition. Now you can start on your way to making some very professional-looking house plans.

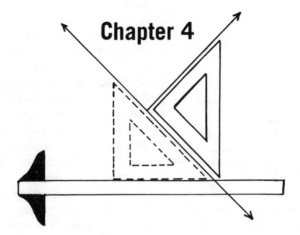

Chapter 4

How to Make Scale Drawings

TRYING TO DRAW HOUSE PLANS WITHOUT THE proper drawing tools will lead to a lot of frustration and a messy result. But don't worry. The drawing tools you'll need are inexpensive. You'll need only a few to begin with and you can add extras.

TOOLS

You'll need a drawing board, but there's no need to trot to the nearest art supply store and plunk down a bundle for their prefab deluxe model. Just consult the Appendix of this book and you'll find three versions of drawing boards.

Alternatives would be to use a large cutting board or a wide shelf of the proper dimensions. Make sure that the sides of the board are straight so that your T-square will ride properly. Also check the angles at the corners; at least two of them must be 90 degrees (Fig. 4-1).

It's nice to have a drawing surface that slants.

You can use the stands described in the Appendix. If you use an improvised board, you can prop up one end with something of the suitable height. We have found that telephone books or catalogs will work in a pinch. There is no law that you have to work on a slanted board. If you like, you can have your board nice and flat on the table top and we won't say a word.

You can use any kind of paper that's heavy enough to take a nice line and that will allow you to erase. For your sketches and excercises you might like to try regular white duplicating paper. Such paper is usually the least expensive available other than newsprint and light manila, which isn't suitable. For work drawings, you can get regular drawing paper in sheets or rolls. Select paper that has enough grain to take a pencil line readily, a hard surface so it won't be easily grooved by your pencil, and lets you erase your mistakes without anguish or hard labor.

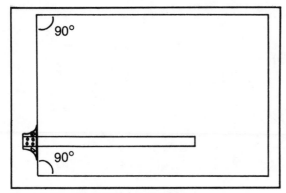

Fig. 4-1. Drawing board and T-square.

You'll need something to attach your paper to the drawing board. You can use thumb tacks, drawing pins or drafting tape. Thumb tacks are readily available and easy to use. If you're careful and use the more expensive ones, with thin heads and steel points, you won't have any problem. Map pins have a tendency to loose their heads at the slightest tug. So use them only in emergencies.

Drafting tape has been designed specifically for the purpose of attaching paper to drawing boards. While drafting tape looks like a twin to regular masking tape, don't be fooled by appear-

ances. Drafting tape comes off the drawing paper easily and cleanly. Masking tape might stick or leave a residue.

The T-square (Fig. 4-2) is the staple of drawing house plans. You can get T-squares in various length, weights, and prices. While a professional draftsman will do well by investing in a super-duper-extra-deluxe version of this basic tool, you can do well with a quite moderately priced one. Expensive T-squares are made out of hardwood and they are often steel edged. The costly models have an adjustable head square that the ordinary person never needs. Some more expensive models are equipped with transparent edges.

On par in importance with the T-square, and used in conjunction with it continually, are the triangles. Triangles are usually made out of clear plastic and they should be stored flat to prevent warping.

We like the kind of triangles that are calibrated; they save a lot of time because you can draw and measure at the same time. We also love the kind of triangles that are marked in inches along one side and in metric on the other. Even if you have never used metric measurements and are only hazily aware of the conversions, you'll find that you can be

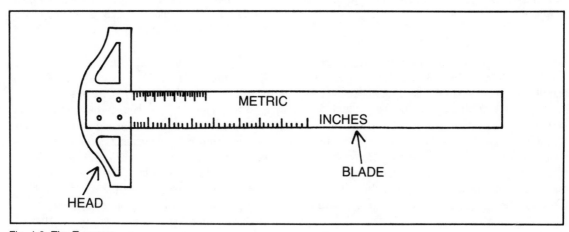

Fig. 4-2. The T-square.

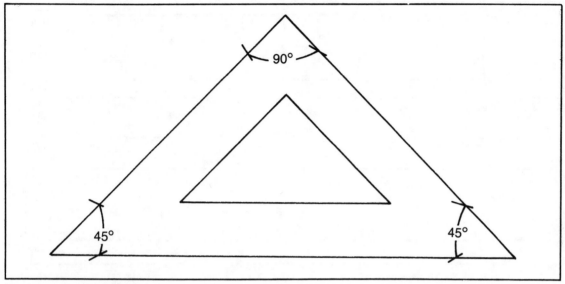

Fig. 4-3. A 45-degree triangle.

much more accurate if you use the metric scale for measuring. The metric increments are much smaller and, because measuring is based on the 10 scale, you never have to experience that sinking feeling that we often used to get when we tried to measure a fifth or a tenth of an inch.

You'll need at least two triangles: one that has 45-degree angles and one that has 30- 60-degree angles. The triangles can be bought in 6-inch, 8-inch and 10-inch sizes. We find the 8-inch size quite satisfactory. See Figs. 4-3 and 4-4.

You'll need what most people term rulers, but what the purists of the drawing world refer to as *scales*. For simple measuring you can use any regular ruler you pick up at a variety store. We do recommend that you select one with steel edges. The plastic kind tends to nick and curve before you have it out of the sack.

Scales refer to the calibration rather than the instrument. In the U.S., we are in the process of converting to metric like most of the rest of the world. In the meantime, you will still find many

rulers marked off in inches along one side and centimeters on the other side. As with your triangles, it is really easier to draw accurately if you use the metric divisions for measuring. If you use your ruler with the dual scale, you'll have an instant equivalent measurement either way (Figs. 4-5 and 4-6).

Architect's scales are usually esoteric to the nondrafting community. Such scales are three sided

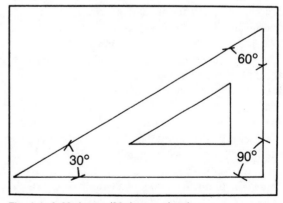

Fig. 4-4. A 60-degree/30-degree triangle.

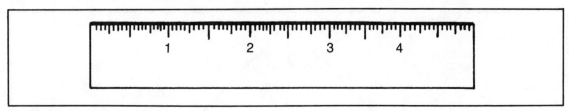

Fig. 4-5. A ruler with inch calibration.

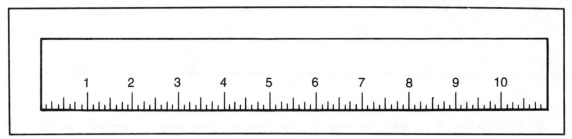

Fig. 4-6. A ruler with metric calibration.

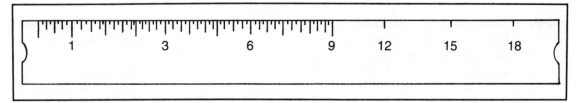

Fig. 4-7. Architects rule with an "open divided scale."

and each surface has its own use. As to calibration, architects' scales are divided into proportional feet and inches. These scales have divisions indicating 1/8, 1/4, 3/8 1/2, 3/4, 1½, and 3 inches to the foot. They are usually "open divided" which means that the units are shown along the entire length, but only the end units are subdivided into inches and fractions (Fig. 4-7).

Civil engineers' scales are divided into decimals with 10, 20, 30, 40, 50, 60, and 80 divisions to the inch. They are used mainly for plotting maps, but they can be used whenever you need to divide an inch by tenth. We feel that a simple metric/inch ruler will do just as well. Other tools that are nice to

have are curved rulers that are usually referred to simply as curves or "French curves." You need them if you want to draw a curved line that is not a circle arc. The pattern of these curves are parts of ellipses and spirals as well as other mathematical curves in various combinations. To use them, you take the peck and hunt approach. You keep trying various portions of your French curve in the space to be drawn until you hit upon the one you need. It's much easier done than said and quite helpful. Also, it gives your drawings that last finished look. The cost for a French curve is only a dollar or so.

To draw a decent circle you need a decent compass. As you very well know, you can pick up a compass at a local drugstore for about 50 cents. These contraptions have a small pencil attached at one side with a small screwed on band. Whatever you do, don't buy one of these. They are an abomination to anybody who strives for even minimal accuracy.

A decent *pencil compass* need not be expensive. Usually you'll find a good one for two or three dollars. A pencil compass, in this connotation *does not* refer to an actual pencil attached to your compass. It means the pencil point that is inserted in one leg of the compass. Often these pencil compasses have an extra steel point that you can put in instead of the pencil point. This transforms your compass into a divider (Figs. 4-8 and 4-9). A 6-inch model is great.

You use dividers to transfer accurate measurements, to divide into segments (particularly on a curve), and to indicate very accurate positions.

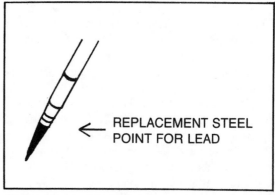

Fig. 4-9. Transforming a compass into a divider by replacing lead with a second steel point.

Some compasses and dividers have extension pieces, cross-set screws called *bows,* and pen attachments. These compasses are usually beautifully made and a joy to use. They are also quite expensive. Because you won't be using the pen attachment or the extension bars, there is little reason for the added costs.

Pencils are graded with a number and a letter. The grading is according to hardness. The H series, that is H, 2H and so forth up to 9H, proceeds logically from medium hard to hardest. The process is inverted when it comes to the B series. This series goes from 6B (very soft) through B, HB, and finally F (which is the middle). Then you pick up good old H and sanity again.

The soft B grades are primarily used for sketches and rendered drawings. The H family is preferred for instrument drawing. The more involved and exact the drawing the higher the H. You will be well equipped if you have one or two specimens from the B line plus a couple of Hs (but not harder than 4H). Even 4H is fairly fine and it leaves a deep mark on the paper when you try to erase it. It does, however, make a nice accurate line.

In addition to the usual wood-encased lead pencils, semiautomatic drawing pencils are available. The lead tips are graded exactly like the ordi-

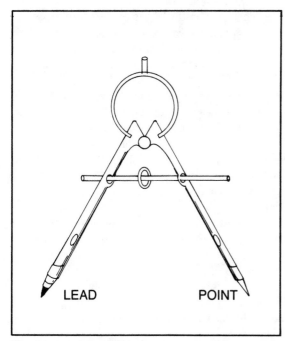

Fig. 4-8. A compass/divider.

nary pencils and are interchangeable within the same pencil. Some of these automatic pencils have a built-in point sharpener. This is a blessing and so is an attached eraser at the other end.

There are some small accessories that are quite inexpensive and they give you a lot of comfort and convenience. The first and most important of those is your trusty eraser. You'll need several erasers for separate functions. A ruby pencil eraser, the large size with bevelled edges, is the standard model. It not only removes pencil lines like a breeze, but is actually more efficient than so-called ink erasers because it will, with a little elbow grease, remove the ink from paper or cloth without chewing up the paper or cloth in the process. The other kind of eraser you'll need is an Artgum eraser to clean up your paper when you're done and remove any finger marks or smears. Another kind of eraser is a secretary's pencil eraser. This type looks like a pencil and you unwind it slowly as needed. The tip can be sharpened. The kind we use has a white eraser base that easily takes off thin and heavy lines. We find it particularily handy for small alterations. You can erase precisely the spot you want without disturbing the rest. It is very useful when you do your lettering.

There is another kind of eraser that comes in a plastic case shaped like a pencil. This one is red gum like the ruby eraser. While the shape is handy, it doesn't do quite as nice a job as our white favorite.

A neat gadget that complements your eraser collection is an erasing shield. It consists of clear plastic that has cutouts on it: curves, straight lines, circles, wedges, what have you. You select whatever shape it is that your mistake resembles the closest, put your shield over the rest, and erase away. Not only does it protect your other lines from becoming extinct by association, but it also prevents extra finger and hand prints on the paper. You hold the eraser shield down with one hand and touch it instead.

You'll need some kind of a pencil sharpener.

We prefer the small hand-held pencil sharpener that has two different-sized openings. While it is a bit more awkward than the wall model, we find we can get just the kind of point we want on our pencils without breaking them off. The trick is to start the sharpening process in the larger opening and then finish off in the smaller one.

If you're really a nut about getting a proper point on a pencil—and those highly trained draftsmen and mechanical drawing specialists will tell you that you need different points for different jobs such as a flat or wedge point for straight line work or a conical point for curves—you'll need two more gadgets. One such tool is a small sandpaper pad with a wooden handle. The other is a file; a nail file will do.

To get a wedge point, sharpen a pencil as usual and then use a pen knife or an X-Acto knife, and make two long cuts, on opposite sides of the pencil, flattening the end of the lead with sandpaper or a file. Then trim in the edges of the tip to make the wedge point narrower than the diameter of the lead.

For a conical point, proceed with the mechanical sharpening and than refine the point with sandpaper or a file.

Keep your pencils sharp. It makes quite a difference in the width of the line. Sometimes you have to worry about such things in a finished plan. Make a habit of it from the start. Get rid of graphite and wood shavings immediately. If you leave them on a desk or drawing table, they can smear your drawings, hands, clothes, and whatever else is in range.

To put paper on a drawing board, use a T-square to ensure that the paper will be parallel to board. This is essential because otherwise you won't have a line parallel to the edge of your paper. If the paper is much smaller than your board move it within 3 or 4 inches of the left edge of the board and several inches up from the bottom edge. A T-square will be most stable and rigid as close to the head as possible while it flips around a bit at the other end.

Get close to the source. As to the distance from the bottom of the board, you need room to slide your T-square down below the edge of your paper if you want to draw a line near the bottom of the paper.

Put your T-square on top of your paper with the head riding on the left edge of your board. Carefully adjust the paper so that the top edge is even with your T-square. Gently pull the T-square down a few inches and secure the top corners with thumb tacks or drafting tape. Repeat the maneuver for the bottom edge of the paper, but this time pull your T-square up instead of down (that is onto the paper not off it) before you secure the bottom corners. Now it should be all nice and square (Figs. 4-10, 4-11 and 4-12).

While you can learn to perform this little drill in a few moments, one of us—who is notorious about trying to find short cuts and absolutely abhors wasting time and energy—has come up with this idea. You proceed as stated, but instead of putting on paper and tape you pull down the T-square and draw a good, dark line along it with a thin-point marker. You do the same at the bottom. Next you measure in 4 inches from the left edge of the board, top and bottom line, and connect the marks with a straight line. Put a piece of drawing paper on the

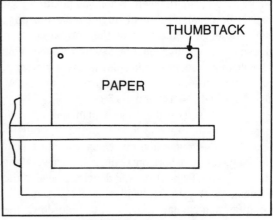

Fig. 4-11. Fastening corners with thumbtacks.

board between the lines and mark off the right-hand edge top and bottom line again. Connect these marks. Presto! You have a permanent frame in which to position your drawing paper without going through the entire routine each time. It works like a charm if you're extra careful when you put your lines on the board and make the lines as thin as possible.

A variation on the theme is to proceed as above, but use colored plastic tape for the framing.

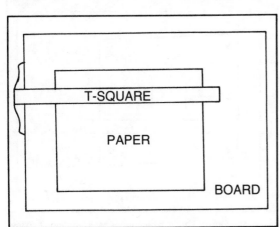

Fig. 4-10. Aligning paper with a T-square.

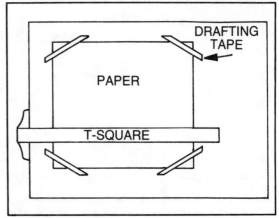

Fig. 4-12. Fastening paper with drafting tape.

Make sure it adheres well. When you position your paper, be consistent about aligning the top edge with top edge of the tape or the bottom edge. It doesn't matter which, but don't switch around. This is even more crucial on the sides where a quarter of an inch can certainly cause your paper to be askew. See Figs. 4-13, 4-14, and 4-15.

Your T-square does more than line up your paper on your drawing board. Actually, your T-square is the foundation on which you start your drawing. All your horizontal lines are drawn along the T-square. To do this, hold down the head of the T-square with your left hand, slide the T-square in position, and change your hand to hold down the extension while the right hand holds the pencil and draws the line along the edge of the T-square.

When you draw a line along the T-square, slant the pencil in the direction you are drawing the line (to the right) and keep the point of the pencil as close to the T-square as possible. This is important. Hold your pencil lightly, but close to the edge of the T-square and do not vary the angle at which you hold it till you come to the end of the line. It's always amazing to us how far off you can get from the straight and true by not observing the above proce-

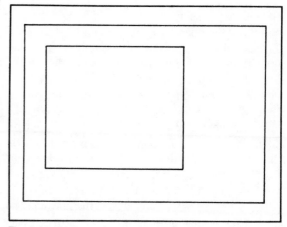

Fig. 4-14. Taping a drawing board for paper position.

dures. That can mean a lot of erasing and doing things over.

If you're left handed just reverse the procedure. Put the head of your T-square along the right-hand edge of your board, draw your lines toward the left—again slanting your pencil in the direction in which you're drawing—(to the left), while keeping the point of the pencil as close to the T-square as possible.

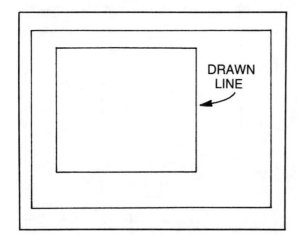

Fig. 4-13. Putting permanent position lines on a drawing board.

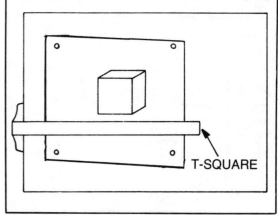

Fig. 4-15. Oops! That's what happens if you don't follow directions.

88

T-squares do more than help you draw horizontal lines. They provide a base for drawing verticals as well. To do this, use your triangles. Let them ride on top of your T-square with the perpendicular edge nearest the head of the T-square and toward the light. (Don't try to draw in the shadow of your hand). Draw your perpendicular or vertical lines from the bottom (of the T-square) up to the top. See Fig. 4-16.

When you draw these verticals along the straight edge of your triangle, you have to anchor your T-square against the board with your left thumb and little finger while the rest of the fingers of your left hand adjust and hold the triangle in position. Your right hand, of course is occupied with holding and guiding the pencil. To make sure that you have the proper contact with the board before you start your line, listen for the double clicking sound that means that the board and T-square head have connected. It will take only a slight pressure of the thumb and little finger toward the right to hold the T-square in place. When you draw that vertical line, the pressure of all your fingers will not only

hold the T-square, but also the triangle in place. Actually it's all quite simple. In this case a try is worth a thousand words. So go do it.

Be sure that, as you draw your vertical line, you keep your pencil point as close to your triangle as possible. Just as with the T-square, the triangle has to be securely aligned with its guiding edge, which is the T-square. Please don't let it flop around and expect exact work. Another trick to ensure accuracy is to keep the T-square below the lower end of the line that you are drawing. That avoids working at the extreme corner of the triangle.

There's quite a lot more that your good old T-square and triangle combo can do. If you want to draw lines at a 45-degree angle to the T-square, all you have to do is put your 45-degree triangle on the T-square and draw along the angled end. For your 30-degree and 60-degree angle, proceed likewise with your 30- and 60-degree triangle. See Figs. 4-17 and 4-18.

If you want to be really fancy and draw 15-degree, 75-degree, or even 105-degree angles, you can do that too. You can draw any angle that is a

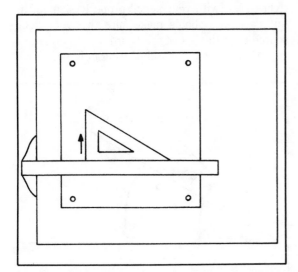

Fig. 4-16. Using a T-square and a triangle to draw perpendicular lines.

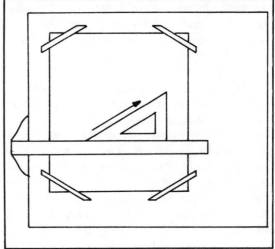

Fig. 4-17. Using a T-square and a 45-degree triangle to draw slanted lines.

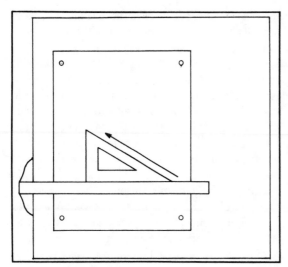

Fig. 4-18. Using a T-square and a 60-degree/30-degree triangle to draw slanted lines.

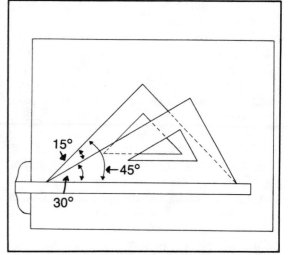

Fig. 4-19A. Constructing a 15-degree angle.

multiple of 15 degrees by using your two triangles in combination with your T-square. See Figs. 4-19A, 4-19B, and 4-20.

You can draw any number of parallel lines by using your T-square and your triangle. Hold your triangle against the line you want to make a parallel line to, hold your straightedge as a guideline, and slide your triangle along the guideline until it is in position for drawing the new line. See Figs. 4-21 and 4-22.

To draw a perpendicular line, place the triangle with one edge against the T-square. In a tight place it is sometimes easier to place the triangle against another triangle. Keeping the base steady, rotate the triangle and move it into the perpendicular position (Fig. 4-23). A shortcut would be to set the triangle with the hypotenuse against the guiding edge, fit one side to the line, slide the triangle to the required point, and draw the perpendicular as in Fig. 4-24.

When working with triangles be sure that your light source comes from the right or you'll be working in your own shadow. If you're left handed.

reverse all the instructions about holding down the T-square and the triangle so that your right hand is doing the holding against the right edge of the board and your left hand is free to do the drawing from right to left with your pencil properly slanted. In this case, you should make sure that your light source is to the left of the board.

Measuring and marking accurately isn't a bit

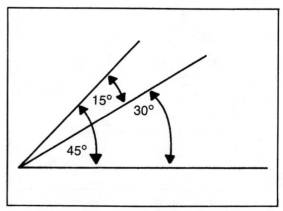

Fig. 4-19B. Detail of 15-degree angle construction.

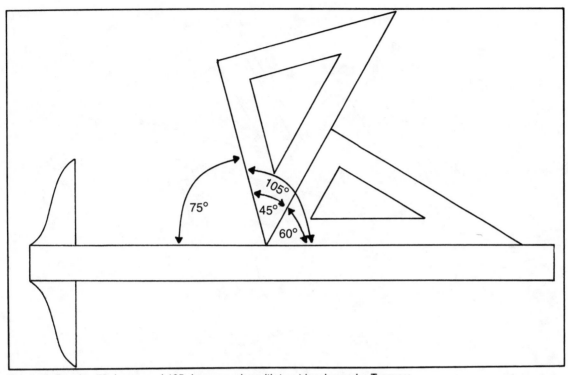

Fig. 4-20. Drawing 75-degree and 105-degree angles with two triangles and a T-square.

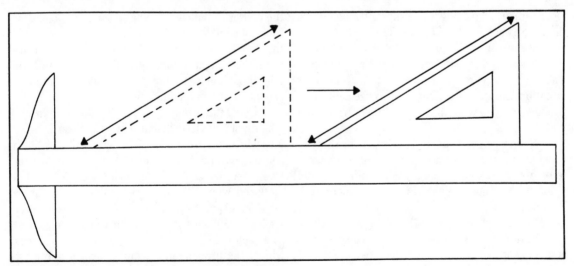

Fig. 4-21. Drawing parallel lines with a triangle and a T-square.

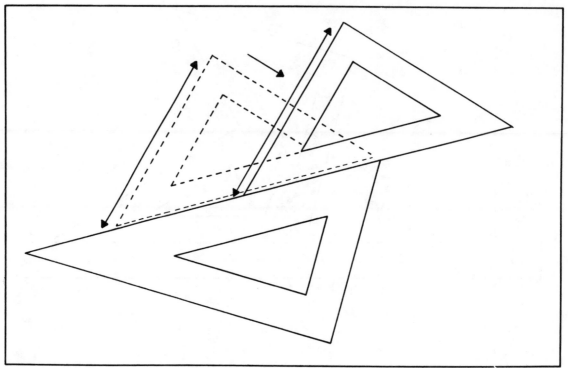

Fig. 4-22. Drawing two parallel lines with two triangles.

more tedious than doing it in a slipshod manner and the results are vastly different. The trick to doing accurate measuring is to have a sharp pencil to do the marking and to mark with a fine line—not a dot. Take your measurements directly from your ruler or calibrated T-square. It is best to use calibrated triangles so you won't have anything extra to fool with.

When it comes to using a compass, the thing to remember is that the pencil lead should be adjusted to be of the exact same length as the pin or needle point so that your compass is vertically centered. For measuring, set your compass directly on the scale and adjust there.

To draw a circle, set your compass on the scale and measure off the distance you want for the radius. Next, place the needle point where you want the center of the circle to be. Holding the compass by the handle, draw the circle in one sweep. Hold the handle between thumb and forefinger and incline the compass slightly in the direction of the line. If the line is too dim, you can make it darker by repeating the procedure. See Fig. 4-25.

Using the French curve is a bit different in that you might have to turn and adjust the French curve every little bit to come out with what will look like a continuous and smooth line. If this sounds contradictory, we can't help it. Again a try is worth a thousand words. A good trick to remember is to draw in a proposed curve lightly by hand after you've established the points that are your guides. Then apply the curve to it after selecting a part that will fit the proportion of your proposed line most closely. Be careful to place the curve in the right

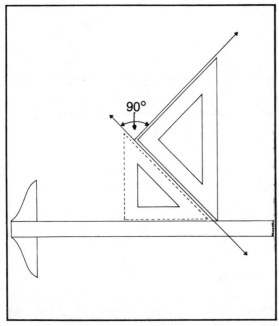

Fig. 4-23. Drawing a perpendicular line (method number one).

direction. If your curve increases, use the end of the curve on your French curve that increases (not the other end that will decrease). Stop just a tad short of the point where the curve and the line will meet and shift to another little space on the curve that will make the transition smoothly. See Figs. 4-26A and 4-26B.

When you shift a curve, be sure that you always adjust the new portion of the curve you plan to use so that it will coincide with the end of the curve already drawn. Fooling around with curves can be a lot of fun and some people get to be quite expert at finding the right curve at a glance. Don't worry if you don't get the hang of the French curve. You can do an awful lot of great plans and other drawings without ever having to cope with the curve.

Plastic templates are a great help when it comes to making house plans. This is particularly true for electrical plans and plumbing plans. What you do is simply to use the cutout places on the template as stencils and run your pencil point around the inside rim. Be sure to keep your pencil

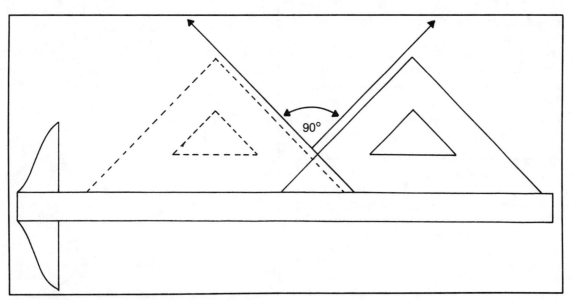

Fig. 4-24. Drawing a perpendicular line (method two).

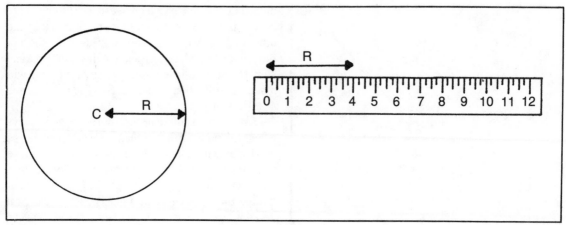

Fig. 4-25. Drawing a circle with a compass.

point in contact with the edge of the stencil or you won't get the benefit of regularity in size and line.

There are a number of these templates available and you can pick and choose from among them. Some people get a lot of fun out of working with templates; it's a bore and a bother to others. Suit yourself as far as templates are concerned. They are definitely not essential and you can do a fine job without them.

ERASING TECHNIQUES

A soft pencil line you want to eliminate or change is the simplest to work with. Just rub a soft pencil eraser lightly over the offending line. For heavier lines, use your ruby pencil eraser. If the paper is

grooved by the line, it helps to run your thumbnail over the line to smooth out the paper. If your thumbnail isn't used to this kind of work, use a tongue depressor, a round ballpoint pen (with the

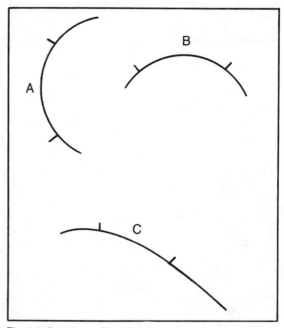

Fig. 4-26B. Using a French curve.

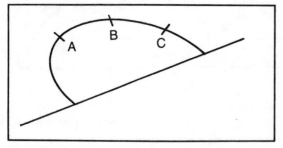

Fig. 4-26A. Drawing a curve using a French curve.

tip down, naturally) or any other like instrument that will flatten the groove. If you'll slip your triangle under the paper, you'll have an extra-fine backing surface.

If your offending line is close to some that you intend to keep, use your eraser shield. First of all make sure that the eraser shield is clean on both sides. Horrible things can happen if graphite or eraser shavings are still sticking to it when you use it.

Select the opening that fits your problem and rub through the shield with your eraser, holding the shield down firmly. If you need to erase an ink line, which you won't have to do if you follow our format, use your ruby pencil eraser. Work the eraser along the line and across it patiently until the ink is off. Use your triangle as backing. Use correction fluid sparingly if at all. It really does show up as a blob on the paper and then by the texture of the line drawn on top of it. Try as you might, the line won't match exactly in thickness or tone.

Whether you erase pencil or ink, be sure to get the eraser crumbs off your drawing. Blowing is the

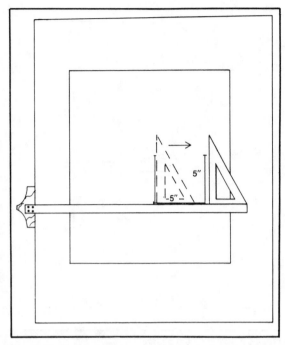

Fig. 4-28. Drawing square, horizontal, and perpendicular lines.

old-fashioned way, and not highly recommended. A soft, clean cloth or a small paint brush is best.

ITS TIME TO DRAW

Put your paper on the drawing board with thumb tacks or drafting tape (Figs. 4-13 through 4-15). Now follow our step-by-step procedure for drawing a square, a rectangle with lines in it, various kinds of lines you'll be using for different purposes, circles, and a cube.

Drawing a Square

Your square will be 5 inches by 5 inches.

Put your T-square on the board and draw a horizontal line where you want your square bottom to be.

Measure off 5 inches and mark a line on both ends with a small vertical line, as in Fig. 4-27.

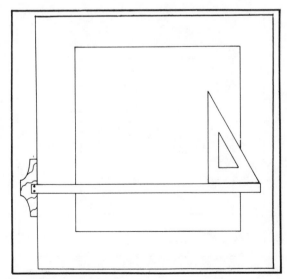

Fig. 4-27. Drawing a square.

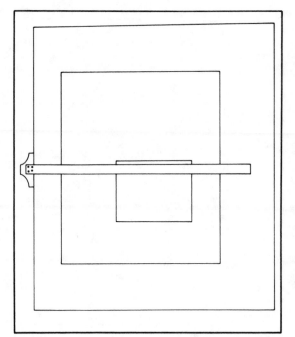

Fig. 4-29. Finishing the square.

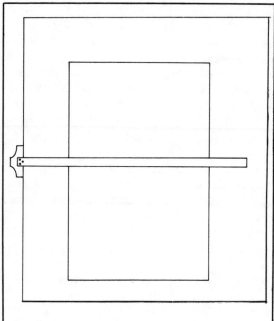

Fig. 4-30. Drawing a rectangle.

Put your triangle on top of your T-square that is now a bit below the drawn line with the perpendicular side lined up with the mark on your line (Fig. 4-28).

Draw a line; then move the triangle down to the other mark and draw the second line.

Measure both lines and mark the 5-inch length.

Move your T-square up to the marks and draw a line between them. Presto! Your first square (Fig. 4-29). Erase any extra length and you're done.

Drawing a Rectangle With Lines In It

Your rectangle is going to measure 7 inches for the horizontals and 4 inches for the verticals.

Construct your rectangle following instructions for the square above, but using the measurements given for the rectangle.

Measure off 1 inch increments along the bottom line.

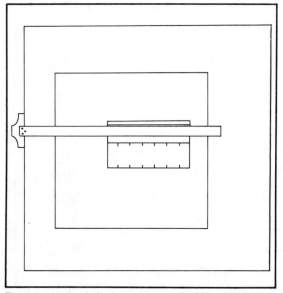

Fig. 4-31. Laying in horizontal lines with T-square.

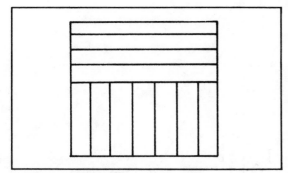
Fig. 4-32. A finished drawing of rectangle.

Measure up 2 inches from the bottom and draw a line across the rectangle (Fig. 4-30).

Measure off 1 inch increments on that line to match the bottom line.

On the remaining 2 inches of the vertical, measure off ½ inch increments.

Using your T-square, lay in the horizontals along the ½-inch marks (as shown in Fig. 4-31).

Using your T-square and triangle, lay in the verticals on the 1-inch marks.

Make sure that the lines meet exactly in the corners and other junction points. Erase any other lines. Your finished drawing should look like Fig. 4-32.

Various Kinds of Lines

When you draw lines, do them first horizontally using your T-square. After you have some practice, draw the same lines vertically using your T-square and triangle together. Then try drawing the same lines at a slant following the hypotenuse of your triangle.

Draw horizontal lines. Vary the lengths from 2½ inches through 4, 5½, and 7¼ inches (Fig. 4-33).

Repeat the excercise with vertical lines (Fig. 4-34).

Once more with feeling on the slant (Fig. 4-35).

Next is the broken or dashed line that is used to indicate things present, but not visible from the viewing angle. Try to keep the dashes the same length (Fig. 4-36).

Practice dashed lines on the horizontal, vertical, and slant.

Next comes the center line that is indicated in Fig. 4-37. Practice this one.

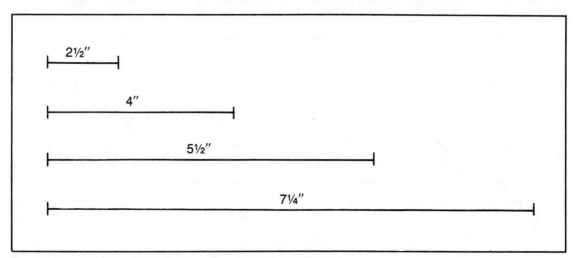
Fig. 4-33. Measuring and drawing horizontals with a T-square and a ruler.

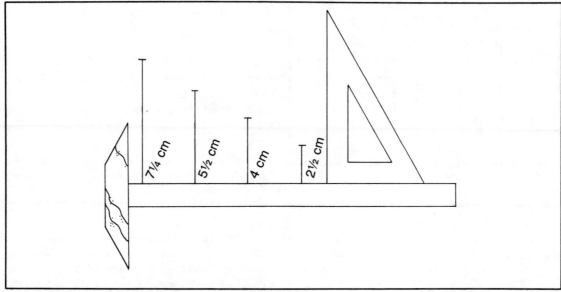

Fig. 4-34. Measuring and drawing verticals (perpendiculars).

This is the dimension line that is easy so you'll only have to do it in one direction, your choice. See Fig. 4-37.

There are other lines that can be done and they are used for various purposes. There's the dotted line and the dot-dash line and any combination of the two you can use if you feel the need. They look like Fig. 4-38.

The convention that architects observe in regard to the thickness of a line, thick for outlines and short break lines is medium for hidden outlines (that's those dashes) and thin for center, extension,

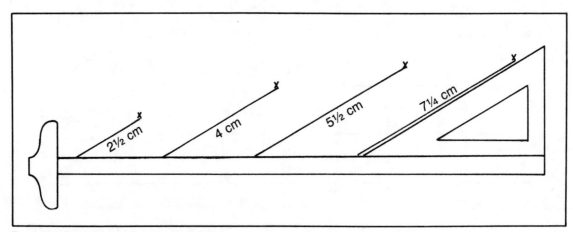

Fig. 4-35. Measuring and drawing slanted lines.

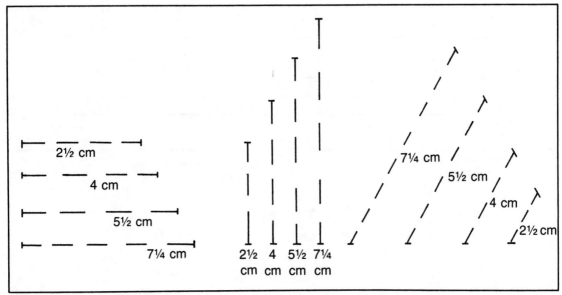

Fig. 4-36. Measuring and drawing broken lines.

and dimension lines. But this is getting a bit too professional for us. We recommend that rather than going by the thickness you pay attention to the different kinds of line and use them.

Circles

Draw a series of circles with your compass. Start with a 1-inch radius and work up to 3 inches by ½ inch. See Fig. 4-39A and 4-39B.

Draw a series of concentric circles (same center point) using 1-inch, 1½-inch, 2-inch, 2½-inch, and 3-inch radii. See Fig. 4-40.

Repeat the exercise above, but use dashes instead of lines. See Fig. 4-41.

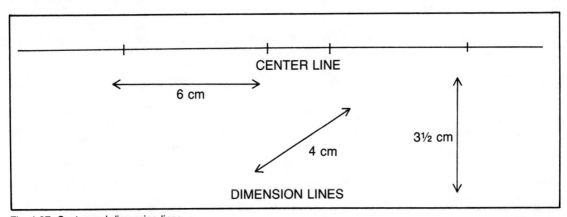

Fig. 4-37. Center and dimension lines.

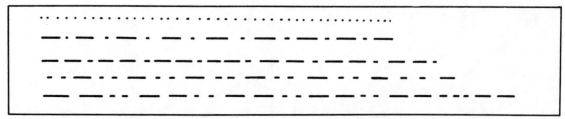

Fig. 4-38. Various kind of lines used in plans.

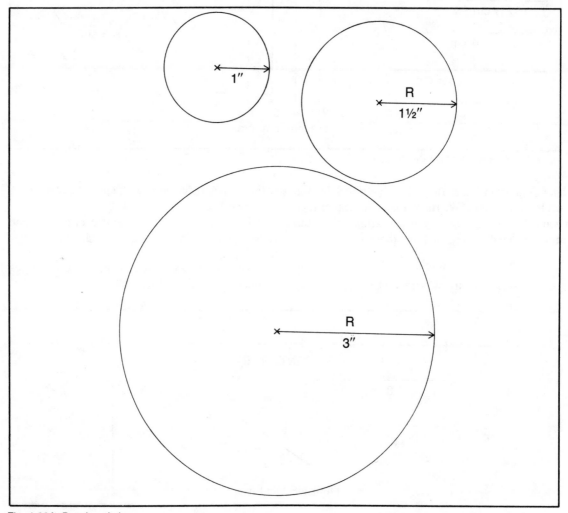

Fig. 4-39A. Drawing circles.

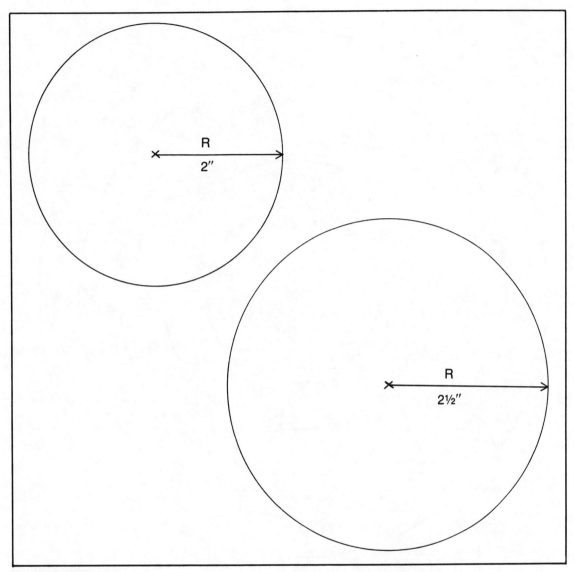

R
2"

R
2½"

Fig. 4-39B. More circles.

One more time and use dashes for all the whole numbers. See Fig. 4-42.

The Cube

We are going to do that cube as an *isometric draw-ing,* which is a simple way to do it.

Where you want the bottom of your cube to be, draw a horizontal line with your T-square.

Mark off a point where the corner of your cube will be and draw in a 4-inch vertical.

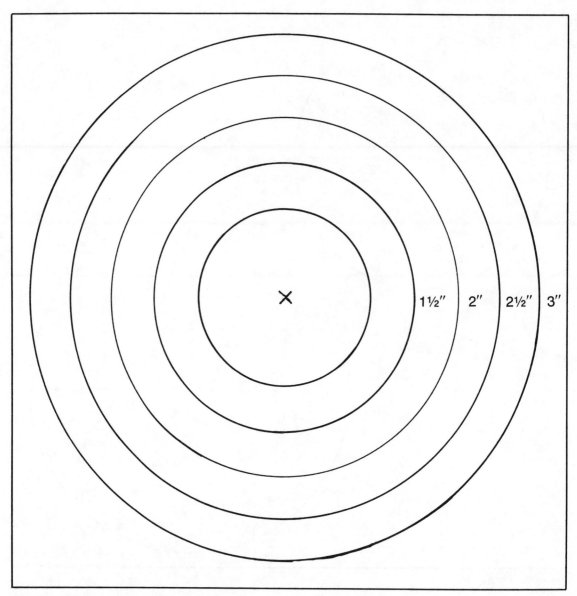

Fig. 4-40. Concentric circles.

With your triangle on your T-square, using the 30-degree angle, draw a line to the right of your vertical and one to the left. See Fig. 4-43.

Measure off 4 inches along each of these lines and put in verticals at those points, also 4 inches long, by turning your triangle so you'll have the

90-degree angle. Use your T-square and the horizontal line for a base. See Fig. 4-43.

With your triangle, connect the verticals parallel to the bottom lines. See Fig. 4-44.

Using the T-square and the triangle, now draw parallel lines, one to each, forming a square on top. See Fig. 4-44. If you'd rather, you can use two triangles, but the T-square is safer.

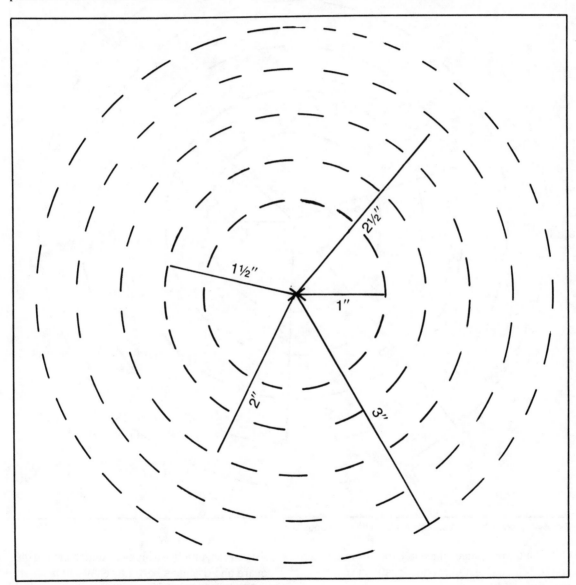

Fig. 4-41. Concentric circles drawn with broken lines.

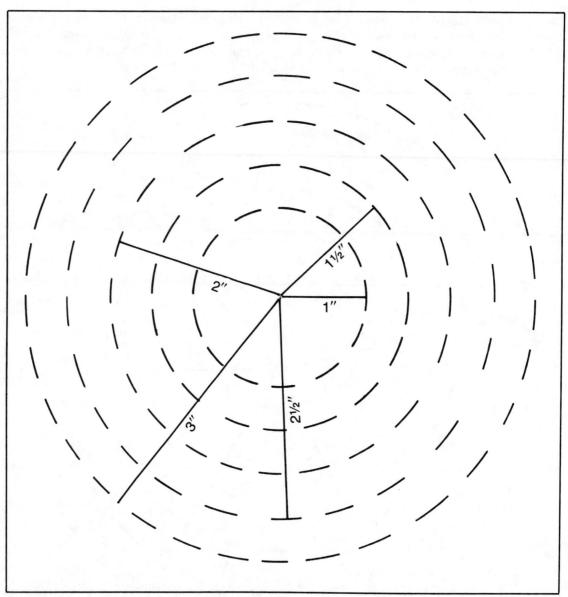

Fig. 4-42. Concentric circles, broken lines, and continuous lines.

Put in your hidden lines, the fourth corner, and the bottom square. Congratulations! You've done it. See Fig. 4-44.

If you can, practice a bit more until handling the T-square and triangles becomes easy and familiar. Calibrated triangles and T-squares surely speed up

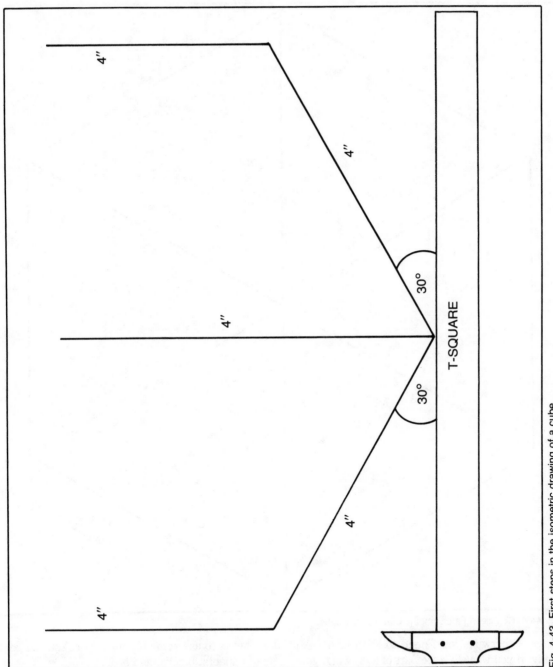

4″

4″

4″

4″

4″

30°

30°

T-SQUARE

Fig. 4-43. First steps in the isometric drawing of a cube.

105

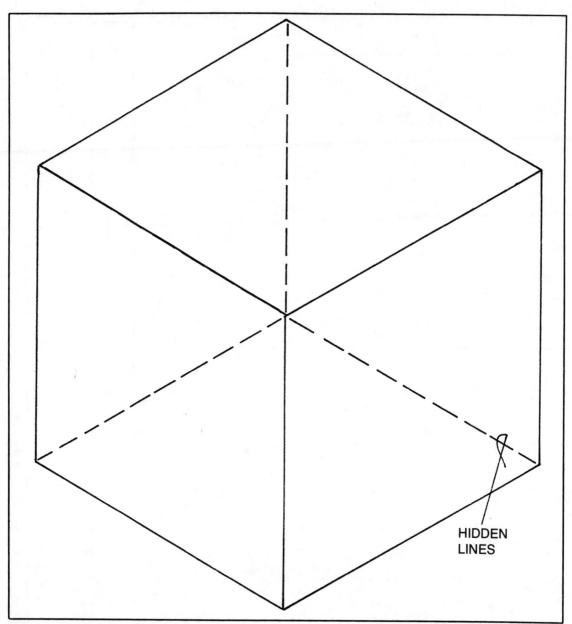

HIDDEN
LINES

Fig. 4-44. Completing an isometric drawing of a cube.

things. Otherwise you'll need to keep your ruler handy. If you want to trace part of a drawing, your best bet is to use some tracing paper. You can get this in sheets, blocks, and pads.

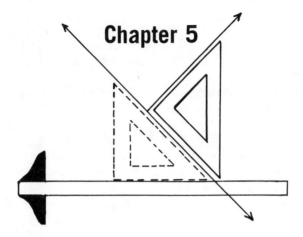

Chapter 5

How to Read Architectural Drawings

EVEN IF WE COULD SEND PICTURES TELEPATHI-cally into the minds of construction workers. there would be many important details that would need filling in and many questions would have to be asked of the designer. Construction drawings represent a precise way for the building designer to communicate with the building builders and the owners of the building so that they all have the same pictures in mind. Architectural drawings are representations in picture form that show just exactly how the new or remodeled structure is to appear. This kind of communications by drawing is called *descriptive geometry* because it describes the form of everything in pictures. These drawings show all the important details of construction and what materials are to be employed. They are the ultimate in step-by-step, how-to-do-it instructions.

Architectural drawings are the end result of "thinking on paper." An architect or building designer will begin by making rough sketches and discussing them with the owners of the building. Once ideas are generated and worked out in trial plans, a draftsperson will make a finished drawing of the designer's final plans. Because you will be doing your own house plans, you will be both designer and draftsperson. You will also need to be part engineer. Any house or remodeling job requires some engineering drawings to indicate such things as the locations of electrical outlets, air-conditioning and heating ducts, etc.

In order to show all the work required for construction or remodeling of a structure, a whole series of drawings is necessary. These are called *working drawings* or *construction plans*. The series is known as a *set* that usually consists of at least the following.

Plans. These are drawings that describe what the designer has in mind, as seen from above, if you sliced off the top part of the structure. A *floor plan* will indicate sizes, shapes, and arrangements of rooms, kitchen equipment, bathroom fixtures, windows, doors, etc. A *survey* and *plot plan* will give information about the site on which a structure is to be built and show where it is to be located on the site. A *landscape plan* gives a view from above of all the plants and small structures that make up the landscape surrounding a structure.

Sections. Technically, a plan is a horizontal section, but the term is usually applied to drawings used to show the interior construction of various structural parts.

Elevations. Elevation and plan views are the two most important drawings in the set. Elevations show what the exterior of a structure is to look like. A separate drawing is required for each side of the structure. Most house plans have four such drawings. Elevation drawings always contain much information and many instructions about how a structure is to be built.

Details. Any information that cannot be shown on plans, sections, or elevations is put into detail views. These are drawings of the details of structural assembly, trim, special equipment, etc. Sometimes detailed information about electrical, heating, air-conditioning, and plumbing work is shown on a separate set of drawings called-*mechanical detail* drawings.

Perspectives. This is a drawing that will look almost like a photograph of the finished structure. It is used to show people who cannot read the mechanical drawings what the designer visualizes as the finished and landscaped structure. Perspective drawings help builders and contractors visualize what their finished job is suppose to look like.

Because one set of drawings would not serve to communicate to all of the persons concerned with building a structure, the original set of drawings must be duplicated several times. These copies are usually black and white and they are called simply prints. They used to be called *blueprints,* after the blue-line method of printing them. Any color combination that shows contrast works fine. Often the term "blueprint" is used just to describe a copy of a set of drawings that might actually be copied in black and white.

When you have completed your set of drawings for your remodeling project or your new house, you will need copies of the complete set of drawings for the contractor, the builders (carpenters, masons, etc.), the estimators, and the financier of your project.

Architectural drawings will also include written *specifications* (or *specs* as they are called for short) for all phases of the work. The specs are put right on the drawings and they include instructions about all materials, methods of construction, standards of construction, and manner of conducting the work.

SYMBOLS USED IN HOUSE PLANS

Learning to read architectural drawings is mainly a matter of learning the language of conventions and symbols. These are the standardized methods of representing walls, windows, doors, stairs, fireplace and chimney, kitchen and bathroom fixtures, etc.

On a plan of a frame house, Fig. 5-1 shows exterior and interior walls drawn as two parallel lines. These lines are 6 inches apart on exterior walls and 4 inches apart on interior walls. This convention pictures walls as they are actually constructed.

Figure 5-2 shows a detail of the actual wall framing of a house at a corner and at a partition junction. Wallboards are nailed to the outside faces of the 2-×-4 inch wall studs. On the inside faces of the studs, plasterboard is nailed. The studs, wallboard, and plasterboard—together with exterior siding and interior paneling—will add up to approximately 6 inches. Partition walls, on the other hand, have only a 2-×-4 inch stud with paneling or plasterboard on each side and the thickness of the wall adds up to approximately 4 inches. (The 2-×-4 inch studs actually measure only 1½ × 3½ inches

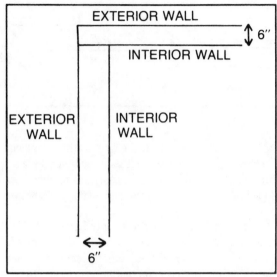

Fig. 5-1. Drawing a complete wall for a floor plan.

when dressed and installed.) The triple studs at the corners and where partitions meet are not drawn in on the floor plan because the floor plan scale would be too small to clearly show the detail.

Windows. The convention or symbol for a window (double-hung) is shown in Fig. 5-3. It can be drawn exactly as wide as the window or it can be drawn as wide as the rough opening to accommodate the window, which will be slightly larger. We recommend drawing the window the width of the rough opening because this gives the builder the information he needs. Window manufacturers always supply the information on the size of the rough opening needed for their windows. This information is available to you when you pick out your windows. The location of the window in the wall is determined by a measurement from the outside face of the stud at the corner of the structure to the *middle*

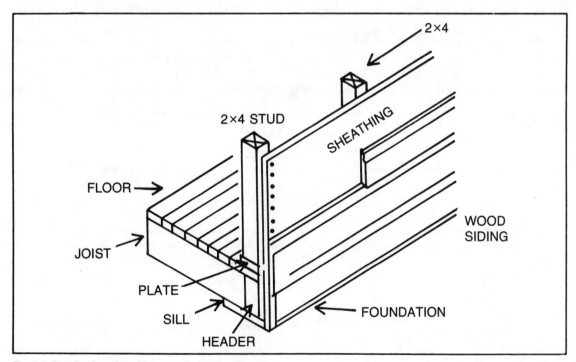

Fig. 5-2. Details of section of frame wall with wooden siding.

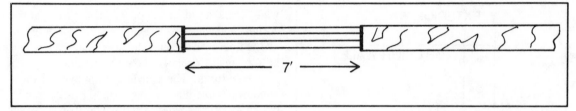

Fig. 5-3. Drawing in a double-hung window.

of the window. This is indicated by the dimension lines.

Doors. Doors are represented by the symbols in Fig. 5-4. The line that is drawn off at an angle represents the door and indicates its angle of swing. The size of the door is often written on the line representing the door. If not, there will be a circled number near the door that refers to a table known as a door schedule on which you will find the dimensions of the door. On exterior doors, an additional line is drawn across the opening on the outside of the door opening to represent the door sill.

Fireplaces. Figure 5-5 shows the standard convention for drawing in a fireplace. There also might be a flue venting the central heating plan drawn in as a circle or a square. The hearth line will

be drawn 18 inches from the face of the fireplace. Firebrick is always used in the lining of a fireplace. Firebricks are made of heat-resistant material far superior to ordinary brick and usually of larger dimensions.

Stairs. Stairs are represented on scale floor plans as indicated in Fig. 5-6. An arrow drawn through the center of the treds indicates whether the stairs go up to the second floor or down to the basement. The number of risers is also given. If one stairway is on top of another as is often the case with basement stairs down and second story stairs up a line is drawn at an angle across the stairs to separate the up-stairs from the down-stairs.

Bathroom Fixture Symbols. Figure 5-7 shows some standard symbols for bathtubs, shower

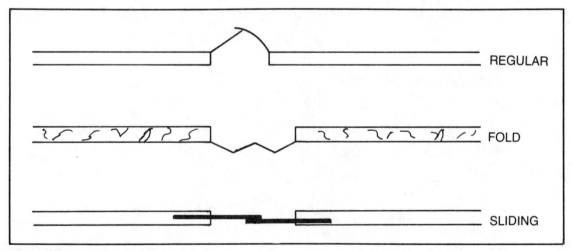

REGULAR

FOLD

SLIDING

Fig. 5-4. Drawing door symbols.

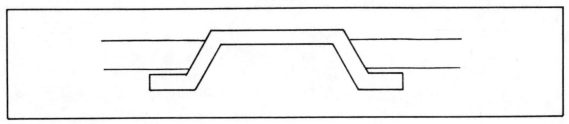

Fig. 5-5. A fireplace.

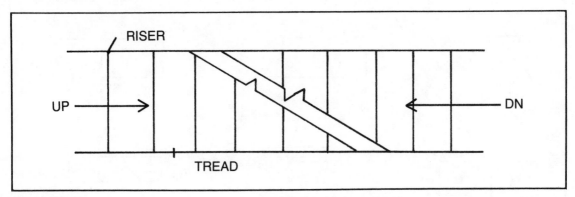

Fig. 5-6. Stairs.

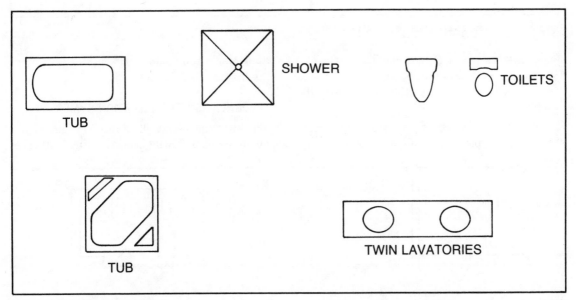

Fig. 5-7. Bathroom fixture symbols.

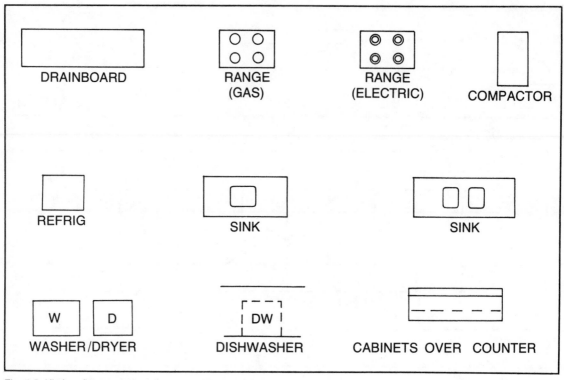

Fig. 5-8. Kitchen fixtures and appliances and their symbols.

stalls, lavatories, toilets, and medicine cabinets. The diagonal lines drawn through the shower stall diagram indicates a floor pitched to drain in the center.

Kitchen Fixture Symbols. Figure 5-8 shows some typical kitchen-fixture symbols, in-cluding single and double sinks.

Closets. See Fig. 5-9.

FOUNDATION AND ELEVATION SYMBOLS

A concrete foundation wall 12 inches wide is indicated on the plan drawing shown in Fig. 5-10. The

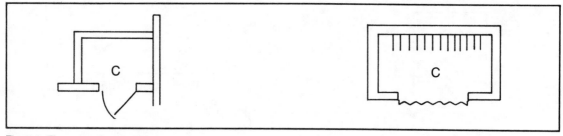

Fig. 5-9. These are the closets.

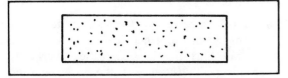

Fig. 5-10. This is how we draw a concrete foundation wall.

small dots represent aggregate or stone in the concrete. Figure 5-11 shows how some other materials are symbolized in drawings. If uncommon or unusual materials are used in the construction of a structure, the plans will include a *symbol key* to indicate how the material is symbolized.

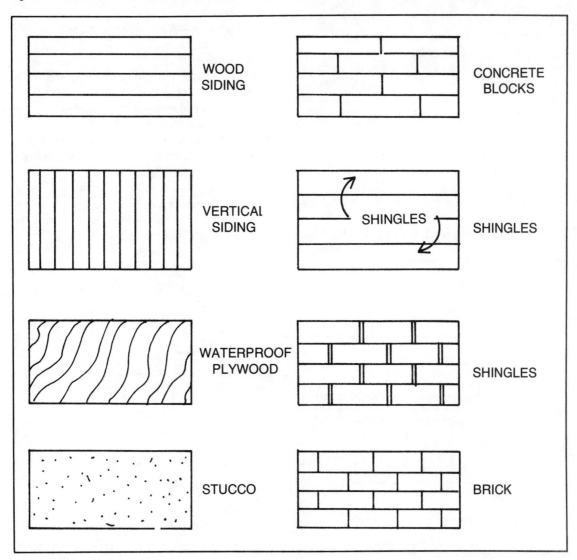

Fig. 5-11. A bunch of material symbols.

It is important to the builder to have the proper representation of exterior wall treatment on the elevation drawings. Figure 5-12 shows horizontal lines drawn close together approximating the width of a brick to indicate a brick exterior wall. Asbestos roof shingles are also indicated by a series of horizontal lines, but these are drawn closer together and fade out near the ends. A lettered notation as part of the drawing further clarifies what is symbolized. These lettered notations have terms and abbreviations with which you should become somewhat familiar. Here is a list in alphabetical order of some of the most common terms. Table 5-1 lists typical abbreviations. Also see the Glossary.

apron—A finishing board placed beneath the base at the bottom of a window.

architrave—Another name for *trim*.

ashlar—The cut-stone facing on the outside of a wall.

awning window—A window that opens out from the top, as does an awning.

batten—A piece of wood used to fasten other pieces of wood together.

board and batten—Wide boards used vertically as siding with battens over the cracks between boards.

casement—Any hinged window.

cement plaster—A mix of cement and sand used as fireproofing or waterproofing on the exterior of foundations.

clapboard—Long, thin siding that is graduated in thickness.

clerestory windows—Small windows in the walls between roof segments.

concrete block vent—A vent made in a concrete block wall by leaving a hole the exact size of a concrete block.

corbel—An arch formed by building out successive courses of masonry.

corner boards—Finish boards used to trim the outside corner of a frame house.

Fig. 5-12. Elevation with finishing materials indicated by symbols.

Table 5-1. House Plan Abbreviations.

Asph.	Asphalt	Ht.	Height
Bldg.	Building	L.	Center Line
B.R.	Bedroom	L.P.	Low Point
Br.	Brick	L.R.	Living Room
B.S.	Bevel Siding	Lt.	Light
Cem.	Cement	Mldg.	Molding
D.C.	Drip Cap	Mull.	Mullion
D.G.	Drawn Glass	No./#	Number
D.H.	Double Hung	Obs.	Obscure
Diag.	Diagonal	O.C.	On Center
Diam.	Diameter	O.C.	Outside Casing
Dim.	Dimension	O.S.	Outside
Div.	Divided	Pl.	Plaster
Dn.	Down	Pl.	Plate
Do.	Ditto	Cond.	Conduit
D.R.	Dining Room	Cop.	Copper
Dr.	Door	Corn.	Cornice
Dr.C.	Drop Cord	Csmt.	Casement
Drg.	Drawing	C.T.	Crock Tile
D.S.	Downspout	Crys.	Crystal
Ea.	Each	Pl. Ht.	Plate Height
El.	Elevation	R.	Radius
Ent.	Entrance	Rm.	Room
Ext.	Exterior	R.W.	Redwood
Fin.	Finish	Scr.	Screen
Fin. Ceil.	Finished Ceiling	Sdg.	Siding
Flash.	Flashing	Specs.	Specifications
Fl.	Floor	T and G	Tongue & Grooved
C.I.	Cast Iron	T.C.	Terra Cotta
Clg.	Ceiling	Th.	Threshold
Clr.	Clear	Typ.	Typical
C.O.	Cased Opening	Ven.	Veneer
Conc.	Concrete	V.T.	Vertical tongued
Cond.	Conductor	and G.	and grooved
Ft.	Foot/Feet	W.	Wide
Ftg.	Footing	W.C.	Wood Casing
Gar.	Garage	Wd.	Wood
G.I.	Galvanized Iron	W.G.	Wire Glass
Gl.	Glass	W.I.	Wrought Iron
Gr.	Grade	Wp.	Waterproof
Gyp. Bd.	Gypsum Board	Yd.	Yard
H.P.	High Point		

cornice—That part of a roof that projects beyond the wall below it.

course—One continuous row of bricks or other masonry material.

dormer—A structure projecting from a sloping roof to provide light and air under the roof.

drip—A projection over a window to drain water away from the window.

fascia—The outside, flat member of a cornice.

finish strip—Used with a crown molding as part of a cornice.

finished ceiling—Term used on elevation drawings to indicate ceiling height.

finished first floor—A term designating the first-floor level on elevation drawings.

fixed wood sash—Windows that do not open.

flashing—Sheet-metal strips installed to prevent water leaking into doors, windows, and roof openings.

flat roof—A roof with almost no pitch.

frieze—A piece of trim used just below the cornice.

gable—A triangle formed by a sloping roof in an end wall.

gambrel roof—A roof that slopes up at two different angles.

grade—The level of the ground around a building.

gutter—A trough, usually metal, for carrying water from roofs.

hip roof—A roof that slopes up from the corners of a structure.

hood—A small roof over a doorway.

jamb—The inside vertical face of a window frame.

lally column—A support for beams, usually a cylinder of steel, sometimes filled with concrete.

leader—A conduit, usually metal, used to carry water from gutter to the ground.

lintel—A beam used to support a wall over window and door openings.

louver—An opening for ventilation covered by angled slats to exclude wind and rain.

meeting rail—The horizontal center rails of the sash in a double hung window.

metal caps—Waterproof flashing over doors and windows.

millwork—Finished and partly assembled wooden parts.

miter—The beveled surface cut on the ends of a molding.

mullion—The vertical division of a window opening.

muntin—That strip of wood that separate the panes of glass in a window frame.

nosing—Overhang of a stair tread.

panel—A framed piece of wood.

parting strip—That strip in a double hung window frame that separates the upper and lower part of the sash.

pitch of roof—The amount of slope displayed by a roof.

rake board—That board that runs down the slope of a roof from the top of the gable. Also called a *verge board.*

ridge—The top edge of a roof where the slopes meet.

riser—The vertical portion of a stair step.

rowlock course—The course of brick that is set on edge under a window.

R.W. siding—Redwood siding.

saddle—Build-up metal around a chimney to throw water away from the chimney.

sash—The moveable part of a window in which the panes of glass are set.

sheathing—The rough boards nailed to the outside of the studs in an exterior wall over which is laid the siding, shingles, or brick finish.

sidelights—The fixed windows on each side of a doorway.

sill—The bottom member under a window or a door.

soffit—The under side of a cornice.

soldier course—Bricks laid on their ends with edges exposed.

stool—The support at the bottom of a window.

stringer—The supporting member at the sides of a staircase.

structural glass—Special glass, available in colors for use inside or outside.

T and G siding—Tongue and groove boards used as siding instead of flooring.

tread—The horizontal member of a stairway.

trim—The finish around openings or ajoining parts.

valley—The groove where two roof slopes intersect.

verge board—That board that runs down the slope of a roof from the top of the gable. Also called a *rake board.*

water table—A shelf of masonry or wood projecting from the top of a foundation to protect the foundation from rain water.

weather strip—Any strip of any material used to keep drafts and dirt from entering a building. Used to cover joints and cracks.

window wall—Fixed glass windows with large panes that form one wall or nearly all of one wall of a structure.

window water table—A *drip* over the top of a window to throw rain water away from the window.

PLUMBING SYMBOLS

Typical plumbing symbols are shown in Figs. 5-13 and 5-14. You should become as familiar with these symbols as with the words that describe plumbing fixtures and accessories. Plumbing symbols are drawn accurately to scale so that the builder will allow sufficient room for their installation.

HEATING AND VENTILATING SYMBOLS

Heating and ventilating symbols, like plumbing symbols are drawn to scale so that the builder will know exactly how much space to allow for the equipment. Figure 5-15 shows the most-used symbols.

SOLAR AND WIND GENERATOR SYMBOLS

New innovations in energy generation and distribution have brought about whole new designs relating to heating, air-conditioning, and electrical work described on house plans. Some of the solar energy extractors also have a great deal of plumbing connected with their construction. Figure 5-16 shows some of these new symbols as they are generally represented on plans being drawn to include these new ideas in the capture and conservation of energy.

ELECTRICAL SYMBOLS

Electrical outlets are always indicated on floor plans in their approximate locations. Fixture type is indicated by an uppercase letter in the symbol. Lowercase letters designate switch control. Numbers identify the circuit. In the switch symbol, there will be a letter indicating the device that switch controls. The electrical symbols shown in Fig. 5-17 are typical of the variety of symbols used by architects. Once you learn to recognize these, you will be able to recognize variations that will appear on plans from time to time.

Be sure to pay careful attention to all notations you find on drawings. Most good drawings contain printed instructions relative to many of the details of construction. These notes will give information

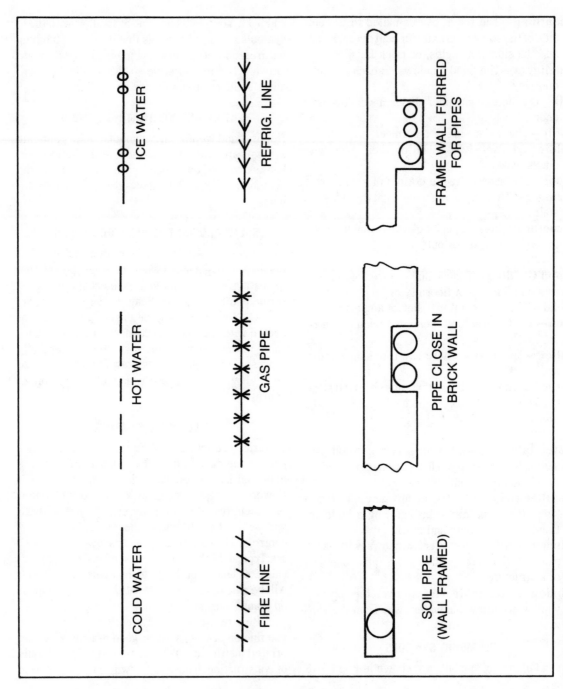

Fig. 5-13. Plumbing Symbols.

118

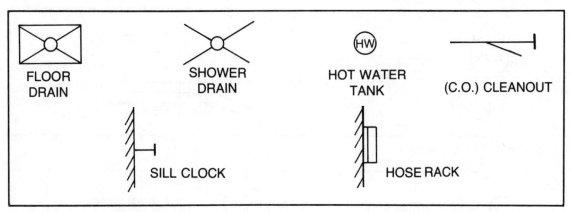

Fig. 5-14. Plumbing symbols.

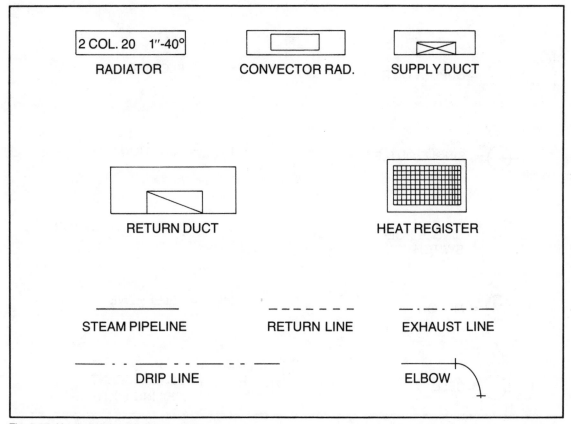

Fig. 5-15. Heating and ventilating symbols.

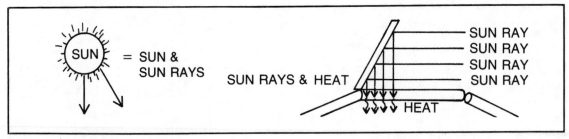

Fig. 5-16. New solar energy symbols.

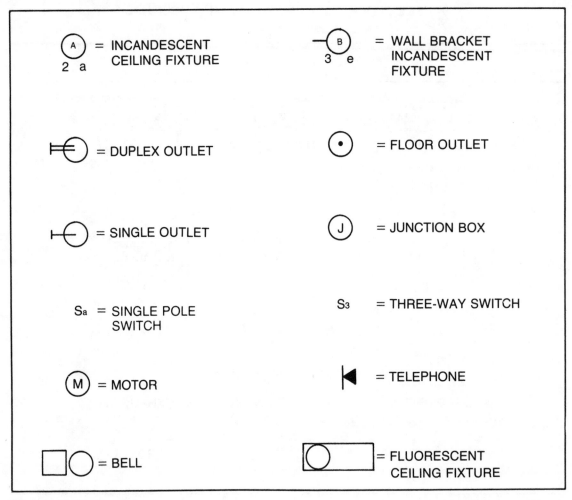

Fig. 5-17. Electrical symbols.

directly or refer you to other parts of the set of plans where you can find more information. When drawing your own plans, don't hesitate to explain details of what you have in mind by making notes on your plans. There are times, believe it or not, when a word is worth a dozen pictures!

LINES ON PLANS

When you are learning to read construction drawings—and later on in your own drawing of plans—you will need to pay close attention to the variety of special types of lines used for specific purposes on all architectural drawings. There are four types of lines with which to become familiar.

Invisible Lines. This is a line made up of a series of short dashes. It is used to indicate parts of the drawing that cannot be seen or to indicate hidden edges.

Broken Lines. A broken line is to indicate that parts of the drawing have been left out or that the full length of something is not shown. This line has an uneven break in it at intervals.

Section or Reference Line. This is a solid line with an arrow head at each end pointing in the direction of a detail drawing on another sheet of the set of plans. Reference letters or numbers may be shown at the ends of the lines.

Center Lines. Dash-and-dot lines are drawn lightly. They are used to indicate the centers of things.

Figure 5-18 should be studied to familiarize yourself with the various kinds of architectural drawing lines and what they indicate.

SECTION VIEWS AND DETAIL DRAWINGS

While plan and elevation views are the basic and most important drawings in a set of construction plans, they often cannot show enough information to enable the builders to see exactly how to build or assemble some parts of a structure. For example, the plan and elevation drawings might show that the exterior walls of a house are to be constructed using 2- x -4 inch studs, with plasterboard on the inside and sheathing, covered with building paper and clapboard, on the outside. And that's about all the information you get. No indication about the location of the studs or what type of sill construction or method of bracing is to be used. This information will appear in *section views* and *details*.

Section views and details are more picture-like drawings than are plans and elevations; They usually contain more information in the form of symbols, abbreviations, and terms. Details and section views also show how things are assembled,

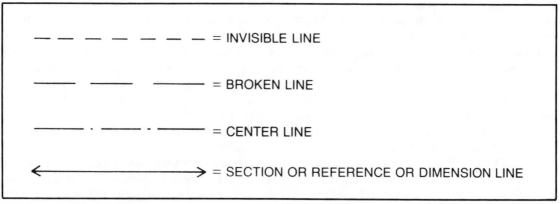

Fig. 5-18. Some architectual lines.

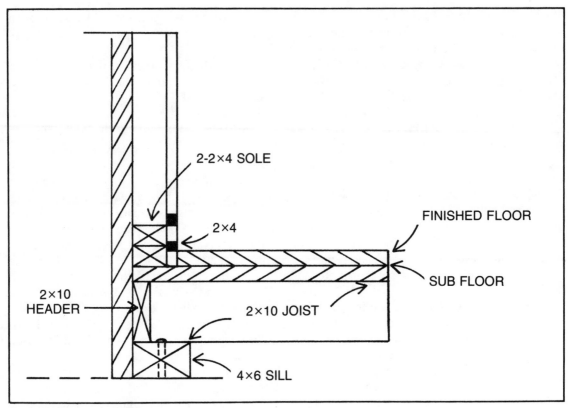

2-2×4 SOLE

2×4

FINISHED FLOOR

SUB FLOOR

2×10 HEADER →

2×10 JOIST

4×6 SILL

Fig. 5-19. Section of a wall.

how they relate to one another, and how they relate to the structure as a whole.

In general, section views and detail drawings are drawn to a much larger scale than plan and elevation drawings. This allows for a "close up" look. Sections and details are also often drawn isometrically. This makes them more picture-like and dimensional than the flat, two-dimensional plan and elevation drawings. This added dimension means that much more information can be included.

Staircases and fireplaces are good examples of structures that need additional drawings to show carpenters and masons how many stringers to use, and their size, or how brickwork over the fireplace opening is to be supported. Section views are used primarily to indicate the interiors and arrangements of individual or related structural parts. Detail drawings are those section views that show blow ups of items too small to be represented by the scale used for plan and elevation drawings. We will treat them as section drawings from now on and refer to both as *sections*. These sections are drawn carefully to scale (a larger scale) just like all the rest of the construction drawing set.

When you visualize a section, you imagine that the structure or part of the structure, has been cut through *vertically* as shown in Fig. 5-19. This is a section of footing and foundation wall; it shows how the two are tied together. Just imagine that you can use a saw and cut the header, sill, and footing on the line *xy*. The dashed line *fg* shows that the saw cuts the footing and foundation wall vertically. Now, imagine that once we get the saw all the way through the footing, we can swing the *a* and *b* corners backward.

We can see "inside" the anchoring arrangement between footing and foundation and visualize just exactly how it all goes together. The subfloor is nailed to the joists that are at right angles to the header and the sill. The sill is anchored to the foundation wall that is resting on top of the footing. The header and sill are continuous members running completely around the building. The joists are usually spaced 16 inches on centers at right angles to the header/sill combination.

If you continue to study the sections, you will discover the information needed to construct and finish the walls. Figure 5-20 shows how the sole plate relates to the subfloor in Fig. 5-19. This in turn receives the 2-×-4 inch wall studs. Figure 5-21 shows a frame wall covered with a veneer of brick. The section drawings show such details as the extra width of the foundation wall to accommodate the brick, the sheathing, building paper, etc.

Figure 5-22 continues the wall section up to the second floor to show the studs resting on the

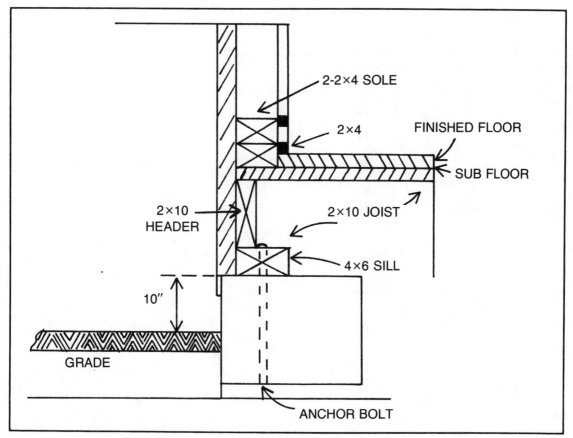

Fig. 5-20. Section of a wall and footings.

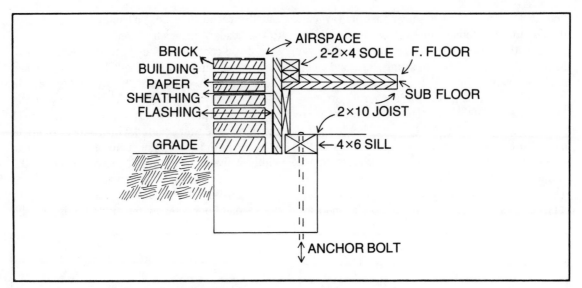

Fig. 5-21. Section of a frame wall with brick veneer.

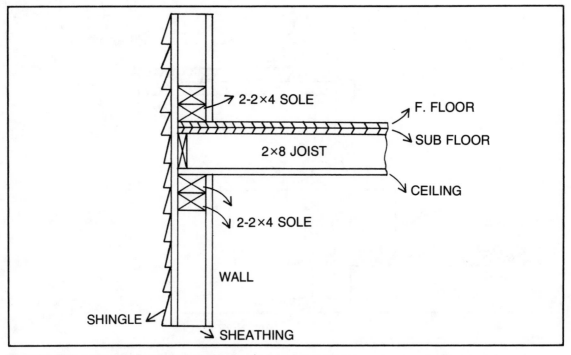

Fig. 5-22. Wall section showing relationship between first and second story.

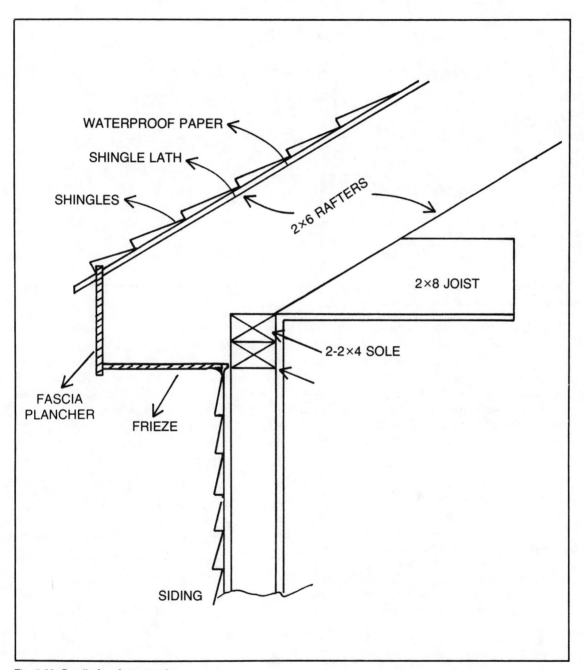

WATERPROOF PAPER

SHINGLE LATH

SHINGLES

2×6 RAFTERS

2×8 JOIST

2-2×4 SOLE

FASCIA
PLANCHER

FRIEZE

SIDING

Fig. 5-23. Detail of roof construction.

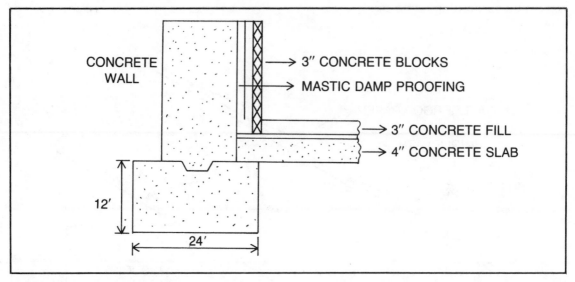

CONCRETE WALL

→ 3″ CONCRETE BLOCKS

→ MASTIC DAMP PROOFING

→ 3″ CONCRETE FILL

→ 4″ CONCRETE SLAB

12′

24′

Fig. 5-24. Cast-in-place wall section.

second floor sole plate and the relationship between those elements of construction and the joists, top plate, and first-floor studs below.

Topping off the structure with a section (Fig. 5-23) that carries you to the roof, you can see how the construction is to be carried out in relation to the top plate on the second floor, the rafters, and ceiling beams, as well as some detail on the finishing of the roof.

Concrete and Masonry Wall Section Views

There are two basic types of concrete and masonry walls: those made of concrete cast in place (Fig. 5-24) and those made of precast units (Fig. 5-25). Most engineers recommend cast-in-place concrete for buildings where external water pressures are encountered, on hillside locations or deep basements where severe side thrust of the soil is a factor, and where load requirements are severe—as in tall buildings. All types of foundation walls should rest on concrete footings to provide an even surface on which to base the wall proper.

Other construction details you can pick up from concrete and masonry wall section views is that concrete walls below grade level are usually 12 inches thick, going to 8 inches above grade. A brick veneer is often applied to the face of the concrete above grade to improve the appearance of the face of the wall. Notice, too, that the floor joists rest on brick rather than on the concrete to insure an even alignment of joists. Be sure to learn the symbol for concrete block and for brick and tile.

A tile wall that can be used in light structures, hollow building tiles come in a variety of sizes. Perhaps the most common size is 12 inches long by 8 inches wide by 5 inches deep. In this type of wall,

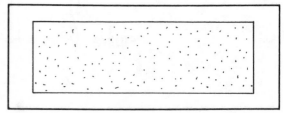

Fig. 5-25. Pre-cast concrete wall.

126

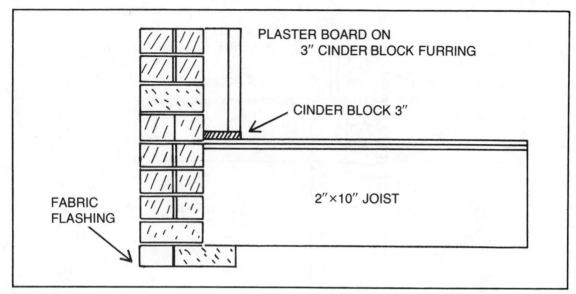

PLASTER BOARD ON
3" CINDER BLOCK FURRING

CINDER BLOCK 3"

2"×10" JOIST

FABRIC
FLASHING

Fig. 5-26. Details of a wall.

fill with concrete any tiles on which floor joists rest (as noted in the detail drawing). Good engineering practice recommends inserting steel reinforcing rods into the tiles before packing with concrete. This construction detail will be shown on the drawing.

Brick walls are bonded every fourth course to the concrete block behind them. Concrete slab floors need to be from 4 to 6 inches thick depending upon the load to be supported and on the pressure of ground water. If soil at the construction site is water-logged, a 4- to 6-inch fill of cinders or gravel needs to be specified to provide a dry base for the concrete slab. The slab is usually placed directly on the earth. Where the slab meets the wall, a little space needs to be provided for expansion.

Study the construction details shown in Figs. 5-26 and 5-27. These detail drawings show a solid brick wall rising from a poured concrete foundation supported by a keyed footing. A 3-inch cinder block is used as furring with air space provided between it and the wall. The basement and first floor are of 4-inch concrete with a 3-inch cinder block on top. The fabric flashing between the foundation and the brick wall prevents moisture from seeping into the structure.

Large-Scale Details

Figure 5-28 shows the details of an ordinary wood double-hung window set into a frame wall. The drawing projects the three distinct components that make up the window construction. The window sash goes into the window frame; in turn, this goes into the rough opening in the wall. Figure 5-29 is a large-scale representation of a small section of the window frame and sash installed in the rough opening. All parts of the window are shown clearly along with the outside wall finish around the window.

Framing Plans

A complete set of house plans does not have to include detailed plans for framing the structure to be built. Most builders are quite familiar with where to place framing members and how they go

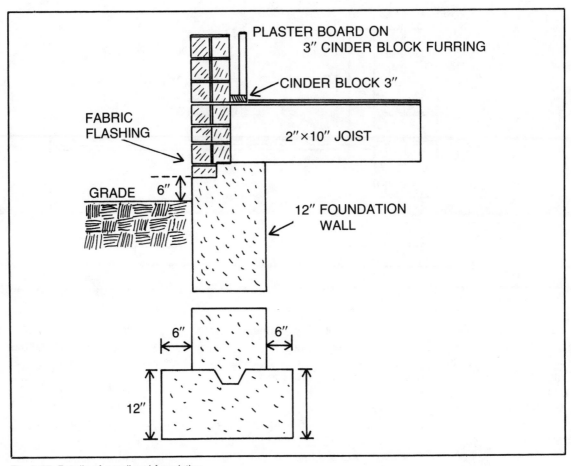

Fig. 5-27. Details of a wall and foundation.

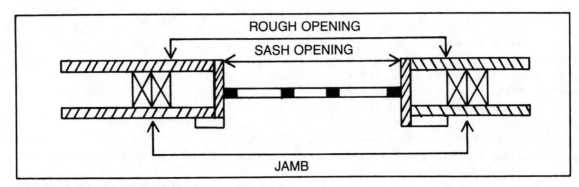

Fig. 5-28. Details of double-hung window.

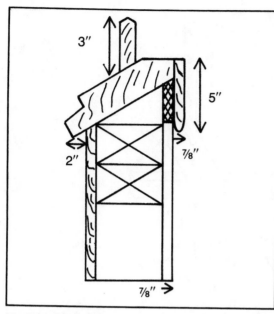

Fig. 5-29. Sill detail of a window.

together. Although you do not need to draw framing plans, it is best to be able to read these drawings and to understand what they illustrate.

Framing members consist of *joists, headers, tail beams, trimmers,* and *bridges.*

Joists. The term joists applies to both floor and ceiling beams as shown in Fig. 5-22. Spacing of joists in both floor and ceiling is usually 16 inches from the center of one joist to the center of the next.

Headers. These are beams used around openings for windows, doors, stair wells, etc. Fireplace and chimney openings also require headers. Headers are placed at right angles to joists and are used to carry the ends of joists that are cut. Because headers carry extra loads, they are usually doubled or tripled. Figure 5-30 shows construction details of headers as well as tail beams and trimmers.

Tail Beams. Tail beams are simply cut joists butting against headers around openings. Tail

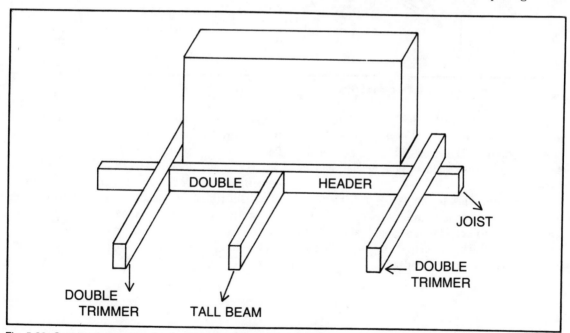

Fig. 5-30. Construction details showing trimmers, joist, and a tall beam.

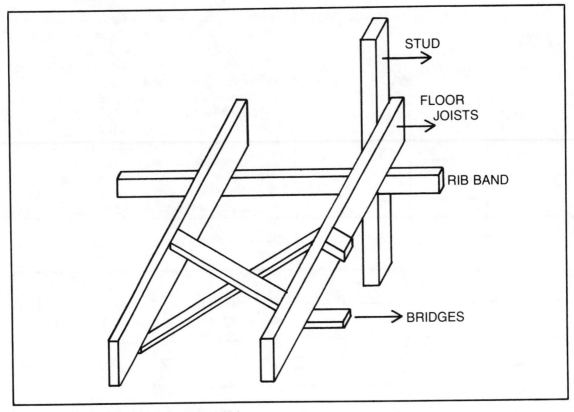

STUD

FLOOR JOISTS

RIB BAND

BRIDGES

Fig. 5-31. Floor construction detail showing bridging.

beams carry their loads to the header. Sometimes they are supported by metal joist hangers.

Trimmers. These are floor joists that are doubled, run at right angles to the header, and are fastened to it.

Bridging. This is the 1-×-3 inch pieces of wood nailed crosswise between joists, tail beams, and trimmers to keep them perfectly aligned with one another. One row of bridging is needed for every 8 feet of joist span. Good builders will use lots of extra bridging to insure sturdy, rigid construction. Figure 5-31 shows cross bridging underneath a floor.

Complete floor and roof framing plans are sometimes included in construction plans. This is especially true if the designer wants to deviate from conventional construction methods. Otherwise, these plans can be deleted from sets of plans for remodeling, build-ons, or complete new construction.

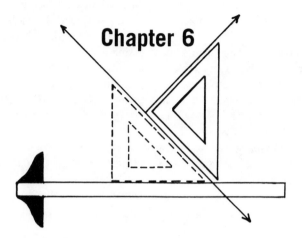

Chapter 6

Scale Floor Plans: Part 1

IF YOU ARE NEW TO DESIGNING PLANS FOR houses you will probably need to get a handle on dimensions. What does it mean that a house contains 2100 square feet? Is that a tiny house or a mansion? If a room is designated on a floor plan as having the dimensions 16′ × 22′, how bit is it really?

Get out a tape measure and start taking the measurements of the house or apartment you are in right now. Look around the rooms and get a feel for their size and then measure them. If you have a room that feels small and cramped, measure it and look at the dimensions. Pick a room that seems large and spacious to you and then measure it. Look at your measurements and remember how the room feels to you. In a very short time, you will develop a good feel for dimensions.

Now measure a few pieces of furniture. If you own furniture that will go into the new room, addition, or house you are going to design, get acquainted with the sizes of this furniture before you

begin to design the rooms it will go into. Then measure the spaces between pieces of furniture and get a feel for these spaces in relation to the way you feel sitting in a conversational area or watching TV. Take a good look at the way you and your family members walk and circulate around the furniture in the rooms where you live now. Tight squeeze? Loose? Associate for yourself dimensions on paper with the way you sense space.

Keep in mind that big is not always better. Small is often great! Service areas like kitchens, baths, and utility rooms need to work well. That usually means small and efficient. Conversation areas are also better if they are small and cosy.

Measuring will also give you some feeling for the proportions of rooms. A room that is very much longer than it is wide will seem awkward and "out of proportion." If you make a room's length more than twice as long as its width, it will feel like a corridor.

There are certain rule-of-thumb sizes for the

various rooms in a house that are helpful to know. These are minimum sizes below which nearly anyone will feel cramped carrying on the normal activities of the room listed.

Hallways. Two people cannot pass one another in a hallway that is less than about 2 feet 6 inches wide. Three feet wide is a better minimum width if the hallway runs beyond about 4 feet in length. A very long hall (10 feet or more) ought to have a minimum width of 4 feet so that it will not feel oppressive. This way it can also be used for a bit of furnishing and to hang some pictures.

Entryways. If you are going to greet a guest and help him or her remove a winter coat, you will need at least a 5-×-5 foot area to move around in. That will not include the area of your coat closet which should always be provided with an entry.

Closets. No closet should be less than 2 feet deep, even if you make it extremely narrow. There is no minimum width unless you are designing a walk-in closet. Such a closet needs to be at least 7 feet wide to allow clothing to be hung on both sides.

Kitchens. Stoves and sinks usually measure 2 feet out from the wall. Custom-built and ready-built cabinets with counters are built to the same dimensions. Overhead cabinets will protrude 1 foot from the wall. With counters and/or appliances on both sides of a corridor kitchen should not be less than 7 feet wide.

Ceiling height is very important in the proportion of any room. Minimum ceiling height should be 7 feet. Standard in most new construction is 8 feet, but exceptionally large rooms should not be designed with the standard 8-foot ceiling or they will look squashed. On the other hand, a 5-×-5 foot entry with a 12-foot cathedral ceiling would give one the feeling of standing in the bottom of a well.

Doors come in standard sizes. They do make a standard door only 2 feet wide, but don't use it unless you have to. This is a narrow closet or bathroom door. Stick to the standard 2-foot-6 inch door even for closets and bathrooms if at all possi-

ble. The front door of any house should be a standard 3-foot door at minimum.

Wall thicknesses follow a design convention of being 6 inches thick if constructed of wood on exterior walls and 5 inches for interior walls. Brick and stone walls are 10 inches thick by design convention. Those are the dimensions you use on your plans on paper. The actual thickness of the finished wall will likely be something else.

You need one more project before you begin to make some trial floor plans and that is to make furniture cutouts to scale. Use the same scale that you will use on your floor plan drawings. Figure 6-1 shows some common pieces of furniture drawn to ⅛-inch scale. You can trace them and cut them out.

MAKING TRIAL FLOOR PLANS

Trial floor plans evolve out of the space needs of the people who will be using the floor plan. Even if you are only planning a simple one-room addition to your present home, you will profit by drawing up a design. Everyone who will use the space should list the spaces they feel they want and need. Then they should tell what function this space will have and describe the atmosphere they would like to create in the spaces. Figure 6-2 is a sample design made by some friends of ours before they drew their plans for a three-room addition to their small house.

The next step in your trial design is to relate your spaces to one another, and to the space you already have if this is to be an addition. Remember that spaces can relate vertically as well as horizontally, and that a two-story building is usually more economical than spreading out over a single story.

You will probably want to make a lot of rough sketches on scratch paper (Figs. 6-3, 6-4, 6-5, and 6-6) before settling on some basic relationship (not necessarily the final arrangement of the rooms yet). Be sure to check with your local zoning regulations to make sure what you are planning can be built. Restrictions in height and area are especially important to take into consideration in these prelimi-

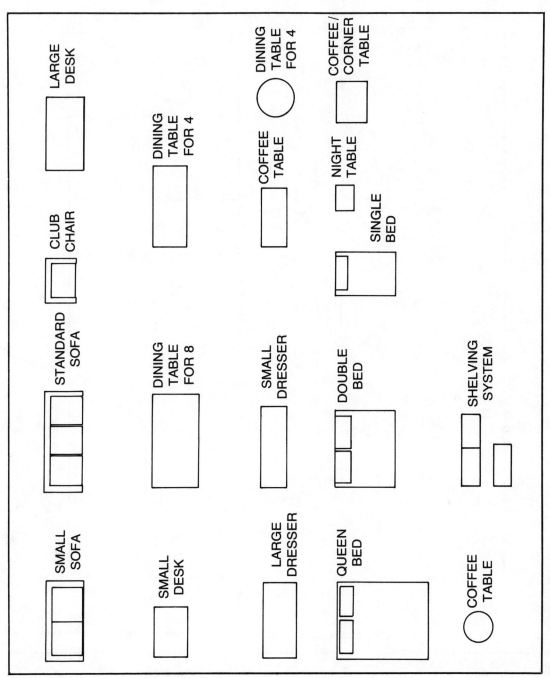

Fig. 6-1. Scale furniture.

133

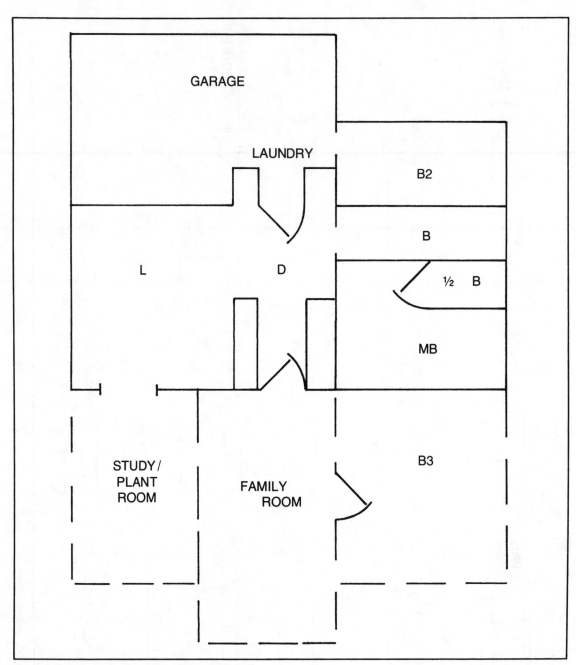

GARAGE

LAUNDRY

B2

B

L

D

½ B

MB

STUDY/
PLANT
ROOM

FAMILY
ROOM

B3

Fig. 6-2. Sample design for a three-room addition.

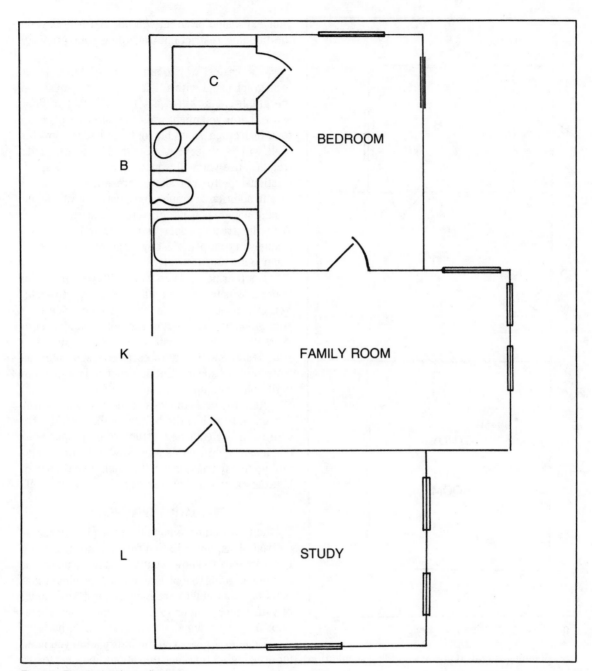

Fig. 6-3. Rough sketch number one.

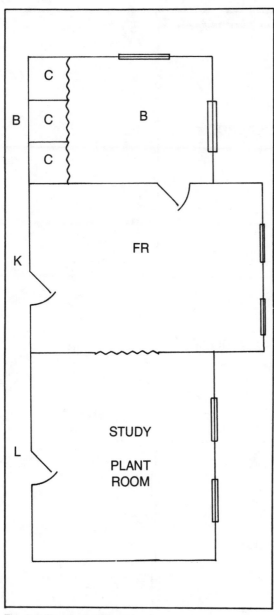

Fig. 6-4. Rough sketch number two.

your expansion program will not take you beyond the building restrictions regarding your property lines.

The easiest way to draw your trial floor plans is on graph paper with a ⅛-inch grid. One square on the graph paper will equal 1 square foot of floor space. Later you might want to scale your plans up to ¼-inch graph paper, but for trial plans the smaller scale will be easier to work with. This is especially true because you will want to establish your space relationships to your site or present yard.

In addition to graph paper, you will want some tracing paper, pencils, erasers, and drafting tape. With the tracing paper and tape, you can make changes in your plans just by taping another layer of paper onto your drawing.

Another neat way to work with your first trial floor plans is to make cutouts of the space to scale. You can move the spaces around on a scale (use your graph paper) layout of your lot or building site. Work out the approximate sizes of all the spaces in your design and then draw each room seperately as a rectangle or square. Cut them out and rotate them until you come up with your first rough plan.

Architectural drawings are drawn with north at the top and south at the bottom of the drawing. Be sure to orient your new structure on property so that it can be drawn this way. Now is the time to go through many trial plans with single-line drawings like the sketches shown in Fig. 6-7, 6-8, and 6-9.

EVALUATING TRIAL PLANS

By the time you have gone through a half dozen or so trial plans, you will find that you are becoming quite anxious to know what your new structure or addition is going to look like. It is a good idea at that point to either build a preliminary cardboard model of your house plan or to draw sections and elevations of it. Our suggestion is that you do both!

Chapter 7 gives you the information you need for drawing sections and elevations and Chapter 13 is on model building. You might skip ahead and read

nary planning stages. If you are building an addition to an existing structure, you will need to be sure

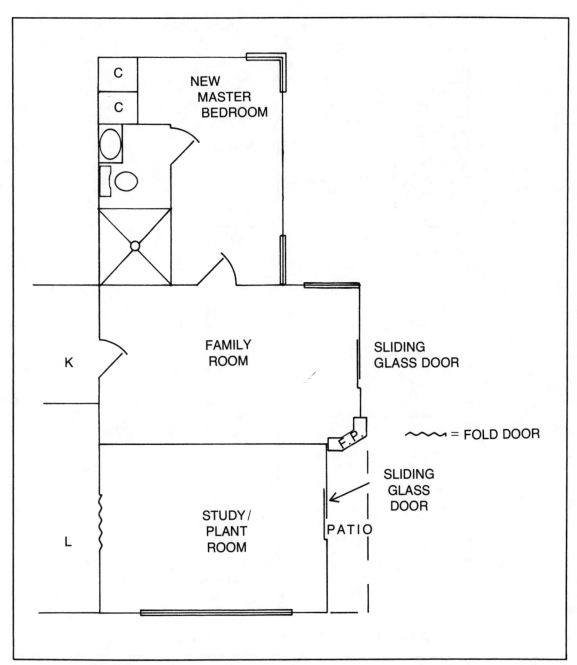

Fig. 6-5. Rough sketch number three.

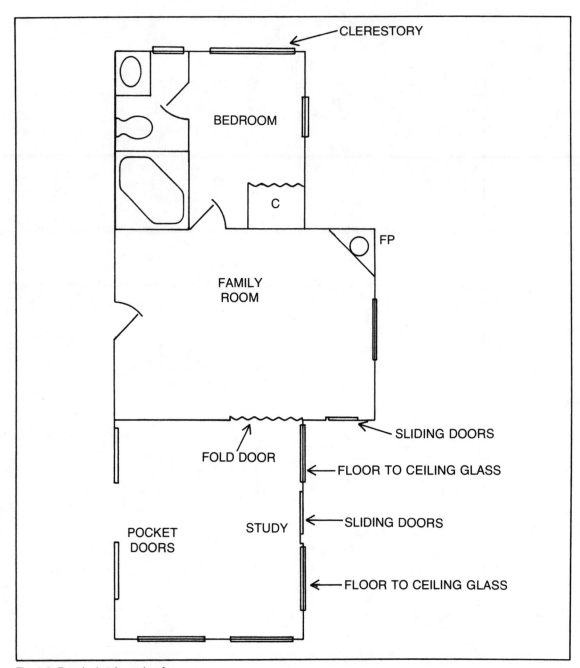

CLERESTORY

BEDROOM

C

FP

FAMILY
ROOM

SLIDING DOORS

FOLD DOOR

FLOOR TO CEILING GLASS

SLIDING DOORS

POCKET
DOORS

STUDY

FLOOR TO CEILING GLASS

Fig. 6-6. Rough sketch number four.

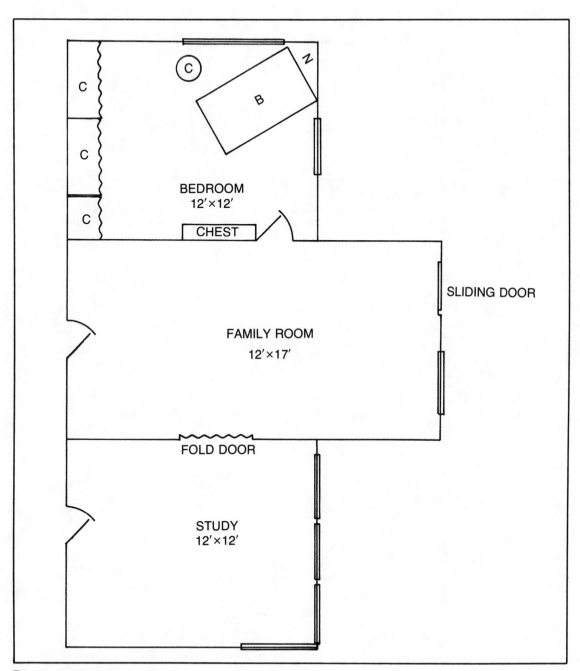

Fig. 6-7. Trial floor plan number one.

139

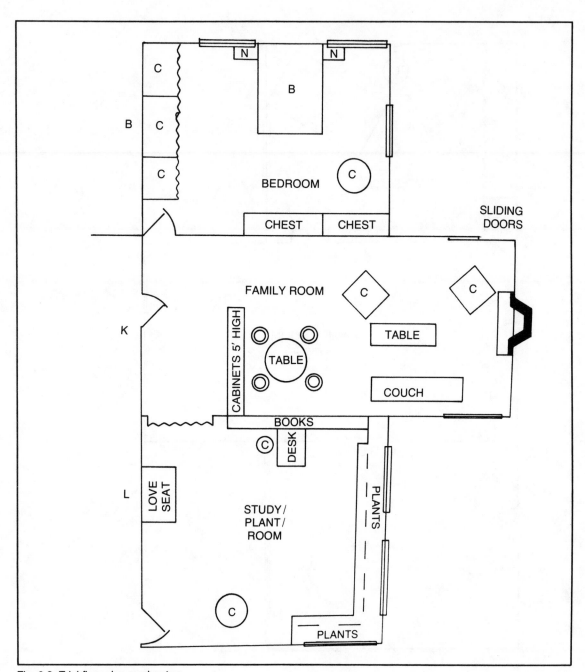

Fig. 6-8. Trial floor plan number two.

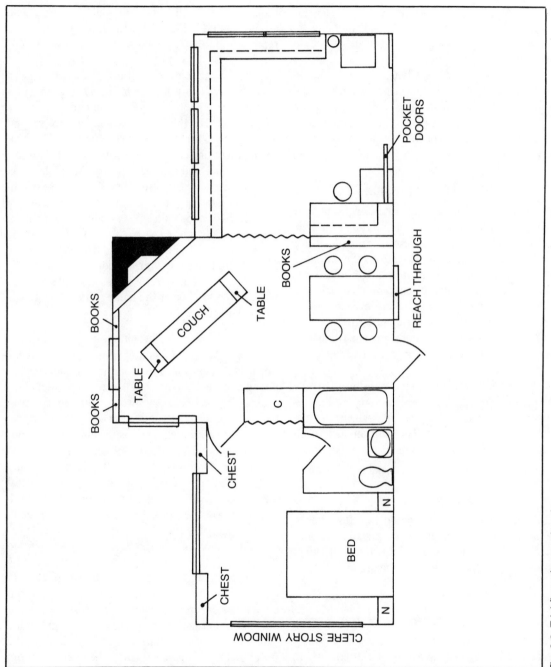

Fig. 6-9. Trial floor plan number three.

141

these chapters and then get in some practice for doing your final drawings and model building by making these preliminary drawings and a simple model of your final trial plan.

In your sections, elevations, and models, you will discover things about the shape of your roof and the height of ceilings. Perhaps you will discover some wasted space you can salvage or some things that seemed to work on paper, but that do not work out in three dimensions.

REVISING YOUR DESIGN

As you revise your design on paper from your evaluation with sections, elevations, and models, you will want to make sure your revised plan fits a standard building module. The most efficient module in a house or addition constructed of wood is the 4-foot module. Virtually all building materials and components come in 4-foot and 8-foot sizes. Lumber is sold in 2-foot increments. Therefore, you will want to layout your revised design on a 4-foot grid and do whatever needs to be done to adapt your plans to it.

You will also want to go to a two-line plan now and draw in the thicknesses of your walls. Remember that your room sizes will shrink by the amount of wall thickness. This will amount to almost 1 foot off the dimensions of the rooms each way.

DETAILED FLOOR PLAN

With your design now translated to a floor-space plan it is time to think about the planning of individual rooms. You will need to plan individual rooms as much as possible for maximum utility in minimum space.

Kitchens

Architects identify at least seven basic types of kitchen arrangements: one wall, U, broken U, L, broken L, two walls, and individual center. These are illustrated in Fig. 6-10 with the shaded-in areas representing the space occupied by the work centers.

A 7-cubic-foot refrigerator used to serve a small family is only about 6 inches smaller in width than a 12-cubic-foot refrigerator needed to serve a large family. But the work-space length would need to be doubled for the larger refrigerator. The sink and dishwashing center in the kitchen will also vary in work space and cabinet capacity. Much depends on the size of the family served by the kitchen. Same goes for the stove and the serving center.

Each of these three separate work centers should be complete with cabinets and counter space, but they can be separated from one another as in the individual center kitchen layout shown in Fig. 6-10. This separation enables several people to work in the kitchen at the same time without tripping over one another.

Bathrooms

The addition of an outer lavatory to a conventional bathroom is a real boon to the family with young children. Figure 6-11A shows this idea. Figures 6-11B and 6-11C shows some other compact bathroom floor-plan suggestions.

Be sure to pick your bathroom fixtures out from the various manufacturers' catalogs before you design your bathroom floor plan. There are many shapes and sizes to bathroom fixtures and you will want to draw yours to exact size. Fitting a bathtub between two closets in another room is a good space-saving design, but you need to know the precise dimensions of the tub before you can plan the closets.

In planning bathrooms, you must give some thought to the placement of fixtures and the economics of running plumbing lines as well as the placement in relation to doors, windows and walls. You will not want a bathtub under a window or a toilet that is in full view through the open bathroom

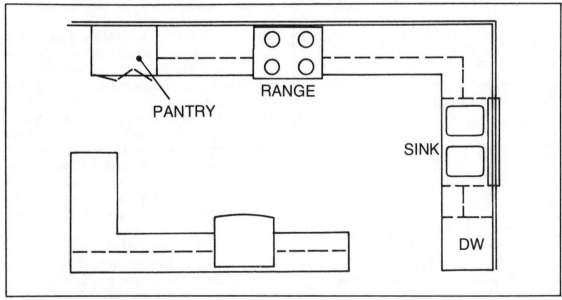

Fig. 6-10. Floor plan of a kitchen.

door. Lavatories need plenty of elbow room around them.

Dining Rooms

Professional house plan designers probably give less thought to dining space than to any other area. Yet families spend a lot of time eating together and a pleasant place to eat is a very important factor in one's quality of life. As long as you are designing your own floor plans, give some extra thought to

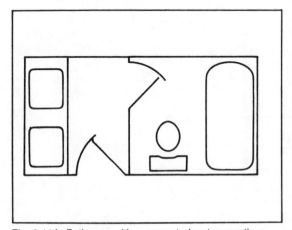

Fig. 6-11A. Bathroom with a separate lavatory section.

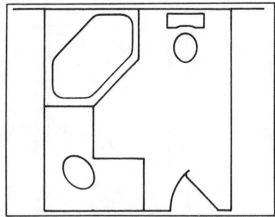

Fig. 6-11B. A compact bathroom with a shower.

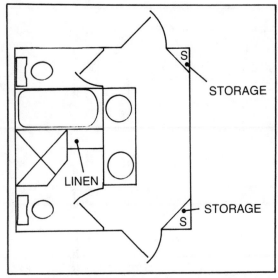

Fig. 6-11C. Triple facilities in a 9-×-9.8-foot area.

your dining spaces. Maybe you'd like several eating areas: a breakfast room, a dining room, and even a lunch counter. Perhaps you'd like a snack area in your bedroom if you are a night snacker or a booth in the family room for snacking while watching TV.

If you like open space with few partitions, but also feel a need for private dining, design in a partition that will fold into a wall or extend to make a wall. High windows (at least 4 feet from the floor) give you more efficient use of floor space. The same is true for built-in hanging cabinets. If you do skimp on dining space, don't skimp so much that tables and chairs crowd diners out of the elbow room needed for minimum comfort. See Fig. 6-12 for some ideas.

Living Rooms

Did you ever notice how little living is done in living rooms of the type designated for the conventional

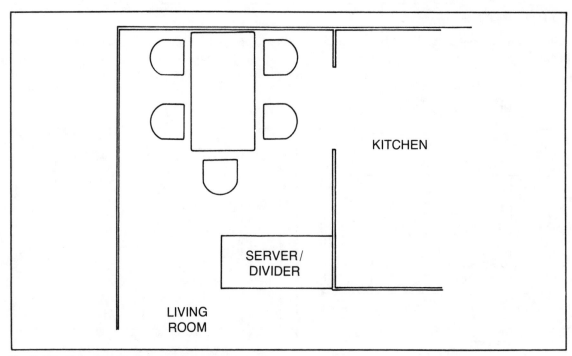

Fig. 6-12A. Dining in a 7-×-9-foot area in comfort.

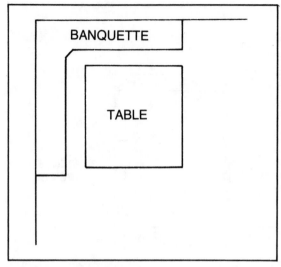

Fig. 6-12B. Dining in a corner.

suburban tract house? Most of the living is done in the family room or game room or on an outdoor patio—weather permitting. Why not design a living room to accommodate the kind of living your family likes to do?

If frequent barbecue parties are your way of living, why not have sliding doors between the living room and patio that can be opened to make your living room an important part of your parties. How about a combination living room and walled garden? Planning a living room that can be used for your style of living can be the most fun of all. Give that space a lot of tender, loving thought. Figure 6-13 shows some unusual living room ideas that will start your creative processes flowing!

Bedrooms

Professional architects have given us two innovations in recent years that are worth hanging onto in most bedroom designs: sliding closet doors and high window sills. Bedroom windows have grown shorter and wider along with the high sill that gives more wall space for placing furniture and guards privacy. These windows should never become too

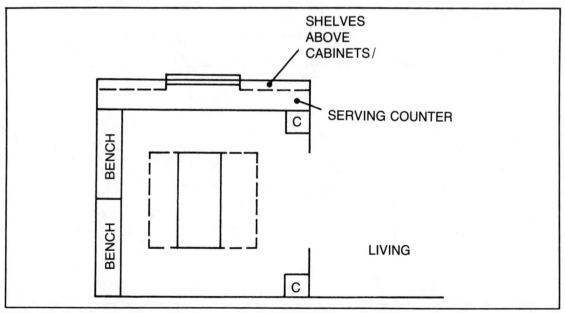

Fig. 6-12C. A small-space dining solution is a drop-leaf table and upholstered benches.

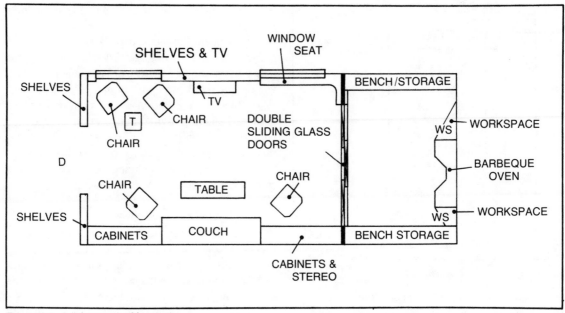

Fig. 6-13A. A living room with a patio.

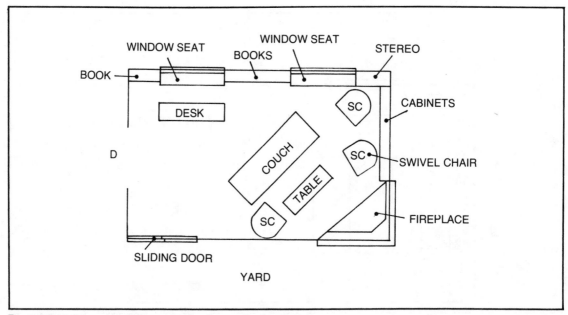

Fig. 6-13B. A living room with a corner fireplace as the focal point.

146

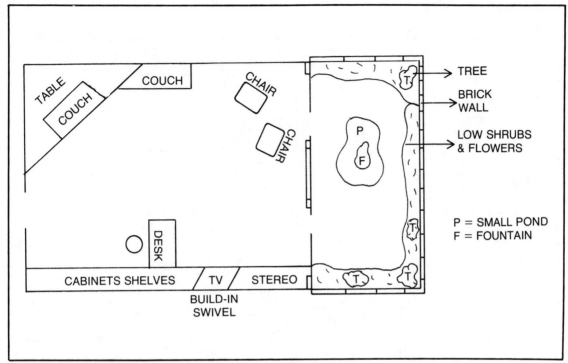

Fig. 6-13C. A living room with a walled garden.

large. Total window area in the bedroom should not exceed about 15 percent of the floor area. Figure 6-14 shows some ideas for window location in relation to furniture placement.

Several conventional bedroom designs can be used. A popular idea is to place two bedrooms side by side and then use the common wall between as a closet wall. Chimney space, a hall linen closet, and two bedroom closets can be designed to fit compactly together. Another good convention is to put a bathroom between two bedrooms. One entrance can be through the hall and the other through the master bedroom.

The master bedroom needs its own bathroom. Even if you do not prefer this arrangement, most people do and a house with a master bedroom "suite" will bring more money when you go to sell it. Chapter 11 provides more designs of the different rooms of a house. Included are some suggestions on laundry and utility rooms and hallways as

they relate to one another when you design an entire house at one time.

While the comments we have made here are mostly appropriate when designing an entire residence from scratch, they are given with the idea that you might be planning a single room or single-wing addition to your present house. If this is what you have in mind, you might still want to skip ahead for our planning comments, room by room, in Chapter 11 before you finalize your plans.

Garages, Porches, and Breezeways

Garages, porches, and breezeways are all popular and easy add-on structures to houses. They are often planned and then left to be added at a future time due to economic necessity at the time a house is first built. We once had a detached, steam-heated garage of well-insulated double-brick construction. You would think that this would be ideal, especially for cold winter nights. But we also had a porte

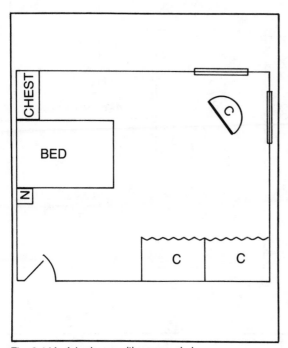

Fig. 6-14A. A bedroom with corner windows.

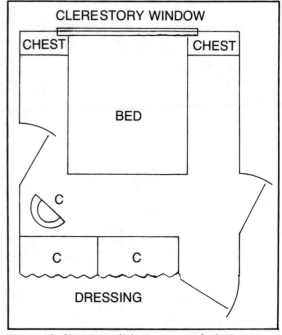

Fig. 6-14C. Clerestory windows are great for bedrooms.

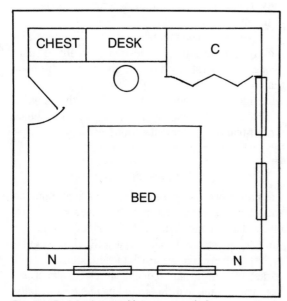

Fig. 6-14B. A bedroom with too many windows.

cochere right by the front door. Where do you suppose the family car spent most of its time? Right there by the front door under the roof of the porte cochere, even on sub zero nights! The moral of that story is that a detached garage standing away from the house is quite an inconvenience. This is especially true in bad weather. Save yourself a lot of money and attach the garage to the house. It almost always improves the appearance of the house and adds to its resale value.

In your preliminary sketches, do not underestimate the size of your garage in relation to the house. A double garage should be at least 20×20 feet square to house even economy cars without crowding.

An attached garage can work with the walls of your house to make a two-or three-wall enclosure for a porch, as shown in Fig. 6-15. Front and back porches make delightful living areas in all climates.

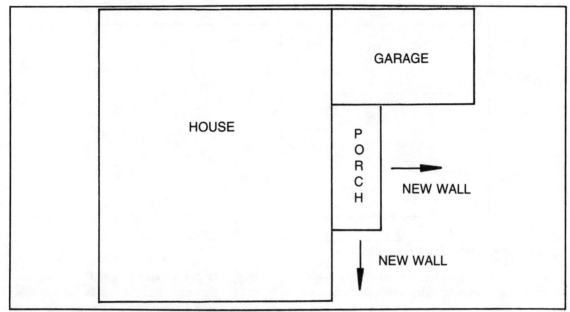

Fig. 6-15A. A porch situated between the garage and house.

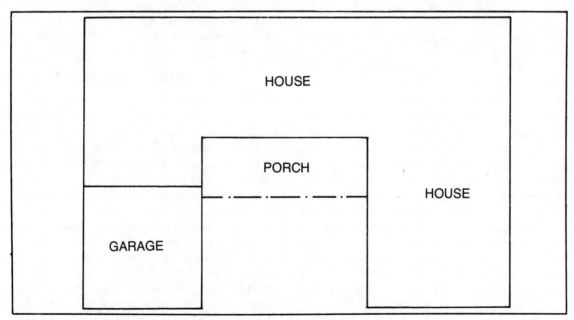

Fig. 6-15B. A porch located between the garage and house (version two).

149

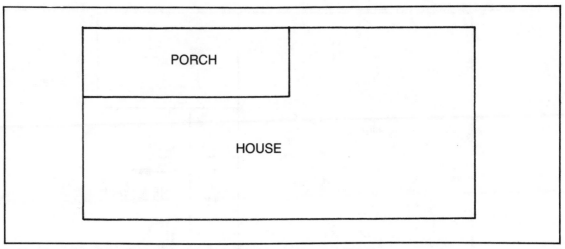

Fig. 6-15C. A porch nestled between two wings of the house.

In one house we rented for a time in Minneapolis, Minnesota, we had an upstairs screened-in sleeping porch. That was the best summer-time sleeping we have ever known. Unheated and storm windowed during the long Minnesota winter, we occupied it every night from about mid-May to mid-September. During some years, we occupied the room into late October—viva porches!

Porches should be designed and oriented so as to be shaded in summer with cross ventilation by prevailing breezes. They should get direct sunlight in winter. With double-glass storm windows, they can be used year round even in severe climates.

The *breezeway* is an old Texas hill-country invention that old-timers refer to as a "dog trot." Most young architects will tell you that the breezeway came into use as a device to attach a separate garage to a house. Actually, it came about as a device to connect the smoke house to the kitchen and to provide a sheltered place where evaporative cooling could take place in the summertime. Built to catch any breeze that was stirring, the breezeway on some of the restored historical houses we have visited will often be 15 degrees cooler than surrounding shaded areas or house interiors.

If attaching a garage to a small house will render one entire side of the house windowless, save the situation by building the garage away from the house and then build a breezeway connecting the two. The breezeway can then be used for family living, dining, or sleeping if it is properly enclosed with combination screen and storm windows on the open ends.

THE FLOOR PLAN WORKING DRAWING

Once you have arrived at a final floor plan and have worked out all the dimensions of all your spaces, draw a single-line floor plan like the one illustrated in Fig. 6-16. Draw the lines in lightly. Remember that the outside single lines represent the outside faces of the wall studs, and that the inside lines cross the centers of the studs making up the partition walls.

Do not put any window or door openings in this drawing. You will do that when you are double lining. That is the next step in your drawing. To double line exterior walls, measure 2 inches outside of the single line and 4 inches inside to make your 6-inch exterior walls. Double line the interior partition walls by measuring 2 inches on either side

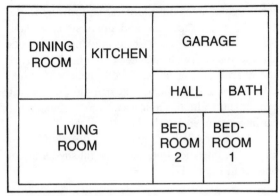

Fig. 6-16. A single-line plan.

of your single line. In almost all frame construction, exterior walls are drawn 6 inches thick and interior walls and partitions are drawn 4 inches thick. Stone, brick, or concrete block walls will be drawn thicker depending on the actual dimensions of the building materials.

Locate your door and window openings along the center lines. Look up the actual doors and windows you will be specifying and make your drawing dimensionally accurate. Be sure that they meet building code requirements for light and air. Most codes call for a minimum glass area in a room to equal 10 percent of the floor area, for light, and 5

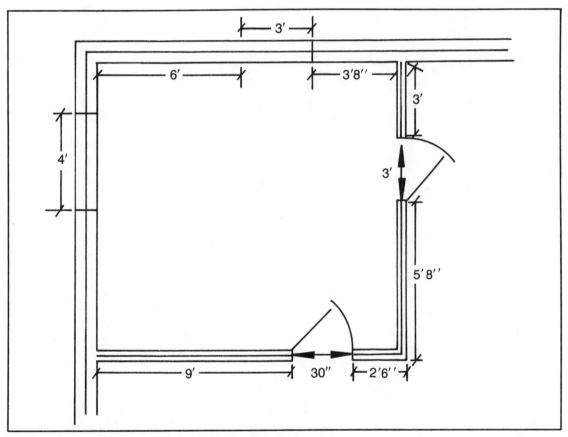

Fig. 6-17. A double-line plan with doors, windows, and dimension lines.

percent of the floor area must be able to be opened up to air.

When drafting your final floor plan, show window and door openings the size of the rough opening required for framing in the window or door. Next draw in the direction of swing on your doors, as shown in Fig. 6-17, and study these swings to be sure you have easy access and good circulation to all rooms, closets, etc.

Now draw in all your fixtures in kitchen and bathrooms. Before drawing in any steps or stairways, make a separate large-scale drawing to determine the exact size and dimensions of your treads and risers. Do a scale drawing of the side view of the stairwell and check your head room and the overall size of the stairwell opening.

Fireplaces should be drawn to show the overall length and width of the brickwork, the flue, and an outline representing the hearth.

Go over all the plan lines and darken them. Place all dimension lines as in the finished drawing shown in Fig. 6-17.

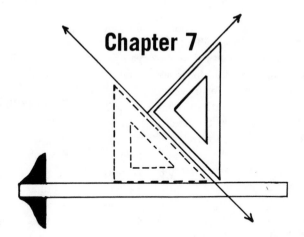

Chapter 7

Sections and Elevations

SECTION AND ELEVATION DRAWINGS ARE necessary to show contractors and workmen how all the structural and architectural parts of a building relate to one another, and to show the expected finished appearance of relating those parts. Generally, sections show relationships and elevations show appearances. Elevations are usually drawn by projecting sections.

CROSS SECTIONS

Section is architectural jargon for *cross section*. A cross section is any view you get when you cut across a structure and look at the "inside" of it. If you have ever looked down on the stump of a freshly cut tree and counted the annual growth rings, you have looked at a section of the tree. That would be a horizontal section because the cut to show it would have been made horizontally. A vertical section of the tree would have a cut up and down the tree and show a different version of its structure.

Technically, a floor plan is a section drawing. It is what you would see if you cut horizontally across the bottom of a house just a few inches above floor level. The difference is that a horizontal section drawing will show, in addition to the floor plan, details of materials used in walls and foundations—structural details. For this reason, it is usually referred to as a *structural section*.

Drawings are made of structural sections that will best illustrate the relationships of all parts of the structure and can be taken through the structure horizontally or vertically. Often small sections are drawn with "cuts" made at any angle. Whatever best shows the desired construction details of stairways, fireplaces, doors, windows, etc., is appropriate.

Structural sections must show all dimensions and such important details as plate height and roof pitch. And they must be drawn to the same scale as the rest of your house plans. It is acceptable, and sometimes necessary, to draw small details on the same sheet as a section to a larger scale, but be sure to note the scale of the detail if it is different from the main section.

Sections should also show points of connection between structural parts and notations about the size and material of structural members. Usually one or two sections is all that is required for plans for a simple addition to a house. Three or four will suffice for a small residence of conventional construction, but anytime there is a change in shape or method of construction a new sectional drawing will be necessary.

Most structural sections are drawn on separate sheets of paper. If your project is not complicated you can combine them with other drawings. Do try to use a fairly large scale so that details can be shown clearly without confusion; ½ inch = 1 foot is a good scale to use.

Instructions in structural systems, represented by sectional drawings, should be applicable anywhere in spite of regional differences in materials and construction practices. For this reason, these construction instructions are usually broken down into five parts corresponding to the way construction usually proceeds:

—Foundation.
—Floor.
—Wall.
—Ceiling.
—Roof system.

You can usually specify any combination of materials you want for any one of the five categories, but you would not usually mix materials within a category. In other words, while you can use masonry materials for your foundation and wood for your floors, you might be in serious trouble trying to use both masonry and wood in your foundation.

There are certain obvious combinations you would not ordinarily use, such as a masonry roof over wood walls. To draw really good, workable section plans, you need to go out and look at the materials and construction practices in your locality and stick to making plans around what is most common in your particular locality. The following information will be helpful to you in your design work and plan drawing wherever you live. It will also help you to recognize what is going on when you visit home construction sites near your home.

DESIGN CONSIDERATIONS

Footings. The purpose of the footing of any building is the same as the purpose of your own feet: to distribute the weight of the building over the ground. The size of the footing varies with the weight of the building and the kind of soil that must support it. In areas where severe winter weather sends frost deep into the ground, footings must go quite deep. The rule is to always go below the frost line. In mild climates, where there is little or no frost in winter, footings can set right on top of the soil.

Footings and foundations are usually made from concrete and masonry. Those are often the *only* materials approved by building codes in most areas. Building codes usually specify the use of reinforcing steel in footings and foundations. We recommend that you show reinforcing rods in the footings of any structure you plan.

Foundation Walls. Foundation walls carry the load of the building to the footings. They also isolate wood construction from water, rot, and insects. The minimum height of a foundation wall should be 6 inches above grade. There is no maximum. The thickness of the wall depends on the weight of the structure, but should be at least 4 inches if it is not specified in your building code. The use of reinforcing steel in the foundation walls will increase strength and make less massive walls possible. You will need to look at your building code and observe building practices in your neighborhood to determine the size and spacing of steel to be used in your foundation walls.

Floors of Concrete. Concrete floors that are on the ground or below grade can be cast as part of the foundation wall or footing or they can be poured separately. The usual thickness is 3½ inches and it is wise to indicate welded wire fabric in your concrete floors to prevent cracking and to add strength.

Waterprooting. Any part of the foundation, footing, or floors that comes in contact with the ground must be protected from water. You will always draw your waterproof membrane on the earth side of any structure or part of a structure that goes below grade. This membrane can be a chemical solution painted on or can be a plastic film. Specify whatever is common and found to be an effective barrier in your locality. Draw in a layer of gravel or crushed rock below any concrete floors you plan (to keep water from being drawn up to it by capillary attraction in the soil).

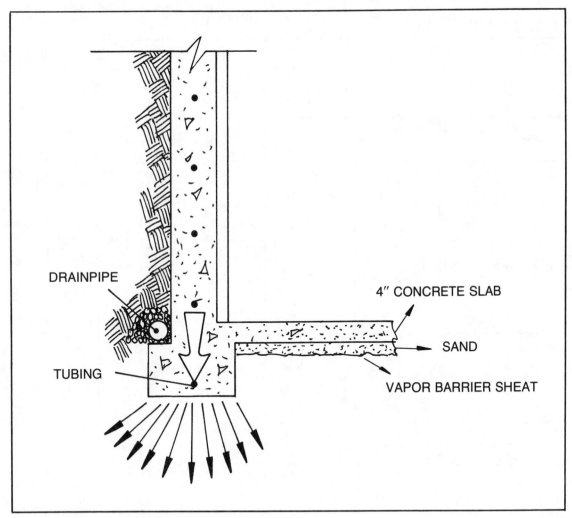

Fig. 7-1. A section with lines showing forces acting on the footing.

As you observe construction in your area, see if builders are fighting excessive groundwater or poor soil drainage. If drainage is a problem, be sure to design drain tiles into your footings to conduct water away from the load bearing bottom surface of the footing. Figure 7-1 shows a section with forces acting on the footings and drain tiles to keep the ground from getting too soft.

Floors. Floors are designed not only to carry their own weight, but to transmit live loads (people walking around) and dead loads (the weight of the building) to the footings. The simplest kind of floor to design (and build) is the common wood-joist floor. Table 7-1 gives the size and spacing of joists for any span and load. The size and spacing of joists is a factor of the load and the span between supports

Table 7-1. Sizes and Spacing for Floor Joists.

	Grade	2×6		2×8		2×10		2×12		Size Span
		12	16	12	16	12	16	12	16	
Ponderosa Pine	#1	10-9	9-0	14-2	12-10	18-0	16-5	21-11	19-11	
	#2	10-5	9-6	13-9	12-6	17-6	15-11	21-4	19-4	
	#3	8-6	7-4	11-3	9-9	14-4	12-5	17-5	15-11	
Red Pine	#1	11-0	10-0	14-6	13-2	18-6	16-10	22-6	20-6	
	#2	10-9	9-6	14-2	12-6	18-0	15-11	21-11	19-5	
	#3	8-4	7-3	11-0	9-6	14-0	12-2	17-0	14-9	
Western Pine	#1	11-3	10-3	14-11	13-6	19-0	17-3	23-1	21-0	
	#2	10-10	9-4	14-3	12-4	18-2	15-8	22-1	19-2	
	#3	8-4	7-3	11-0	9-6	14-0	12-2	17-0	14-9	
Spruce/pine/fir	#1	11-7	10-6	15-3	13-10	19-5	17-8	23-7	21-6	
	#2	11-0	9-9	14-6	12-10	18-6	16-4	22-6	19-11	
	#3	8-6	7-4	11-3	9-9	14-4	12-5	17-5	15-1	
Douglas Fir	#1	12-3	11-2	16-2	14-8	20-8	18-9	25-1	22-10	
	#2	12-0	10-11	15-10	14-5	20-3	18-5	24-8	22-5	
	#3	10-4	9-6	13-8	11-10	17-5	15-1	21-2	18-4	
Western Cedar	#1	10-5	9-6	13-9	12-6	17-6	15-11	21-4	19-4	
	#2	10-1	9-2	13-4	12-1	17-0	15-5	20-8	18-9	
	#3	8-8	7-6	11-6	9-11	14-8	12-8	17-9	15-5	
Hem-Fir	#1	11-7	10-6	15-3	13-10	19-5	17-8	23-7	21-6	
	#2	11-3	10-3	14-11	13-6	19-0	17-3	23-1	21-0	
	#3	9-3	8-0	12-2	10-6	15-6	13-5	18-10	16-4	
Eastern Hemlock	#1	11-0	10-0	14-6	13-2	18-6	16-10	22-6	20-6	
	#2	10-5	9-6	13-9	12-6	17-6	15-11	21-4	19-4	
	#3	9-7	8-3	12-7	10-11	16-1	13-11	19-7	16-11	
Coast Silka Spruce	#1	12-0	10-10	15-10	14-4	20-3	18-3	24-8	22-3	
	#2	11-6	10-0	15-2	13-2	19-4	16-9	23-6	20-5	
	#3	8-8	7-6	11-6	9-11	14-8	12-8	17-9	15-5	

Floor joists   30 PSE Live Load

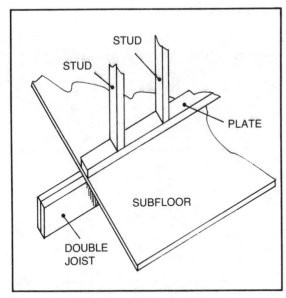

Fig. 7-2. A section of a wood-joist floor.

and the type of wood being used. No fancy floor framing plan need be drawn for this type of floor because carpenters understand this type of construction and could probably build one in the dark! Figure 7-2 shows a section of a wood-joist floor.

A plank-and-beam floor is not uncommon. It differs from the joist floor in that the supporting beams are widely spaced and heavy flooring material such as tongue-and-groove flooring is used to span the wide spacing. Figure 7-3 shows a section of

plank-and-beam floor that would explain what you have in mind to any carpenter.

Walls. Walls support roof loads as well as serve as room dividers and separators in conventionally built houses. Not all interior walls are roof supporters (so called load bearing walls), but all exterior walls are. Figures 7-4 and 7-5 shows a section of a conventional 2-×-4 inch wall. Its components are a bottom plate, studs, and a double top plate. Fire blocking 2×4s are placed between studs as intermediate bracing. The double plates should overlap at all joints and corners. This gives good support to those roof rafters that fall between studs and in general makes a strong ring around the top of the wall. Standard spacing of studs is 16 inches on center. Walls are finished by nailing or gluing finish materials, such as paneling, to the studs.

In post-and-beam wall construction, the bottom plate is the same, but 4×4s are (in place of studs) spaced as much as 48 inches apart. The top plate is one beam, 4×4, 4×6, or 4×8; it depends on the dead weight above and the span of large openings.

Some home designers prefer post-and-beam construction because it saves on materials and labor and results in a building that has a neat modular appearance. Nonbearing walls need not be constructed to carry more than their own weight so it is permissible to use a single 2×4 top plate and place studs 24, 36, or even 48 inches on center. Do not

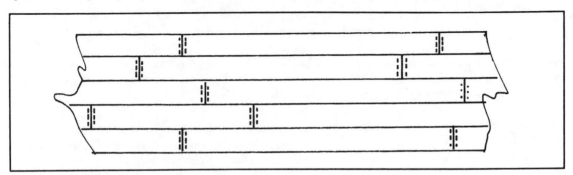

Fig. 7-3. A plan for plank floor.

Table 7-2. Ceiling Joist Spacing and Sizes.

	Grade	2×6		2×8		2×10		2×12	
		12″ c.c.	16 c.c.	12 c.c.	16 c.c.	12 c.c.	16 c.c,	12 c.c.	16 c.c.
Ponderosa Pine	#1	10-9	9-9	14-2	12-10	18-0	16-5	21-11	19-11
	#2	10-5	9-6	13-9	12-6	17-6	15-11	21-4	19-4
	#3	8-6	7-4	11-3	9-9	14-4	12-5	17-5	15-1
Red Pine	#1	11-0	10-0	14-6	13-2	18-6	16-10	22-6	20-6
	#2	10-9	9-6	14-2	12-6	18-0	15-11	21-11	19-5
	#3	8-4	7-3	11-0	9-6	14-0	12-2	17-0	14-9
Western pine	#1	11-3	10-3	14-11	13-6	19-0	17-3	23-1	21-0
	#2	10-10	9-4	14-3	12-4	18-2	15-9	22-1	19-2
	#3	8-4	7-3	11-0	9-6	14-0	12-2	17-0	14-9
Spruce-pine-fir	#1	11-7	10-6	15-3	13-10	19-5	17-8	23-7	21-6
	#2	11-0	9-9	14-6	12-10	18-6	16-4	22-6	19-11
	#3	8-6	7-4	11-3	9-9	14-4	12-5	17-5	15-1
Douglas Fir	#1	12-3	11-2	16-2	14-8	20-8	18-9	25-1	22-10
	#2	12-0	10-11	15-10	14-5	20-3	18-5	24-8	22-5
	#3	10-4	9-0	13-8	11-10	17-5	15-1	21-2	18-4
Hem-Fir	#1	11-7	10-6	15-3	13-10	19-5	17-8	23-7	21-6
	#2	11-3	10-3	14-11	13-6	19-0	17-3	23-1	21-0
	#3	9-3	8-0	12-2	10-6	15-6	13-5	18-10	16-4
Western Cedar	#1	10-5	9-6	13-9	12-6	17-6	15-11	21-4	19-4
	#2	10-1	9-2	13-4	12-1	17-0	15-5	20-8	18-9
	#3	8-8	7-6	11-6	9-11	14-8	12-8	17-9	15-5
Eastern Hemlock	#1	11-0	10-0	14-6	13-2	18-6	16-10	22-6	20-6
	#2	10-5	9-6	13-9	12-6	17-6	15-11	21-4	19-4
	#3	9-7	8-3	12-7	10-11	15-1	13-11	19-7	16-11
Coast Silka Spruce	#1	12-0	10-10	15-10	14-4	20-3	18-3	24-8	22-3
	#2	11-6	10-0	15-2	13-2	19-4	16-9	23-6	20-5
	#3	8-8	7-6	11-6	9-11	14-8	12-8	17-9	15-5

30 PSE Live Load

design in light nonbearing walls where noise between rooms is an important factor.

Ceiling/Roof Structures and Openings. All openings such as windows and doors must be designed with lintels above them to carry the load of the weight above them. You will need to consult your local building code for the allowed material and sizes.

The ceiling and roof structure above the walls ties together walls as well as providing shelter and support. A simple span system with rafters and 1-inch sheathing to form a gable or hip roof is the simplest to design and it is understood by all carpenters. For open beam ceilings, rafters and 2-inch tongue-and-groove decking are quite satisfactory. This type of roof will span up to 24 feet with no engineering problems. Tables 7-2 and 7-3 will help you figure out the sizes of roof parts.

If you go out to observe the construction of large tracts of residences, you might find wholesale use of trussed systems for roofs. Trusses are made and put in place by special equipment in order to speed up construction. We do not recommend that you design trusses into your house plans unless you plan to build homes by the dozens.

Single pitch (shed or flat) roofs are easy to design and construct, but they tend to leak badly after a short time. The same goes for butterfly roofs. We do not recommend that you consider these types in your designs unless it almost never rains where you will be building. Your roof needs a good slope to it and it should be covered with metal

Table 7-3. Rafter Spacing and Sizes.

	Grade	2×4 12"	2×4 16"	2×6 12"	2×6 16"	2×8 12"	2×8 16"	2×10 12"	2×10 16"
Ponderosa Pine	#1	9-10	8-11	15-6	13-11	20-5	18-4	26-0	23-6
	#2	9-7	8-8	14-6	12-6	9-1	16-6	24-4	21-1
	#3	7-5	6-5	11-1	9-7	14-8	12-8	18-8	16-2
Red Pine	#1	10-1	9-2	15-8	13-7	20-8	17-11	26-5	22-10
	#2	9-10	8-6	14-3	12-4	18-10	16-3	24-0	20-9
	#3	7-5	6-5	10-10	9-5	14-4	12-5	18-3	15-10
Western Pine	#1	10-4	9-3	15-8	13-7	20-8	17-11	26-5	22-10
	#2	9-7	8-3	14-1	12-2	18-7	16-1	23-8	20-6
	#3	7-3	6-3	10-10	9-5	14-4	12-5	18-3	15-10
Spruce/pine/fir	#1	10-7	9-7	16-1	13-11	21-2	18-4	27-0	23-5
	#2	10-0	8-8	14-8	12-8	19-4	16-9	24-8	21-4
	#3	7-6	6-6	11-1	9-7	14-8	12-8	18-8	16-2
Douglas Fir	#1	11-3	10-3	17-8	16-1	23-4	21-2	29-9	27-1
	#2	11-1	10-10	17-4	15-4	22-11	20-2	29-2	25-9
	#3	8-11	7-9	13-6	11-9	17-10	15-5	22-9	19-8
Hem-Fir	#1	10-7	9-8	16-8	15-0	22-0	19-10	28-0	25-3
	#2	10-4	9-3	15-8	13-7	20-8	17-11	26-5	22-10
	#3	7-11	6-10	12-1	10-5	15-11	13-9	20-4	17-7
Western Cedar	#1	9-7	8-8	15-0	13-8	19-10	18-0	25-3	22-11
	#2	9-3	8-5	14-7	12-8	19-2	16-9	24-6	21-4
	#3	7-6	6-6	11-4	9-10	15-0	12-11	19-1	16-6
Eastern Hemlock	#1	10-1	9-2	15-11	14-5	20-11	19-0	26-9	24-3
	#2	9-7	8-8	15-0	13-8	19-10	18-0	25-3	22-11
	#3	8-4	7-3	12-5	10-0	16-5	14-3	20-11	18-2
Coast Silka Spruce	#1	11-1	9-9	16-5	14-2	21-7	18-9	27-7	23-11
	#2	10-3	8-10	15-0	13-0	10-10	17-2	25-3	21-11
	#3	7-8	6-8	11-4	9-10	15-10	12-11	19-1	16-6

Size Spacing

Rafters: 3-12" slope; 20 PSE Live Load, PSE Dead Load

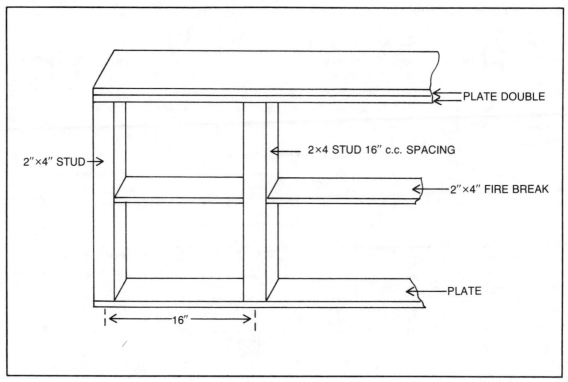

Fig. 7-4. A section of a wooden stud wall.

or one of the many overlapping materials such as singles and shakes, slate, or tiles. Consult your local building code for degree of slope required for these various surface materials.

DRAWING THE STRUCTURAL SECTION

Accuracy and scale are the most important considerations when it comes to drawing structural sections. The sizes, clearances, and spacings of materials and appliances are furnished by manufacturers. They are available from catalogues and standard architectural reference books such as Sweet's Catalogues.

Rough lumber can be drawn to exactly the sizes given. *Finished lumber* must be drawn smaller than given. The actual sizes vary from one area to another, but they usually run ½ to ⅜ inch less than sizes given or quoted. A 2×4, for example, is only a 2×4 when it is rough lumber. Once it is milled it comes down to 1½ by 3½ inches. *Concrete blocks and bricks* all vary in size and nominal size according to locality. *Plywood* will always be the same size as its nominal size. Check around your own locality and make yourself some tables of the actual sizes of construction materials so that you can draw them to scale accurately.

The actual drawing of a section is not at all difficult if you follow these steps.

☐ Decide on the type of foundation, wall, floor, ceiling, and roof you will want to use in the final construction.

☐ Be sure you have or can compute the actual

160

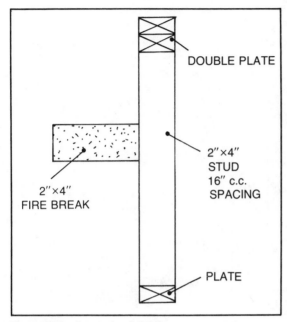

DOUBLE PLATE

2″×4″
STUD
16″ c.c.
SPACING

2″×4″
FIRE BREAK

PLATE

Fig. 7-5. Wooden stud wall detail.

sizes of all structural members to be used in construction.

☐ Establish the grade line. Measuring to scale, draw in a line for the bottom of the footing, top of the foundation wall, finish-floor level, and top plate (see Fig. 7-6).

☐ Establish widths and thicknesses. The total width of your section comes from your floor plan, of course, and the width of the footing and foundation walls, floor joists, wall, roof (and its pitch) all come from Tables or the building code.

☐ Darken all lines representing outlines of structural members. Then draw in all structural connections and all sheathing and finish materials.

☐ Print in all dimensions of structural parts.

☐ Write or print in any necessary notes.

☐ Draw any needed large scale details of structural connections.

Figure 7-6 illustrates all of the above instructions.

PROJECTING SECTIONS FOR DRAWING ELEVATIONS

Although it is entirely possible to make your elevation drawings by a process of transferring measurements from your floor plan and your vertical sections, you can make a more accurate and satisfactory elevation drawing (as a beginner, anyway) by what is called the *direct projection method*. This method avoids the many errors that tend to creep into your drawings when you transfer measurements. It also gives you a better appreciation of the close relationship of the three basic sets of drawings you need to translate your ideas into construction plans: floor plan, section, and elevation drawings.

Your floor plan is really a horizontal section. The structural section you have just learned how to do is a vertical section. By projecting these two sections onto a third drawing, an elevation emerges that will show exactly what the appearance of our section designs will be. Here is how to do your elevation drawings, step by step.

☐ Make sure all drawings (floor plan and sections) are to the same scale.

☐ Place your floor plan directly above the space on your drawing paper where your elevation drawing will appear. One outside wall (the one you want an elevation of) should be facing down. Do not project upward or you will get a mirror image of the wall.

☐ Over to one side, and directly in line with the space where your elevation drawing will appear, place your structural section drawing.

☐ Now project, as a series of light lines, from the floor plan, lines representing the length and all horizontal features of your building such as ends of walls, windows, doors, eaves, etc.

☐ Project lines across from the section drawing that represent height and all vertical features of your building. Don't overlook grade line, floor line, window and door heights, plate line, and ridge line.

☐ Darken all the lines that represent the fea-

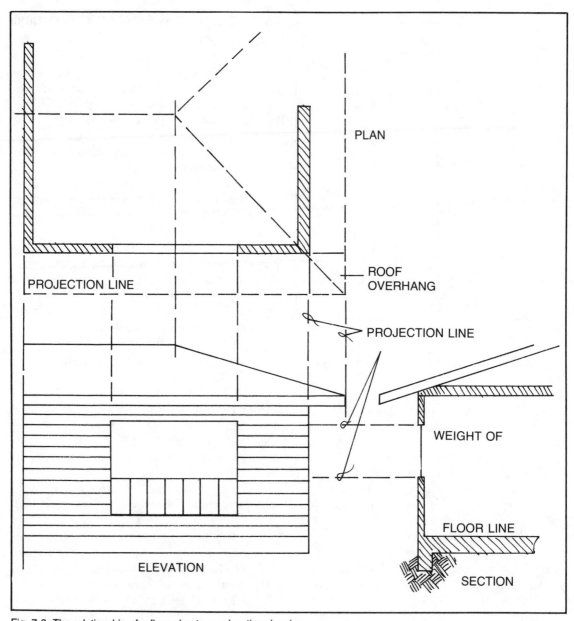

PLAN

ROOF
OVERHANG

PROJECTION LINE

PROJECTION LINE

WEIGHT OF

FLOOR LINE

ELEVATION

SECTION

Fig. 7-6. The relationship of a floor plan to an elevation drawing.

tures of the elevation that are important for you to show. Erase all other lines from the drawing.

Repeat the above steps for all other elevation drawings you need (usually four if you are planning a four-sided house and only two, perhaps, for a dome-type structure) rotating the floor plan for each side and putting the proper section drawing in place. After you have projected these drawings, you will have a set of elevations that lack only the details of porches, chimneys, trim and other details that you might now want to complete.

There are many sources from which you can draw information for the completion of these details. Besides your local building code, that will give you such things as your chimney height, you can consult the sources most architectural draftsmen use: *Sweet's File, Time-Saver Standards, Architectural Graphic Standards*, and good old manufacturers' catalogs. We find large mail-order company catalogs very helpful because they show such details as window and door units, the arrangement of window muntins, etc.

You will want to print in all your notes, reference symbols, title and scale, and perhaps even texture materials on the elevation drawing.

INTERIOR ELEVATIONS

Elevation drawings of interior walls can be very helpful in preventing errors during construction. All interior walls do not need to be drawn. Just draw the important ones such as kitchen and fireplace walls and walls on which there is special cabinet work to be done.

The procedure for projecting elevations can be used on all interior walls, step by step, just as you did with the outside walls. The same sources can be consulted for details of drawing appliances, cabinets, and other interior fixtures.

ANALYZING ELEVATIONS

Elevations should be analyzed to see how the house you have designed is going to fit into its natural environment. The elevation interfaces the environment and shows such important features as roof overhang and angle from which can be determined how much or how little sunlight will strike the house and enter the doors or windows. All of the elements of the elevation will show the relationship of the house, not only to the sun, but to the view, the topography of the site, and the climate of the area. By analyzing the house in relation to these considerations, ways to improve its beauty, economy and comfort will come to you.

CIRCULATION AND LIGHT

Ask yourself some questions and then see how these questions are answered by the elevation and section drawings. How much sun do you want in the interior spaces of your house? How is it allowed to enter and at what time of day? These are important questions to ask of your design. If your elevations show unsatisfactory answers to these questions, change the drawings (working back from elevations to sections to floor plans) until you like the answers you get.

The sun's path in the sky depends on latitude and the season of the year. In most of the United States and Canada, the winter sun stays low in the southern sky, rising in the southeast and setting in the southwest. In the summer, the sun appears to shift to the northeast for rising, arch across the northern part of the sky, and set in the northwest.

Rooms within the house should take into consideration the path of the sun in the sky. You will want your breakfast dining area brightly lighted by the morning sun, for example, but you would not want the sun in your eyes in your study during the afternoon.

Analyze your elevations in relation to the views you get from all directions on your building site. Your window arrangement should be such that it fully exploits the views from your building site.

Building sites with steep slopes call for designs of one kind and flat land requires another. Your elevation drawing will tell the story of how well your design fits the building site.

What do your elevations tell you about your house and its relationship to your climate? Exposures that are very desirable in cold climates can be terribly uncomfortable in hot ones. How are heating and ventilating influenced by your design? Hot and humid areas require houses that are sheltered from the sun, but that remain open to the slightest cool breeze that might happen along. Elevations should show long, wide overhangs to act as barriers against the sun on the western and eastern facades. Air will need to circulate underneath the house.

In climates with extremely cold winters, windows need to be few and small to minimize heat loss, all rooms might wrap around a central chimney, and any large openings would be restricted to the elevation facing south. A row house with only two narrow walls exposed to the outside is a good design concept for energy conservation.

Work with your elevation drawings until you are satisfied that your house blends with its natural environment. Change your sections and floor plans accordingly.

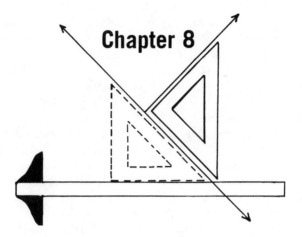

Chapter 8

Appearance

W HILE YOUR ELEVATION DRAWINGS AND FLOOR plans together will give you some idea about what your finished project will look like, these are basically technical or working drawings. To project the appearance of your handiwork, there is nothing quite like a perspective drawing. Drawing to perspective does not take any special talent. You can do it easily once you learn the fundamentals and a few fine points. You will need practice to get really good at it, and you will need to start carefully observing everything you see.

We will be mainly concerned with mechanical (T-square and triangle) perspective, but we will also give you the important principles and "shortcuts" for drawing freehand perspective. Much of architectural drawing is concerned with both.

When you do your practice drawing, you should strive to learn about two things: the form and structure of objects and scenes and, how different view points and conditions of lighting changes the way they appear. It is this appearance of things that

perspective drawing deals with and it is the techniques of representing three-dimensional reality on a two-dimensional sketch pad that one must learn about.

Keep in mind, however, that all pictures are symbolic representations of reality. It is not the purpose of perspective drawing to simulate what the eye can see. The best perspective drawings are limited in size, static, and flat. The eyes, however, are constantly on the move, adjusting for light intensity, changing focus, responding to color and depth.

Perspective drawing is concerned with achieving a sense of the third dimension, space and depth, in order to show what your finished room or house will look like. The first principle for achieving this is the principle that objects appear smaller as their distance from the observer increases.

DIMINUTION

Go out on a street where people are walking and

hold your hand upright with your arm extended forward. Notice that persons close by will be about as tall as the height of your whole hand, but what about people more distant? Some in the middle distance will be the height of your thumb and those in the far distance less than the height of your little finger nail! Now take a large piece of drawing paper and draw the outline of your hand (Fig. 8-1). To one side, draw a series of stick figures: one the same height as your hand, another the height of your little finger, and still another the sizes your finger nail.

With your T-square, draw a straight line across the paper running through the middle of the smallest figure. Put a dot on this line (you have just located a *vanishing point*) and with your triangle draw several lines from the bottom and sides of your paper to this dot. You have just created your first perspective drawing using the principle of di-

minution. Objects always appear smaller as the distance from the observation point increases. You have also made use of *convergence* which is a combination of diminution and *foreshortening*.

FORESHORTENING

Lines or surfaces parallel to your face show their maximum size, but as they are rotated away from you they appear to grow shorter. To demonstrate this, take a cardboard core from a roll of paper towels and hold it at arms length parallel to your face. You would draw this view as a rectangle, perhaps 6 inches long (Fig. 8-2). Rotate the core away from your face about 30 degrees.

To represent what you see now, the top line of your rectangle spreads out into an ellipse and the rest of the rectangle must be drawn much shorter—only about 4 inches long. Rotate the cardboard

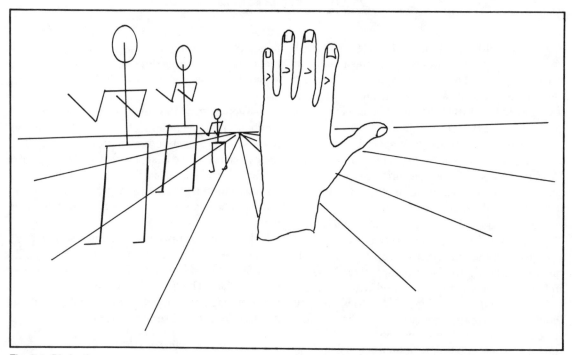

Fig. 8-1. Diminution.

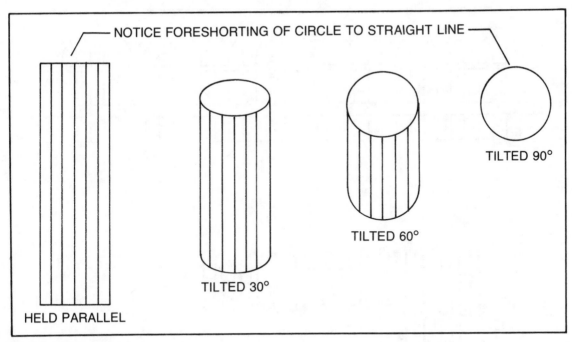

NOTICE FORESHORTING OF CIRCLE TO STRAIGHT LINE

TILTED 90°

TILTED 60°

TILTED 30°

HELD PARALLEL

Fig. 8-2. Foreshortening.

tube another 30 degrees and what you see is foreshortened once more. This is represented by a rectangle only about 2 inches long. Rotate it a full 90 degrees and the rectangle disappears entirely. What you see can now be represented by a circle. The foreshortening is 100 percent complete.

CONVERGENCE

As parallel lines or edges of objects recede from an observation point, they appear to come together. Figure 8-3 illustrates that this convergence is equal to diminution plus foreshortening. Viewed "head on," the pickets are evenly spaced and all the same apparent height. Horizontal lines are parallel. But look at this same picket fence at an angle, down the fence line. How does it look if represented in a two-dimensional drawing? Each picket appears shorter as distance from the observer increases and the width and spacing of the pickets appears nar-

rower. The horizontal lines now angle in such a way that they will eventually converge.

DEPTH AND SPACE

Figure 8-4 shows how the sense of depth and space can be achieved in a drawing by the simple technique of overlapping objects instead of drawing them spaced out and separate. In Fig. 8-5, you can see how it is that shadows give a sense of the third dimension to drawings. Keep in mind that all objects and scenes must be viewed in some kind of light. It is really the shades and shadows created by three dimensional objects in a field of light that gives them their appearance of shape and structure.

Pretend your object or scene is being illuminated by a single source of light and sketch in your shadows accordingly. In real life, pay close attention to how the sun "paints" scenery with its light. Notice how the shade and shadow fall in relation to

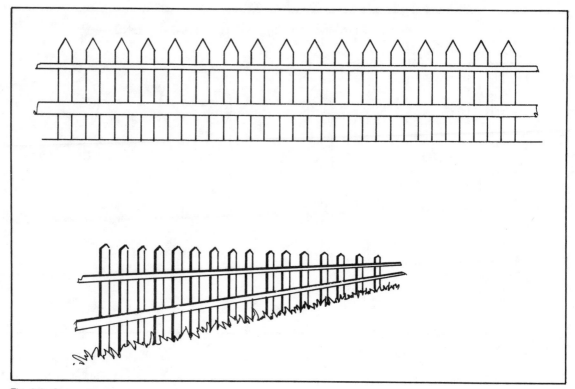

Fig. 8-3. Convergence.

the light. Use color value, or grey values if you are drawing in black and white, to enhance depth in your drawings.

Figure 8-6 illustrates how values (the range of colors, or the range of the grey scale from black to white) are bright and crisp and clear up close and then grow weaker and more neutral in the distance.

Details and patterns are more discernable close up than at a distance (Fig. 8-7) and "focus" is fuzzier or less sharp at a distance away from the observer. Actually, when your eyes focus on objects close to your eyes, background objects become blurred and unclear (Fig. 8-8). This effect can be used to spotlight objects in your drawings.

Figure 8-9 illustrates how *convergence, overlapping, shadow, grey-scale value,* and *pattern* all contribute to achieve the illusion of depth and space in a two-dimensional drawing. We suggest you copy this drawing and be aware of each of the above fundamental principles as you use them.

HORIZON LINES AND VANISHING POINTS

Almost all architectural artwork represents views of something in real life or something that is due to appear in real life when constructed. In this type of artwork, you rarely see horizon lines and you never see vanishing points. Yet these unseen things must be understood and kept in mind constantly. Often you will need to sketch them in temporarily to arrive at a realistic looking drawing.

The *vanishing point* is that point where any two or more parallel lines appear to meet. Figure 8-10

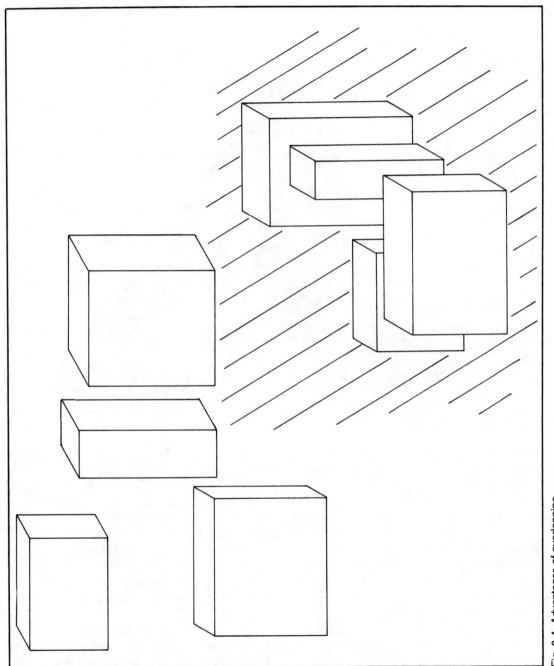

Fig. 8-4. Advantages of overlapping.

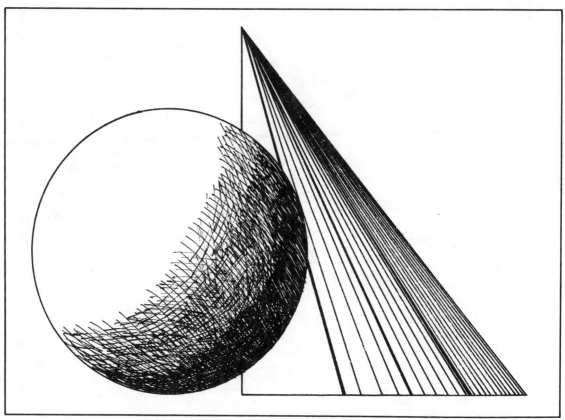

Fig. 8-5. Shadows for three-dimensional effect.

shows the classic example of a vanishing point by picturing a railroad track runing back to the *horizon line*. The rails are parallel, but—as do all parallel lines extended indefinitely—they appear to converge at a single point. Note that this is the point also where a line connecting the bottoms of the telegraph poles and the telegraph lines also meet.

There is one exception to this rule and that is when the parallel lines are also parallel to the observer's face and to the plane of the picture. Such a case is the brick wall shown in Fig. 8-11. Except for that situation, the basic rule of drawing what you see is that all parallel lines meet at a *single* vanishing point.

Most pictures are not as simple as the railroad tracks, shown in Fig. 8-10, with only one set of parallel lines. Most pictures you will draw will have many sets of parallel lines going in different directions. But the rule still applies. Each set of parallel lines will meet at a single vanishing point. You will simply have a separate vanishing point for each set of parallel lines. Some of the vanishing points will exist far away from the picture, but they do exist. Each set of parallel lines will meet at its own vanishing point.

Take any photograph of a building or object and, with a straightedge and pencil, you can extend all the converging lines until they meet at their

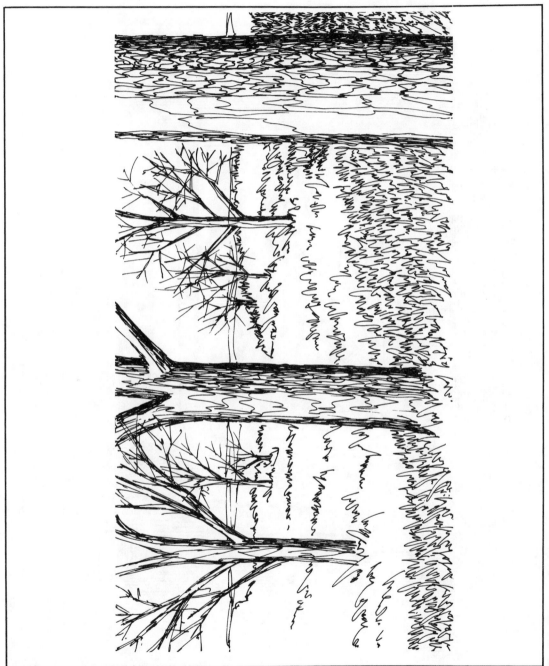

Fig. 8-6. The use of value.

171

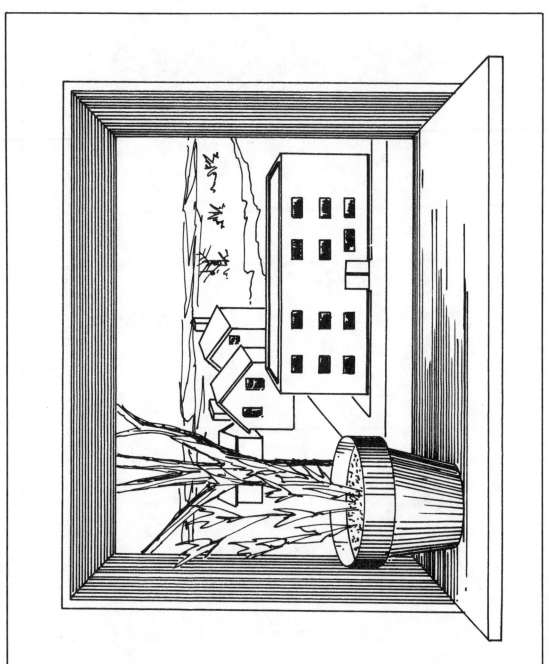

Fig. 8-7. Spotlight effect.

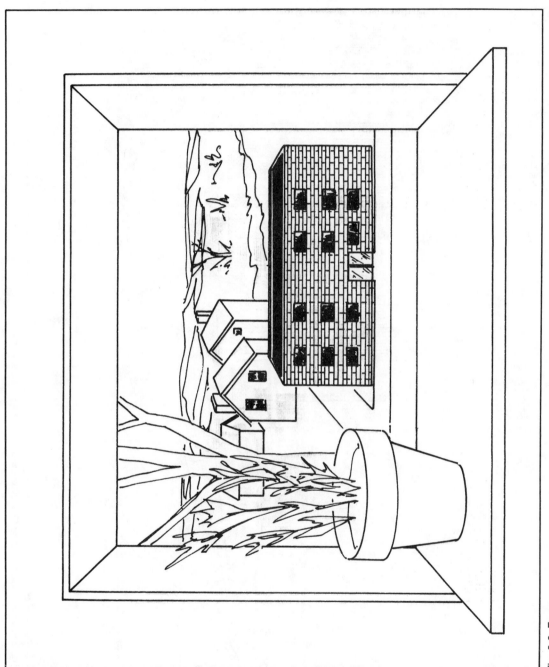

Fig. 8-8. Focus.

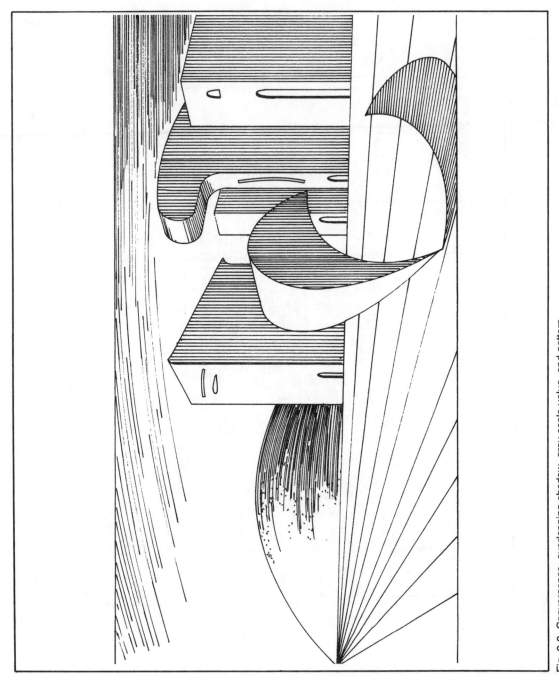

Fig. 8-9. Convergence, overlapping shadow, grey-scale value, and pattern.

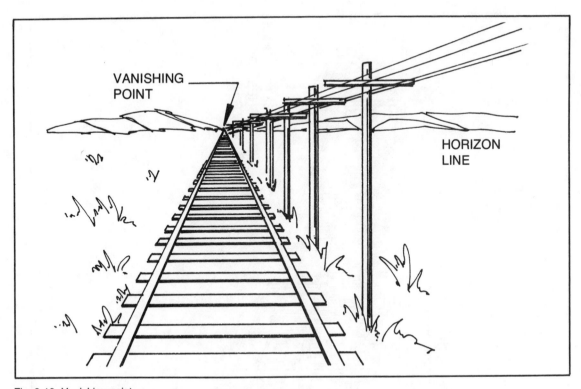

Fig. 8-10. Vanishing point.

Fig. 8-11. The exception to the rule.

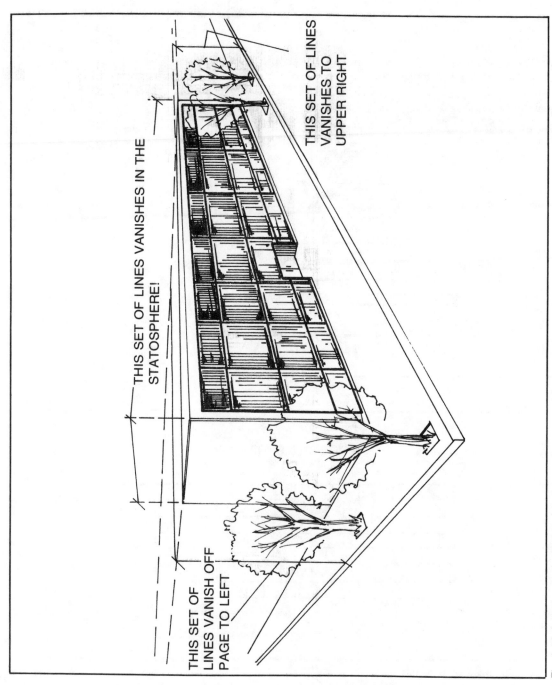

THIS SET OF LINES VANISHES IN THE STATOSPHERE!

THIS SET OF LINES VANISHES TO UPPER RIGHT

THIS SET OF LINES VANISH OFF PAGE TO LEFT

Fig. 8-12. Locating the vanishing point.

176

vanishing point. Try this exercise on the building shown in Fig. 8-12. Locate vanishing points on a large piece of drawing paper. Using your straight-edge, angle back from the vanishing points and draw in all the parallel lines in the building.

With a triangle and a T-square draw in the vertical lines. From the perspective of the drawing, they converge so slightly that you can draw them parallel. They converge somewhere in the strato-sphere. You have now made a perspective drawing of something architectural by mechanically drawing nothing but straight lines. And you probably thought you couldn't draw! You can learn to draw as well as a professional architect if you give it a lot of practice and come to know a few more simple things about horizon lines and vanishing points.

If you will now connect all the vanishing points of all the converging lines that are parallel to the ground (horizontal), you will discover that they line up along a single horizontal line. This is called the vanishing line for all converging horizontals and it will always be at eye level. This eye-level horizontal vanishing line is the secret of good perspective drawing. Where does it come from? How do we use it? How does it change the appearance of a drawing?

What locates the vanishing line in all pictures is the eye of the observer. The vanishing line for a worm's-eye view and the vanishing line for a hawk's-eye view of the same scene will be in two quite different places. It is always the eye level of the observer that determines the location of this important straight and horizontal line. It is an

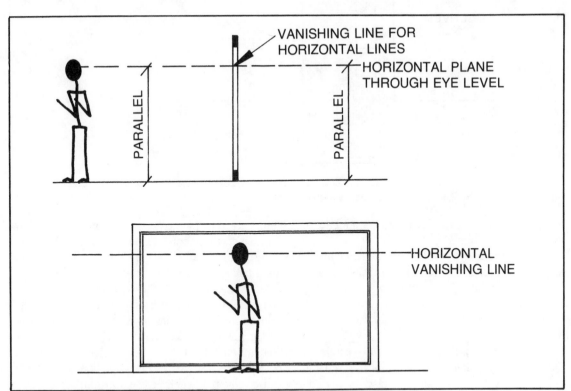

Fig. 8-13. Horizontal and vanishing lines.

177

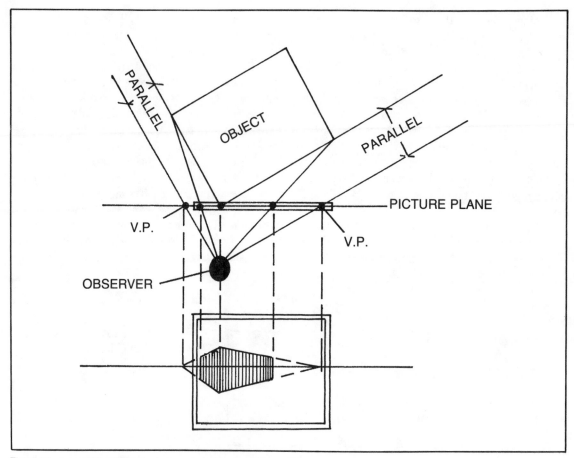

Fig. 8-14. A parallel pointing technique to locate vanishing points.

imaginary plane at eye level and parallel to the ground, as shown in Fig. 8-13.

Because the eye level is the vanishing line for all horizontal lines, specific vanishing points can be located by "pointing" the eyes to a given set of lines. You simply point in the same direction as the lines and discover the vanishing point right there on the vanishing line.

When working with T-square and triangle, the technique of *parallel pointing* to locate vanishing points is very useful. Try the exercise suggested in Fig. 8-14 and you will see what we mean. First construct your plan (top view of an object). Show the object, the picture plane (drawn as a line) and the position of an observer. Now draw your sight lines from the observer "pointing" parallel to the object's lines to locate the vanishing points on the picture plane. The picture plane line will show the relationship of the objects apparent size to the vanishing points. Notice that when you transfer this "measurement line" to the picture it is superimposed on the horizontal vanishing line at eye level. Notice also that whether you draw the object above or below this line, the relationship of apparent size to vanishing points remains the same.

When you begin to observe nature through the eyes of one who draws, you will soon observe that nature always supplies a horizon line right at the eye level of the observer. When you are descending in a roller coaster, the horizon line descends with you. Lie flat on the ground and you observe that the horizon line is still exactly at the level of your eyes. Notice that the big difference in the view from the top of a roller coaster and the view from flat on the ground is the amount of ground seen before you. The amount of foreground in a picture diminishes with a decrease in elevation.

Nature's horizon line, whether you can see it or not, (it is often obscured by people, hills, and buildings) always appears at the eye level of the observer and is the vanishing line for all horizontal lines. On it are located all vanishing points for sets of horizontal lines.

If you continue to observe nature, you will notice that the amount of foreground also changes when you look up, down, or straight out. When you are looking up at something in the sky or at a roof top, you barely see the eye level plane and so the horizon line is close to the bottom of your cone of vision. When looking down, on the other hand, the cone of vision just does include the eye level plane near its top and there is a lot of foreground visible.

From these observations you have discovered the inverse rule for view point. When you place the horizon line high near the top of your drawing paper, you will have to draw a view looking down on your subject. Place the horizon line low, near the bottom of your paper, and you must draw a view looking up. Place the horizon line in the center of your drawing paper and your view will be as if you are looking straight out at your subject matter.

Most of your drawings will probably be as seen by looking straight out. When it is necessary to show the underside or topside of something, you will want to shift your horizon line and thus your vanishing points accordingly.

TRACE-OF-THE-VERTICAL-PLANE DRAWINGS

One of the easiest systems for converting a floor plan to perspective drawings with triangle and T-square is the one illustrated in Fig. 8-15 which we call *trace-of-the-vertical-plane* drawings. It is a system often used by TV and stage set designers to make quick perspective sketches from scale floor plans of their sets. What you draw is what you will get from your scale floor plan. You can even measure to scale back "inside" your drawing. Or you can draw in your vertical scale just the way it will look in reality.

Use the top half of your drawing paper to make your scale floor plan of the room you want to draw in perspective. Orient the scale plan so that the "invisible wall"—the one you wish to "look through"—is at the bottom of the drawing. The line representing this wall becomes your trace-of-the-vertical-plane (TVP) as seen from above. We call this line CD. From points C' and D', drop verticals down to the scale equivalent of the height of the walls in the room you are picturing. Connect the bottom ends of these lines and you have a rectangle ABDC (as shown in Fig. 8-15).

You can now measure to scale on the perimeter of this rectangle as well as on your floor plan. You will need to do this now to establish a vanishing line (horizon) for your drawing. Because most people view a room from an eye level between 5 and 6 feet from the floor, we draw in this line temporarily. Draw lightly because you will want to erase this line later. In Fig. 8-15, line GH is drawn through points G' and H'. These points are measured to scale (6 feet) up from points A and B on the floor line.

We know that the vanishing point (VP) will fall along this line. Its location will depend on the placement of our position of view (PV) along the TVP. In our Fig. 8-15, we have placed it in the exact center of the room. This will make your drawing symmetrical, just as the room would appear viewed from the center of the "invisible wall" by a person about 6 feet tall. Your vanishing point will be any-

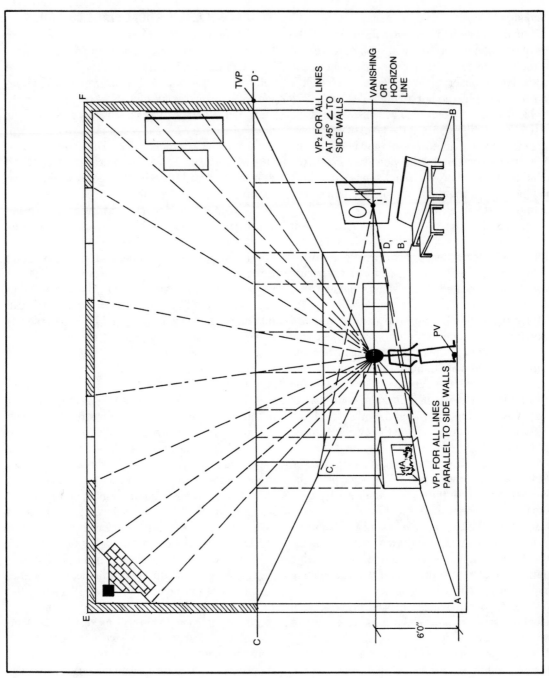

Fig. 8-15. Trace-of-the-vertical-plane drawing.

where along the VL farthest away from the wall you want to emphasize. Figure 8-16 shows what the drawing will look like if the VP is located below a PV far to the left.

Now you are ready to locate all the vertical lines in your drawing. Place a straightedge connecting a point on the floor plan that locates a vertical line (such as point E which is the back corner of the room). Where the straightedge crosses the TVP, make a light line through the TVP and drop a perpendicular line straight down from the point of intersection of the two lines. Do the same from point F to your VP and drop a vertical line perpendicular to the TVP to establish the other corner of the back wall. This is the way you establish the location of all the vertical lines for your drawing.

To locate the horizontal lines, such as ceiling and floor lines, place your straightedge between the appropriate point on the periphery of the rectangle representing the TVP and the vanishing point. In Fig. 8-15, the ceiling lines are established on a line from C' to VP and from D' to VP. The floor lines are drawn from points A and B to the vanishing point. The back ceiling and floor lines connect the points of intersection with the perpendicular line you dropped from the TVP EE' and FF'.

Follow this same procedure to establish the location and size of the windows on the left-hand wall and the large painting on the right-hand wall. Then establish the outlines of the furnishings and accessories in the room the same way. To establish the height of anything in the room, measure the actual height of the object on the outside lines of your picture frame (the rectangle ABD'C' representing the TVP) and locate it along a horizontal line between that point and your vanishing point. Its position "in depth" in the room will be determined by the vertical lines you drop from your TVP line. Study the lines in Fig. 8-15. You can study this further by using your straightedge on the drawing in Fig. 8-16; Most of the trace lines have been erased.

Figures 8-15 and 8-16 show what architects call *one-point perspectives*. All horizontal lines converge on one vanishing point. Sometime, in architectural drawing it is desirable to draw a room or a building in *two-point perspective*. Two-point perspective drawings often look more natural and tend to emphasize the focal point in a room.

In our one-point perspective drawing (Fig. 8-15) with a vanishing point in the center of the drawing, the focal point becomes the couch. Yet the focal point of the room is not the couch at all, but the painting above the table on the right-hand wall. The other one-point drawing (Fig. 8-16) with the vanishing point moved to the far left does tend to emphasize that wall more and it is more suggestive of the focal point of the room. But the VP is so far to the left that the horizontal lines that run parallel to the TVP tend to appear distorted. They should all converge on another vanishing point to the far right of the picture frame.

Figure 8-17 shows the same room in two-point perspective with one point several inches off the page to the right and the other falling correctly within the picture. Notice especially the change in perspective of the table top and the ceiling tiles and fixtures. Some would say this is a more "honest" representation of the finished room.

To make these two-point perspective drawings, simply extend your vanishing line and locate another vanishing point to the far right or left off the picture along this line. Draw your back ceiling and floor lines and all other lines parallel to your TVP so that they converge on this distant vanishing point.

Other vanishing points along the vanishing line can be used for accurate rendering of objects sitting at oblique angles in the room (such as the corner fireplace). Each *set* of parallel lines will have its own VP; remember? For all practical purposes, however, you can sketch freehand. Keep the other vanishing points in mind. Locate them mentally once the position of the object is established by the TVP method.

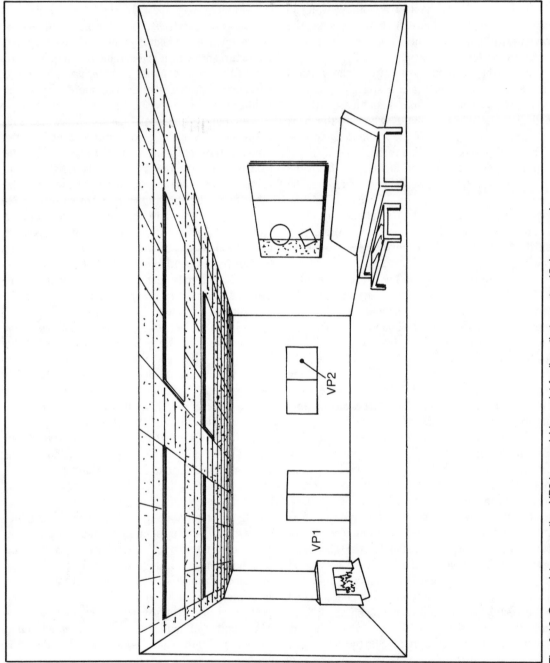

Fig. 8-16. One point perspective; VP2 is a vanishing point for lines that run at a 45-degree angle.

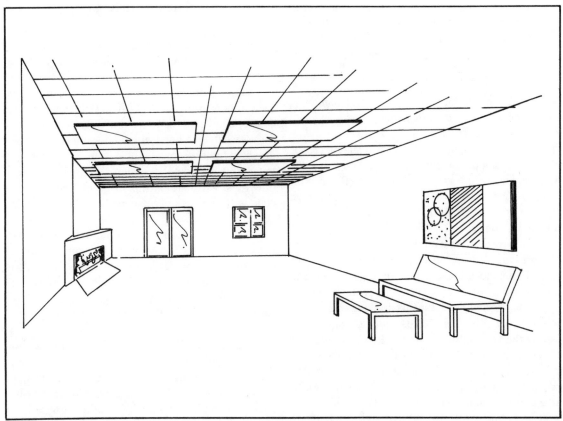

Fig. 8-17. Two-point perspective.

Technically, all of your vertical lines should be converging on a common vanishing point. In drawings of rooms and small structures, this vertical convergence is so slight that it can be ignored and all lines can be drawn parallel just as you do the set of horizontal lines parallel to the TVP in one-point drawings. If you were making a drawing of city skyscrapers from a low angle, however, their vertical lines would converge noticeably on a vanishing point far above them.

OVERCOMING DISTORTION

Distortion in perspective drawings relates to the spacing of vanishing points. Placement of vanishing points also relates to the distance effect in the drawing. Placing vanishing points close together tends to distort the edges of a drawing and pull the viewer in close to the subject matter. Spreading out the vanishing points will eliminate the distortion and give the effect of the observer having backed off for a more distant view.

Distortion due to excessively close vanishing points is the most common because it is easier to work with vanishing points that are close together. If you work with your vanishing points spread too far apart, however, your drawing will go "flat" and appear to have little dimension due to minimal convergence of lines.

Generally, convergence is less near the center of the drawing and increases toward the edges. If you try to draw too wide an angle of view, distortion at the edges of your drawing becomes unacceptable.

DETERMINING HEIGHTS AND WIDTHS

When drawing in furnishings and wall hangings, doors and windows, etc., most heights can be found by relating to your wall height. The standard wall height is 8 feet. Measure off eight equal lengths, or 8 feet to scale, on the outside vertical edge of your wall and use this as a guide to find the proper heights. As in Fig. 8-18, a 7-foot high door is drawn by using the line from the 7-foot mark back to the vanishing point.

A door knob 3 feet off the floor is located on the three foot to VP line. If you want to draw a 6-foot grandfather clock in the foreground, the dotted line from the 6-foot mark provides you with its height.

The vanishing line for this drawing was picked at the 4-foot level. This makes our clock four-sixths below the two-sixths above eye level. Notice that this ratio remains the same in all parts of the drawing. A six-foot high cabinet against the back wall will appear much smaller than the grandfather clock in the foreground, but four-sixths of the cabinet will still be below eye level and two-sixths above.

Drawing a three-foot chair at the same "depth" as the door knob requires carrying the door knob height across the room to the place where you want the chair. A 1-foot diameter lamp hanging from a 1-foot long chain directly over the chair is measured by "chasing the 6- and 7-foot lines in to the "depth" of the door knob then coming out with parallel lines to a position over the chair. (See Fig. 8-18).

The width of objects is similarly gauged by measuring to scale across the bottom of the picture frame and "chasing" lines back to the vanishing point to get the attenuation of the width of objects. The grandfather clock is 3 feet wide and so is the door on the back wall. Notice (Fig. 8-18) how the width attenuates as objects are placed farther back.

FINISHING TOUCHES

Don't forget that round objects and circles will foreshorten and appear to be ellipses when drawn in perspective. The only exception is when the circle is exactly parallel with the face of the observer (when seen "front face"). Cylinders tend to become cone shaped in perspective drawings. This will not be noticeable in vertical cylinders unless you are drawing huge storage tanks from a worm's eye view. But horizontal cylinders, even in room-size drawings, will take on the shape of a section of a cone with the apex of the cone being the vanishing point.

Shade and *shadow* make up the final touch to a good perspective drawing of any kind. Shade is defined as darkening that exists when a surface is turned away from the source of light. Shadows exist when a surface is facing the light source, but receives no light due to the presence of an intervening object.

The shapes in Fig. 8-19 all have several surfaces in light and some surfaces in shade. The surface they are sitting on is all turned toward the light, but is in shadow where the shapes intervene between the surface and the light source. Each object casts its shadow on the lighted surface.

Notice that there is always a *shade line* separating those portions of the objects that are in the shade from those that are in the light. Shade lines are important to an artist because they determine the shape of the shadow.

Artists make a distinction between sunlight and a point source of light such as a light bulb or firelight. Sunlight illuminates a scene by what appears to be parallel rays because of its great distance (93 million miles) from the Earth. Shadows of figures in sunlight, therefore, are drawn parallel with one another (as in Fig. 8-20). The closeness of point sources of light causes shadows to diverge into radial patterns around the source of light (as shown in Fig. 8-21).

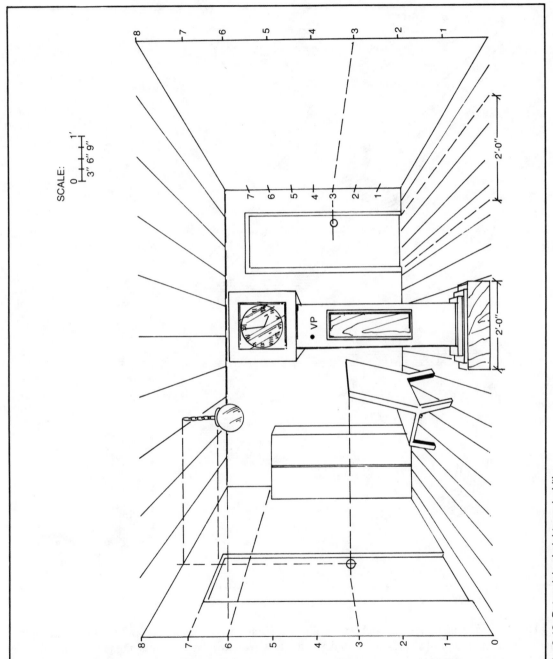

Fig. 8-18. Determining heights and widths.

SCALE:

0   3" 6" 9"   1'

185

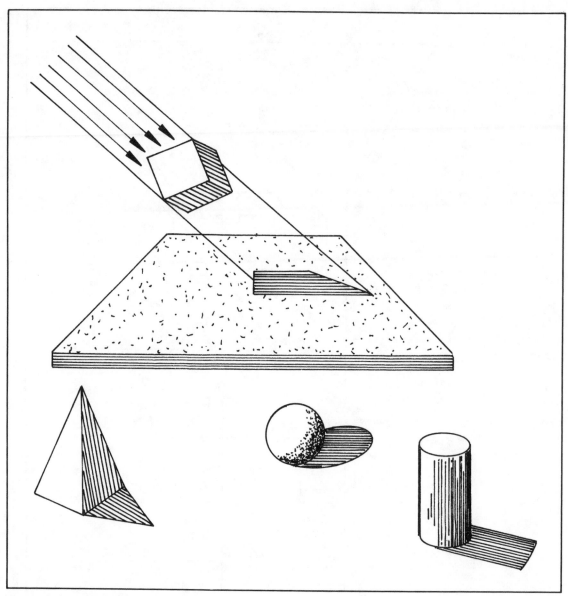

Fig. 8-19. Shade and shadow.

The vanishing point for the light rays illuminating your drawing will always be located at the light source. Therefore, the vanishing point for sunlight is 93 million miles away. The shadow, however, will have a vanishing point of its own. It will follow the rules for any other object: all sets of

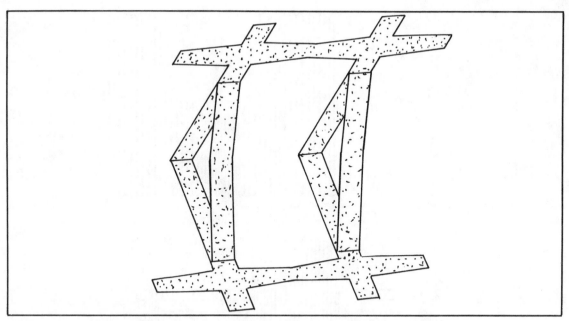

Fig. 8-20. Drawing sunlight shadows.

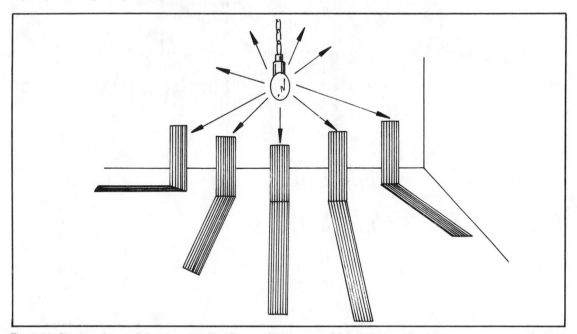

Fig. 8-21. Shadows in a radial pattern resulting from a close source of light.

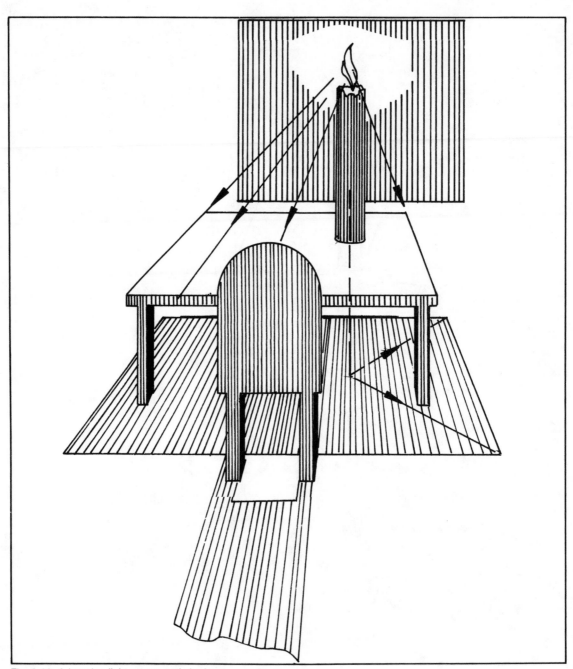

Fig. 8-22. A hanging light source and shadows.

188

parallel lines converging on a common vanishing point lying along a vanishing line that is always at the eye level of the observer.

Study the shade and shadow created by the point source of hanging light above the chair shown in Fig. 8-22. Single-arrowed lines are used to indicate diverging light rays used to locate shadows. Dotted lines represent guidelines that project the light source onto floor, wall, and ceiling surfaces, etc. Double-arrowed lines (coming from large dots) are guidelines to determine the directions of shadows cast by shade lines (perpendicular to the surfaces).

From studying Fig. 8-22, you can set down this rule about shade and shadow: a point source of light can be thought to be radiating diverging rays which locate all shadow points. Shadow direction is determined by lines diverging from a point that is directly below the source of light.

Observing shade and shadow in sunlight and under artificial light and sketching what you see is the best way to develop expertise at finishing off your drawings with neat and professional-looking shading and shadowing.

SIMPLE RECTANGULAR ISOMETRIC DRAWING

Another way to represent the appearance of what you are drawing is through the use of isometric drawings. The principles can be stated in three rules.

☐ All vertical lines in your section or elevation drawings remain vertical in the isometric drawing (Figure 8-23).

☐ All horizontal lines in your section or elevation drawings are drawn 30 degrees to the left of the horizontal.

☐ All vertical lines in your plan view drawings are drawn 30 degrees to the right of the horizontal.

Figure 8-23 shows a plan view and an elevation

represented in an isometric "perspective" in which you can identify lines AB, CD, EF, BC, etc. A 30/60/90-degree triangle and T-square are essential for making isometric drawings. You can use dividers to step off distances on your plan and elevation drawings. You can then transfer them directly to the isometric drawing which will then turn out to have the same scale as your orthographic plan and elevation drawings. Proportional dividers can be used to transfer distances if you want to change the scale of your isometric drawing.

To transfer lines that are neither vertical nor horizontal from orthographic to isometric drawings, you must first find the end points of the line in terms of a vertical and horizontal line and then connect the end points with a straightedge.

To make a practical application of drawing nonisometric lines in isometric drawings, make an isometric drawing of a rectangular house by projecting the roof plan and front and side elevations (as suggested in Fig. 8-24). The hip roof construction will give you four lines that are neither horizontal or vertical in the plan and elevation drawings. To transfer them to the isometric drawing, do the following step by step.

☐ Using your dividers, step off the vertical distance measured from the ground line to point C, level with the roof ridge shown in the side elevation.

☐ Using this vertical distance, locate point C in your isometric drawing.

☐ Find point A on the isometric by stepping off distance CA on your plan view.

☐ Connect points A and B.

☐ Use the same procedure and transfer the other three roof ridges to your isometric drawing.

Isometric drawings are not as "true to life" as perspective drawings and they have a "mechanical" feel, but they are true to scale and they do a beautiful job of communicating information to the builder.

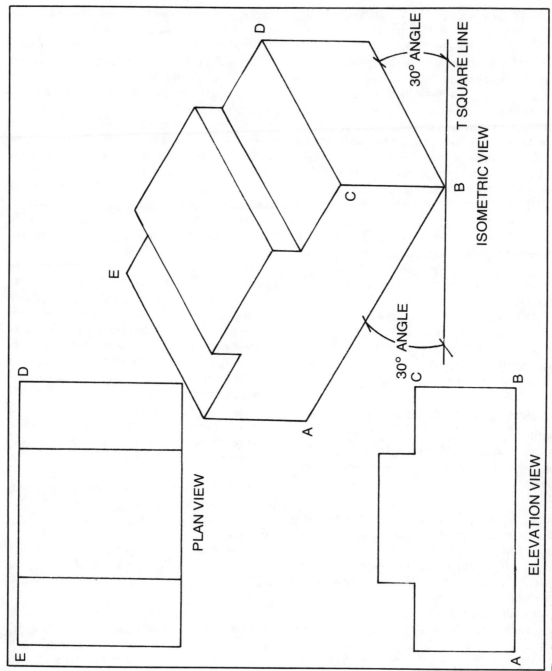

PLAN VIEW

ELEVATION VIEW

ISOMETRIC VIEW

30° ANGLE

30° ANGLE

T SQUARE LINE

Fig. 8-23. A simple rectangular isometric drawing.

190

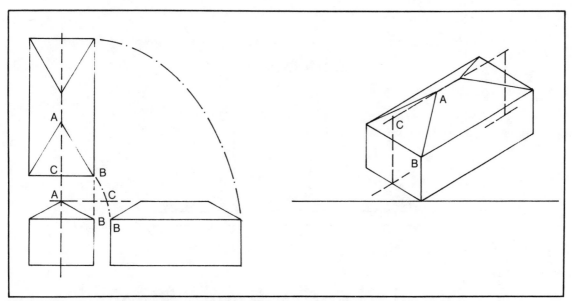

Fig. 8-24. Drawing non-isometric lines on isometric drawings.

As a rule, you use isometric drawings to communicate details about the house plans and perspective drawings to communicate the feeling you want to design into your plans.

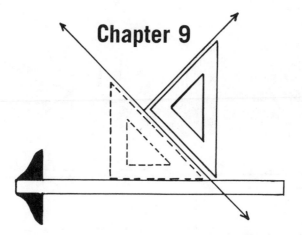

Drawing Entire House Plans

THE GOOD FEELING THAT YOU GET WHEN YOU open your front door and walk inside your home is one of the most important single things your house can offer you. That feeling is part of the mystique of owning a home. Part of that mystique is to have your guests feel welcomed when they cross your threshold.

ANALYZING YOUR SITE

That good feeling that comes with the opening of your front door must really begin before your front door is reached. You have to feel good about the environment in which you choose to live. You will not long maintain a homey atmosphere inside your house if you despise the neighborhood in which you live.

We have some friends who found a beautiful, big, wooded lot the whole family fell in love with. The price was right and they bought it without giving a thought to the neighborhood except that it seemed quiet and nice.

After much excitement and planning, they built their dream house and moved in. Slowly they discovered that their neighbors were almost all retired folks living on pensions of one sort or another. Our friends had four boisterous children, a big dog, and two cats. The older residents didn't really hate urchins, but they did appear to resent their intrusion. Living on fixed incomes, they predictably voted down every bond issue that came up for school improvement for the very good reason that they could not afford the higher taxes. Our friends just simply could never feel "at home" in that neighborhood even though their site and house were otherwise ideal.

The moral is clear. Pick your community first. That is of vital importance. Where do you and your family feel most at home? On a desert island away from it all? Smack in the middle of the city with a pulsing social life? How do you feel about high taxes to support good schools and long commutes? Once you have searched your soul and found a suitable community then, and only then, are you ready to look for a building site around which you can draw your house plans. Make up a check list and then check out each and every item on the list. It should include answers to the following questions.

☐ Are there children nearby you will be happy to have your children play with?

☐ Are your future neighbors, those with children, satisfied with the schools?

☐ If you are active in community affairs or politics, do your prospective neighbors share your interests? If not, will you be happy proselytizing or miserable without a support group?

☐ If you are connected with a religious group, is there a place of worship nearby?

☐ Does the community provide for garbage disposal or is this on their do-it-yourself list?

☐ Are there parks and playgrounds and free library services nearby?

☐ How does the tax rate stack up against the services your taxes pay for?

☐ Is the police protection good and efficient?

☐ Is the fire department well organized and can they get to your site in less than 10 minutes?

☐ Are the roads and streets well maintained? Who pays for this? Is the snow plowed in winter? Is the area fogged for mosquitoes in summer? Who pays?

☐ What about mail? Is it delivered or will you have to pick it up every day from the post office?

☐ Are there non-noxious industrial plants nearby to provide jobs for residents, customers for stores, and to carry a big share of the community's taxes?

☐ Study the houses in the neighborhood and notice how they are maintained. Is this a community once deteriorated, but now being revitalized? If so, you can very often find a real land bargain. Check to see if there is any reason why the community might be disrupted in the future. An example would be the building of an expressway or highway.

HOW MUCH LAND?

The amount of land you purchase is usually determined by how much money you have to spend or how much you can afford to pay down. But it should also include enough space for any special activities such as gardening, basketball or tennis practice areas, or a swimming pool. It should also afford privacy and, if possible, a view. All of these things need to be considered when it comes to making a site plan. The amount of land, however, is not nearly as important as some other site considerations such as available utilities, access, sunlight, wind, and zoning. A small lot with good, workable physical characteristics is a more livable and satisfying homestead property than a lot of acreage you can get to only on foot, or one that would require a thousand-foot well to bring up that life sustaining necessity, water!

WATER AND DRAINAGE

Most home sites in or near a city are supplied with water and sewage disposal as utilities. Out in the country, neither are usually available as utilities; you are on your own. You will have to dig a well for your drinking, bathing, and washing water. Before buying any rural property, always inquire of neighboring land owners how deep they had to go to find safe drinking water and what the cost of such wells might run to. If you must go to a depth of a hundred feet or more, the cost of a well can run to thousands of dollars. And that is just for the hole and casing. You will still need a pump and plumbing lines to get the water to where you need it.

You will want a home site that gives you a slope to build on. All water should drain away from your house so you do not end up with a swimming pool in your living room. Building at the crown of a gentle slope is also the most economical way to go for several reasons.

☐ You need no expensive drainage system because rain water will run off in response to gravity.

☐ No fancy machinery for excavation is needed when building on a nearly flat site.

☐ No elaborate underpinnings are needed to support your structure such as might be necessary when building on a steep site.

☐ There is more leeway in making use of the sun and wind.

SUNLIGHT AND WIND

Building on the crown of a slope will keep you warmer than building at the bottom of a valley. Warm air rises because it is lighter than cool air so the tops of hills and slopes are always several degrees warmer than where the cool air "pools" in the valleys.

You might want to build just below the crown of the slope in order to protect your home from the prevailing wind in winter. If your piece of land is on the windward side of a hill or slope, you will get the full force of the prevailing winds. If you locate your building site on the leeward slope, you will have some protection from the wind.

In addition to finding out the direction of the prevailing winds, you need to find out how the sun travels across your site. Are there tall buildings, a ridge, or a mountain that will put your home in shadows for most of the day? If so, is this desirable? How will the sunlight and shadow patterns change with the seasons? Can you build so as to have the shade in summer and the sun in winter? Architects have sworn to us on a stack of house plans that if you build so as to take full advantage of the sun and wind (both use of and protection from seasonally) you can cut your energy bills by as much as 75 percent!

ACCESS AND SOIL CONSIDERATIONS

Roads cost a lot more to build than houses. Even the crudest of roads will cost you an arm and a leg. This dictates that those great building sites off the beaten track with such a splendid view will not be worth the price even if they are selling for a dime an acre. Not only is the access road expensive to construct, it will cost you lots more money to get your materials and machinery onto your building site if it is 10 miles from nowhere.

Keep in mind that land is not nearly as stable as we tend to think. There are lots of desirable land and beautiful building sites now being offered for sale that are disappearing by inches per year. This erosion can whittle your property down considerably in the time span of a single generation. If the area is subject to flooding and severe storms, this erosion can come in quantum leaps of acres per year in the form of mud slides.

Find out about any flooding and erosion problems that neighboring property owners have experienced. Try to determine the rate of erosion. It may be that the erosion is so slow that you will be long dead and buried before there is any problem. If so, you might decide to partake of the "temporary" charm and advantages of a magnificent waterfront location.

Other soil considerations may not be so easy to deal with. If you are really serious about a piece of property, by all means have the soil tested by a soil-analysis lab. Get a surveyor to supervise percolation tests, borings, installation of a well point, and to determine if there are large boulders under the topsoil. If there are large boulders present, excavation for a foundation can be expensive and excavation for a basement might be extremely difficult.

If you do plan a basement, then your well point will give you the fluctuations in the water table that will tell you if you are going to have flooding problems in your basement. If the level of water is only a foot or two below ground, you might decide you don't want to deal with the problems a basement under water will entail.

Percolation tests will tell you how porous your

soil is and thus how well it can absorb water and sewage effluent. There are almost always city or county—sometimes even state regulations—about the soil conditions in relation to sewage disposal systems such as septic tanks or evaporative transpiration installations.

The strength of the soil is another important factor that you will need to determine. If the soil is weak, you will face a choice of enlarging your foundation, at considerable added expense, or risking serious settlement and cracking problems in your future home. Very poor bearing soils require putting your house on stilts or piles of tapered, rot-resistant telephone poles.

The best kind of soil to look for is compacted sand and gravel or a sand and clay combination. Clay alone and silt and noncompacted sand are less desirable. Clay without sand is very slow to absorb water and tends to puddling and flooding. It does absorb the water after a while, however, then it swells to a much greater volume than when dry. This can give your house quite a ride.

Don't forget to have your drinking water tested if you will be needing a well. Pollution is showing up everywhere and you will want to assure yourself that the level of pollution you must deal with is within safe limits.

Don't overlook the value of trees for their shade and cooling effect. Then again, if you are a sod busting gardener or a lawn fancier you may prefer few trees. Keep in mind that they do give you the best insurance against erosion you can buy.

ZONING AND COVENANTS

Three terms you need to become familiar with, before you sign on the dotted line and write a check for your building site, are *zoning laws*, *covenants*, and *easements*.

A trip to the planning department of your city, town, or community will get you all of the information you need. If anything seems unclear or confusing, it never hurts to pay an attorney a small legal fee to counsel you before making your committment. You will want to check especially any recent amendments to zoning laws to be sure that an airport or anvil factory has not been just approved for your prospective neighborhood.

Zoning laws are, in general, a very good tool for protecting a community from mixing up homes, factories, offices, massage parlors, convenience stores, etc., without regard to the effect that one might have on the other. But zoning is not forever and the laws are often bent to accommodate large land developers. Neighborhood associations have been formed in cities and towns all across the country to fight for maintaining the zoning they had when they first bought their property. If there is a neighborhood association operating around your proposed building site, by all means consult with the members to get as much information as you can.

Once you are satisfied with the zoning situation around the property you are thinking of buying, take a good look at how the zoning relates to your building plans. Zoning regulations restrict the height of what you build in order to keep the neighborhood in scale. They will also tell you the minimum distance from the street or from your neighbor's house that your structure must be built. These *set-back* lines will determine the shape and dimensions of your yards—front, sides, and back. Always be sure your building site is large enough to accommodate the size house you plan to build once these set-back lines have been established. Is there enough room left to add on a new room, a car port, a tool or a storage shed?

After the planning department, the next place to visit is the building department of your local community government. These folks will issue you your building permit and they will be concerned about your plans to use approved materials and techniques of installation. You will be required to conform to their minimum standards for electric wiring, heating, plumbing, etc.

Keep in mind that you might be able to get a

variance of the zoning laws and building restrictions to suit your special needs if you can show good cause and no harm to the community. You will need to check out the procedure with the town clerk and go before the town council or planning commission. You would be well advised to seek legal council.

In some small communities where you find no planning departments or commissions, you might find that the zoning and building restrictions are established by covenant. Restrictions are established by covenant and apply to all the property within the boundaries of the town or village. A covenant is simply an agreement between buyers and sellers of property. Sometimes they require some off-beat things such as that you may only paint your house you build on this property some shade of pink—no other color—pink!

Covenants are legally binding no matter how serious or silly they might seem. Be sure to check out any covenants that are in effect on the property you are buying.

Beware of easements. Almost all deeds have clauses written into them giving someone else the right to make use of your property. This might be the government, a utility company, another landowner needing access to his property through yours, etc. Even though you own the property, you can do nothing that will interfere with the access necessary to the other party having the easement right.

Other deed restrictions might be written into your deed.

MAKING A SITE PLAN

Once you have done all of the preceeding, you are ready to draw a site plan. The surveyor, who measured your parcel of land and set stakes marking the exact corners of your property, will give you a site map (or plot plan) from which to work. Figure 9-1 illustrates a site map we received on a piece of property we once bought. It was while drawing plans for this building site that we discovered some simple ways to save money.

If you order your survey of the lot for a line drawing before purchasing the property, you not only can use the drawing for buying the property, but also as a *topographic map* with which to build and as a mortgage survey. Your mortgage company will require a final survey before giving you your money. Be sure to give them a copy of your topographic map early on. Otherwise they will order a *mortgage survey* and you will pay double for your drawing. Maybe it will cost you more than double if they use a surveyor unfamiliar with the area where your property is located. If at all possible, employ a surveyor who has worked on the boundary properties. He can save you money by using his previous notes and check points.

The mortgage company will be satisfied with a simple line drawing of the lot with the house located on it (Fig. 9-2). Your construction people and local building department, however, will want something more elaborate such as Fig. 9-3. To arrive at such a finished site plan, first lay a piece of tracing paper over the surveyor's drawing and trace it off with a soft pencil. Trace off the contour lines that show the elevations of the property. Practice visualizing the shape of the land from these contour lines. A good exercise for this is to imagine pulling the plug in the middle of a lake and then imagine drawing lines at different levels as the water receeds. See all this happening from directly above the lake and the lines you draw will be contour lines.

As you trace off the lot lines, recognize that your surveyor laid them out using polar coordinates. Each line is described by *distance* and *bearing*; these are its length and its angle in relation to true north and south. The distance is measured in hundredths of a foot (instead of inches) so that, for example, 16.25 feet would equal 16 feet 3 inches. Bearings are measured with true north and south reading 0° (Fig. 9-4). Although your surveyor should have noted bearings down to minutes and seconds (there are 60 seconds in a minute and 60

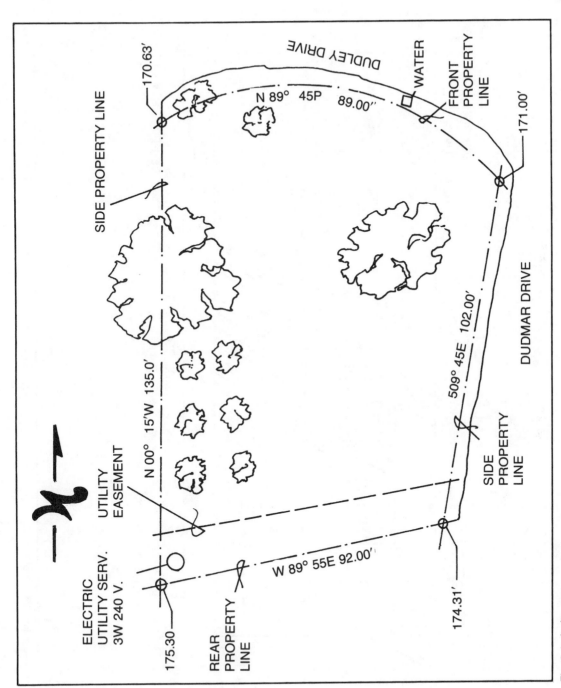

Fig. 9-1. A site map.

197

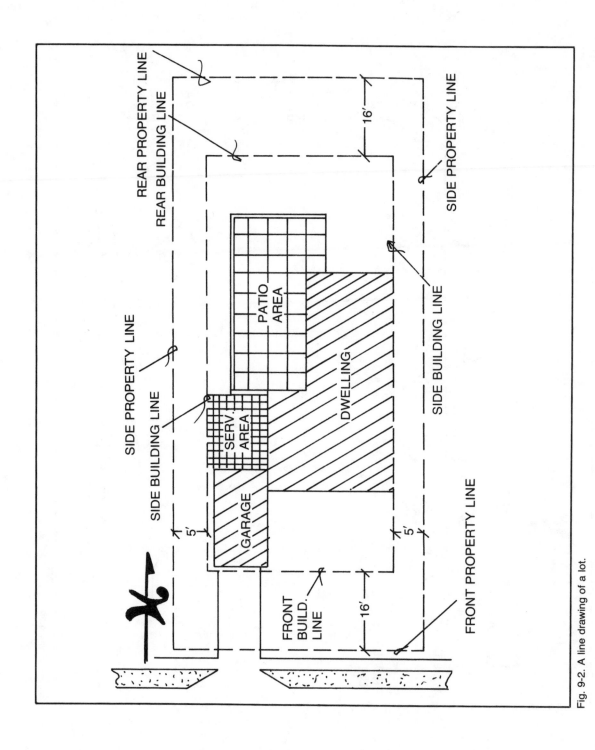

Fig. 9-2. A line drawing of a lot.

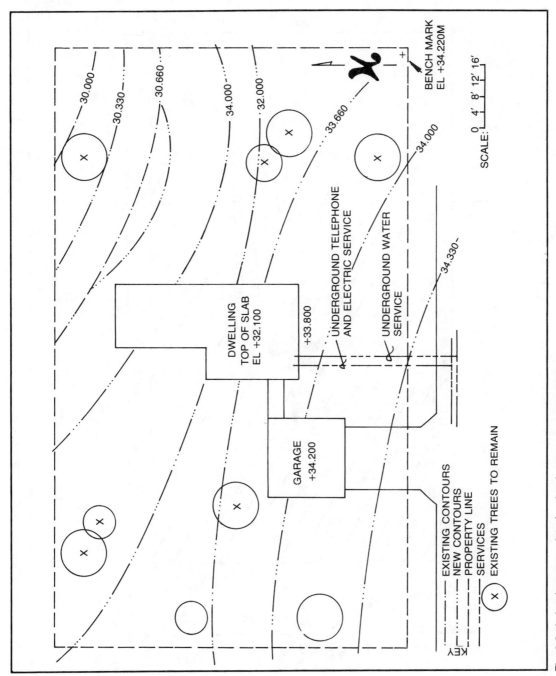

Fig. 9-3. A drawing appropriate for showing to a mortgage company.

199

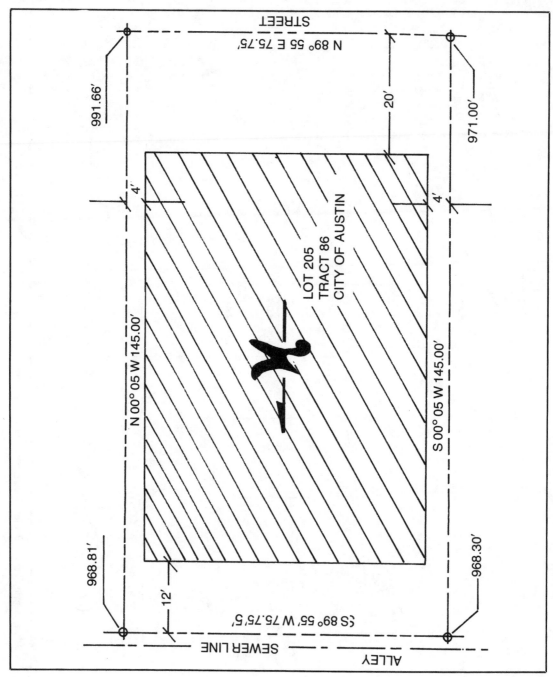

Fig. 9-4. A sketch with distance and bearing notations.

200

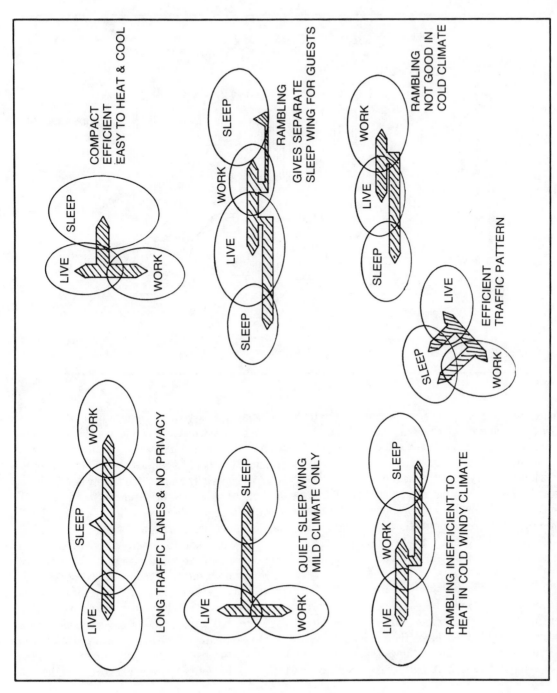

COMPACT
EFFICIENT
EASY TO HEAT & COOL

RAMBLING
GIVES SEPARATE
SLEEP WING FOR GUESTS

RAMBLING
NOT GOOD IN
COLD CLIMATE

EFFICIENT
TRAFFIC PATTERN

LONG TRAFFIC LANES & NO PRIVACY

QUIET SLEEP WING
MILD CLIMATE ONLY

RAMBLING INEFFICIENT TO
HEAT IN COLD WINDY CLIMATE

SLEEP
LIVE
WORK

Fig. 9-5. Flow diagrams.

201

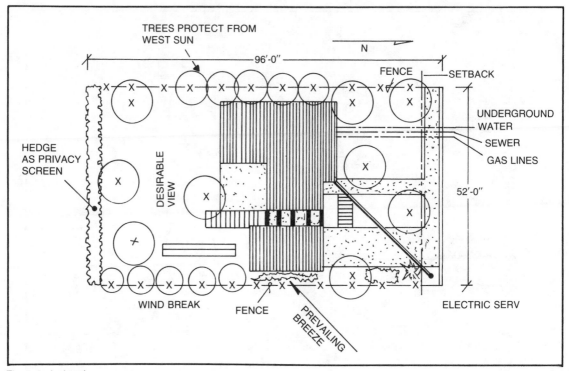

TREES PROTECT FROM WEST SUN

96'-0"

N

FENCE

SETBACK

UNDERGROUND
WATER

SEWER

GAS LINES

52'-0"

HEDGE
AS PRIVACY
SCREEN

DESIRABLE VIEW

WIND BREAK

FENCE

PREVAILING BREEZE

ELECTRIC SERV

Fig. 9-6. A site plan.

minutes in a degree) you can round them off to the nearest half degree. That is all the accuracy required on a site plan and it is about as small as you can measure with an ordinary protractor anyway.

Now trace in your setbacks and easement lines so that you will know where you cannot build. Use a symbol or notation for any prominent landscape features such as trees or wild flower beds you want to preserve. Take your tracing to a gathering of the whole family and get them involved.

LISTING DESIGN GOALS

Encourage your family to visualize the property from memory and your tracing. Try not to get hung up on details, but do keep them in mind. Get everyone thinking about the things that matter the most to them. As you think and discuss, doodle out a

flow diagram on your tracings (Fig. 9-5).

What kind of view would you like and from where? How will you and your family likely move around? How best to get onto and off of your property? Where will the quiet areas likely be? Where is the action? Who has preferences for what? Will there be a vegetable garden? Rock garden? Pool? Badminton court? Tennis anyone?

You will begin to generate some ideas for a floor plan with your flow diagram, but for right now concentrate on the family flow in and out of your future home and around the property. Make a list of these design goals. Take your time and make a long list so you will have a lot of choices when it comes time to pick and choose what you feel you must have in relation to what you can afford. Keep in mind the feeling of the entire space you and your family will occupy—inside and out—and the good feelings you want to create.

At this time, you should settle on the dimensions and shape of your house in order to be able to draw your final site plan.

DRAWING THE SITE PLAN

When drafting your site plan, it is a good idea to draw the project in the order of its construction.

☐ Pick a scale large enough to show detail; 1/16 = 1 ft is a scale most architects use.

☐ Lay out the lot showing everything your surveyor showed on the site map he gave you. Include contour lines (unless it's a flat lot). Be sure to place the north arrow accurately.

☐ Draw in all streets and alleys.

☐ Show locations of all utilities: electric, water, gas, sewer lines, etc.

☐ Draw in the shape of any existing structures that are not to be torn down during construction. Use dotted lines to draw in any existing struc-elevations of ground at both property and building corners. If your planned structure is multilevel, show the elevation of each floor. Identify all areas.

Landscape templates are available from drafting supply stores and they are neat to use. They will speed your work along and make it look more professional.

tures that are to be demolished. Make a margin note stating by whom this structure is to be removed.

☐ Using a hard-lead drawing pencil, rule off light lines representing front, rear, and side setbacks required by ordinance. Lay off the boundaries of any easements that cross the property.

☐ Using a soft-lead drawing pencil draw in heavier lines the outlines of all buildings and roof overhangs.

☐ Track down and locate on your drawing all the little details like fences, gates, plumbing vents, air-conditioning compressors, and the like.

☐ Draw in all areas of gravel, rock, or concrete work.

☐ Draw in dimension lines as shown in Fig. 9-6. Always draw dimension lines parallel or perpendicular to lot lines. Two dimensions are needed if the lot lines are 90 degrees to each other and the building is parallel to one of them. If the building is not parallel to a lot line, then you will need to locate one corner of the building in relation to two dimensions at a corner of the lot (Fig. 9-6).

☐ Draw your trees and shrubs to the size they will be when they are mature. Use circles to mark the locations of tree trunks.

☐ Identify all plants or planting areas in your notes right on the site plan. Note also the thickness of concrete and paving. Identify all utilities. Show

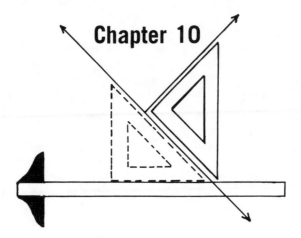

Chapter 10

Unusual Design Solutions

THE FIRST CONCEPT FOR APPLYING UNUSUAL design solutions is to make use of every inch. A dome shape will enclose the most space with the least material and it will present less surface through which heat is lost in winter or gained in summer. Next up the scale is to build square, two-story, or as near a cube as possible. This will give you much less wall area than a long, low rectangular house. These structures also require a smaller building lot and leave more room for things like gardens, woodlots, and recreation areas. Enclose only the space you need and use every inch of space you have enclosed.

Take a run out to your nearest housing development under construction and take a look at the wasted space. Useless roof trusses are one example. Why not use the sloping area under the roofs, like our early settlers did, for a sleeping loft? Nothing could be cozier. But there are other uses for this space. It is almost always heated by rising

convection currents so why warm the trusses? Why not use it for a children's play area, always-needed extra storage space, or tuck away a solar hot-water heater or even a small auxiliary furnace. If you design for underground or passive solar effects, such a small auxiliary furnace is all you will need, even in cold climates. Figure 10-1 shows a cross section of such an idea.

Small spaces can be designed so as to flow together and increase their apparent size. This flow can be designed either vertically or horizontally. An example is the cross section of a small house illustrated in Fig. 10-2.

If you combine your kitchen, dining, and living room areas you will make the entire space more flexible for living and much more economical for heating and cooling. Long, low, rectangular houses—so-called ranch houses—are designed that way primarily to provide adequate daylight to all parts of the house. But the design is inefficient

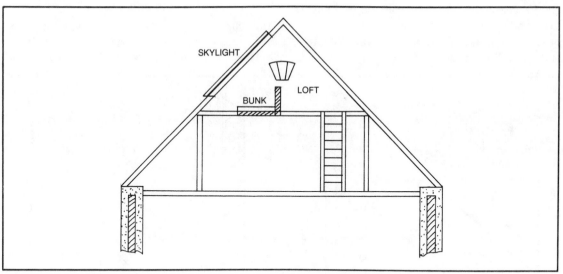

Fig. 10-1. A sleeping loft.

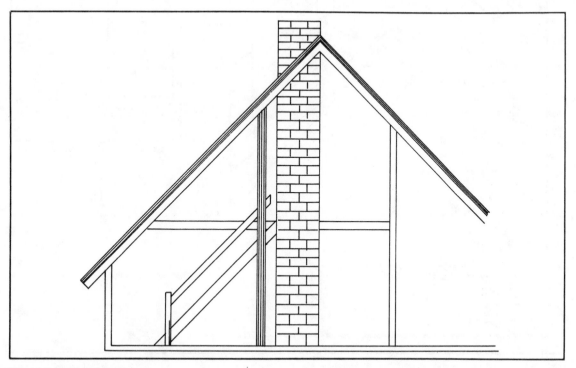

Fig. 10-2. Vertical flow of space.

and lot consuming. A better solution is skylights. You can plan compact and make any interior space usable. Do include them in your design solutions and you will not have to waste an inch of space.

USE BUILD-INS

You can design smaller rooms if you make good use of build-ins. Why not build your bed 3 or 4 feet off the floor. Who said beds have to be low to the floor?

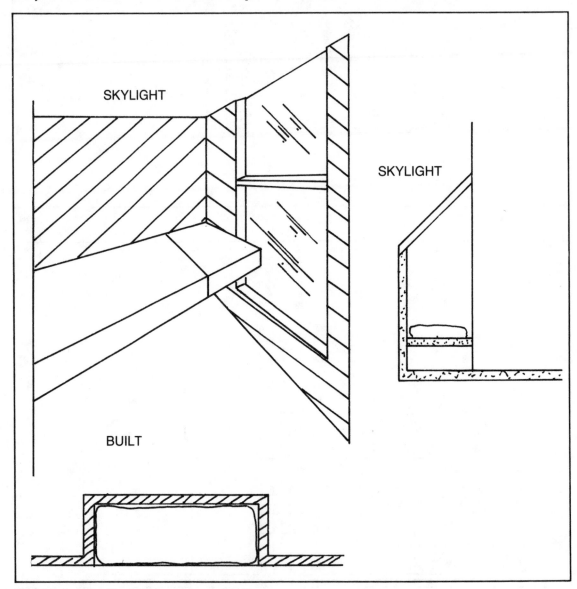

Fig. 10-3. A niche with a build-in couch and skylight.

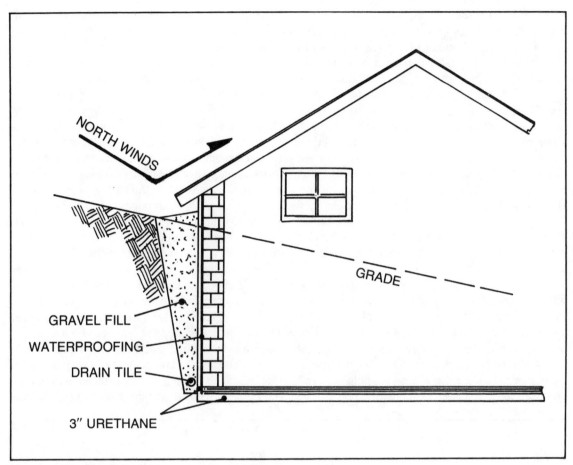

Fig. 10-4. Geothermal solution elevation.

Look at all that lovely storage space you have just created! You can even design in chests of drawers on the sides and hinge the bottom boards in the center of the "bed board" to have easily accessible storage. With your bed, chests of drawers, and storage chest all built into one unit, think of the space and money you have saved.

Couches are expensive items you can build in.

If you design something like the alcove couch shown in Fig. 10-3, it can double as a guest bed—complete with storage underneath.

SPECIAL REQUIREMENTS AND SOLUTIONS

If you are designing a house for a cold climate, by all means turn your back on the north wind. Use your building site in such a way as to make your north wall solid and mostly underground if at all possible. A hillside lot is ideal for this kind of design solution, provided, of course, that the hill is not just one big rock. This would require some expensive blasting. Still you can bury your north wall after it is built on top of the rocky hill and still get protection from the north wind as well as the geothermal "flywheel" effect of the constant temperature of the earth. Figures 10-4 and 10-5 illustrate these ideas. You can still let in a good amount of north light, through a skylight or a high triple-insulated strip window. Just be sure that your contractor has had experience building underground walls and can follow your specifications on insulation and waterproofing.

Using a lot of masonry inside your house will allow the house to store its own heat. A brick, concrete, or stone floor will feel warm in winter and cool in summer *provided* you design it so that it is very thoroughly insulated around its perimeter. Designing in a large masonry fireplace and chimney is one way to put solar heat storage into a house. Place the chimney so that the sunlight will fall on it a good part of the day and put it all inside (not outside) the structure.

A solar greenhouse on the south wall of a house will store a lot of heat. If you use large areas of glass to take advantage of solar heat, remember to design some means of covering the glass with an insulating material at night to avoid sudden and massive heat loss when the sun goes down. Consider using double or triple glazing in the windows to help cut down on heat loss. If you are designing for a home to be built in Alaska, quadruple glazing is recommended.

If you are designing for the special requirements of a hot climate, there are special design solutions to keeping a house cool without excessive energy consumption. Window design and placement can be one of the crucial factors in these solutions. During the summer months in temperate climates and even during the winter months in hot climates, 90 percent of the sun's heat can be transmitted through window glass. This calls for no windows or only very small windows on the east and west side of the building. An east/west window can admit as much heat through 1 square foot as an insulated wall admits through 225 square feet!

The best control of heating can be had by admitting most of your light from the south, either through skylights or large south-facing windows. These skylights and windows should be designed to make use of roof overhangs and projections so that the high-angled summer sun is shaded from them. The low-angled winter sun can then be admitted for passive solar heating. See Fig. 10-6. Research has shown that such an arrangement can keep the same room at about 77 degrees in summer without air conditioning with an outside temperature of 92 de-

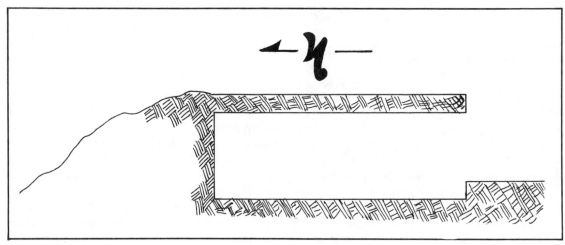

Fig. 10-5. Geothermal solution floor plan.

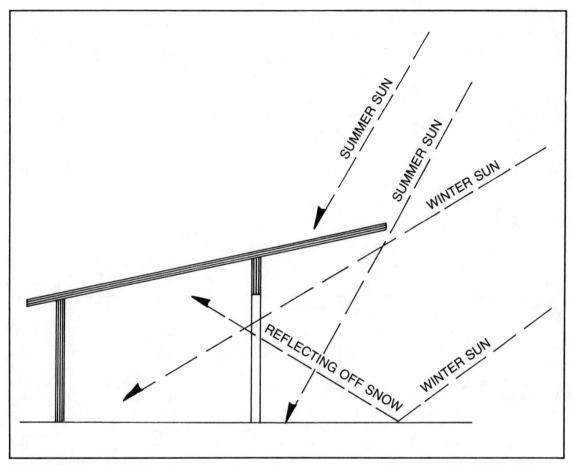

Fig. 10-6. Passive solar heating.

grees. In winter with an outside temperature of 32 degrees, the room can be kept at the same comfortable 77 degrees.

Whether your special problems are heat or cold—or both—special design solutions can result in energy savings of between 50 and 80 percent.

DOME HOMES

A dome home is probably the most economical structure to build and maintain. It is by nature an energy saving structure. If you ever had a course in geometry, you might remember that a circle with the same area as a square has a much smaller perimeter. See Fig. 10-7.

In conventional square or rectangular housing, it is around that perimeter where energy is lost whether you are heating or cooling. The heat loss factor of a typical 40-foot diameter dome, for example, is only about 15,000 Btu compared to something like 25,000 Btu for a rectangular structure of the same area with comparable insulation. There is a gain over and above the reduced perimeter of the

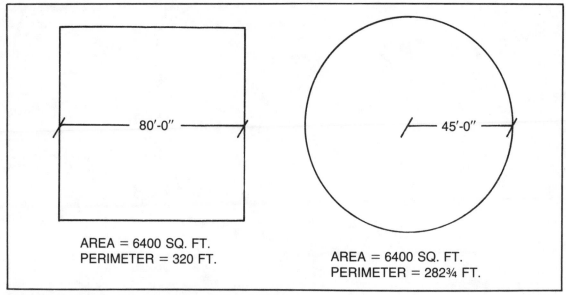

AREA = 6400 SQ. FT.
PERIMETER = 320 FT.

AREA = 6400 SQ. FT.
PERIMETER = 282¾ FT.

Fig. 10-7. Comparison of the perimeter of a circle and a square.

dome that recent research has brought out. The right insulation in a dome can save you more money than the same insulation in a nondome with the same floor space.

Don't let the unusual mathematics of dome design put you off. The complex equations can be left to the contractor or factory fabricator to figure out. Designing in the round is just as easy as designing with four sides. And it's a lot more fun. Dome homes have now become so popular that there are contractors in nearly every community capable of executing your dome plans. If you decide to do your own contracting or building, there are lots of instruction manuals to instruct you on the translation of mathematics to construction modules. There are also lots of dome home kits on the market that will furnish you the dome shell and then let you design and finish the interior spaces. These shells come in a variety of sizes from diameters of 26½ feet (with loft about 525 square feet of living space) to 45½ feet (nearly 3000 square feet on two levels).

Foundations

Standard foundation techniques apply to all domes regardless of type. The geodesic dome, popularized and invented by Buckminster Fuller, has grown into many variations. Some are nongeodesic, but all will sit on standard foundations. Standard floor framing is used for the first floor of a dome and post-and-beam framing is used for the second floor or loft. Box-beam risers make ideal chase channels for plumbing and wiring.

Steps in Building a Dome

The construction of most domes involves the assembly of either 2-×-4 or 2-×-6 panel frames. One-piece exterior panels are nailed or glued to the frame's exterior. After this framing and "skinning" is completed, skylights, windows, and doors are installed. Windows and often doors are of standard dormer construction; these are the type where the window or door framing projects through the framing of the sloping roof. The dormers are then sealed

210

with a special adhesive and all other seams are sealed.

A four- to six-mil poly or kraft paper vapor barrier is then installed on the inside of the frame and plumbing and electrical wiring is put into place. Furring strips are then applied.

All of the interior work, including the installation of a second floor or loft, is begun usually at the same time the roof is going on.

Roofing, like the foundation, can be quite conventional. Often used are strip shingles or cedar shakes with two layers of felt paper underneath. Keep in mind that a well-constructed dome will be as leakproof and watertight as any other traditional structure. All structures will feature indoor rain if not constructed properly and many domes were constructed during the 1960s and early 1970s without attention to proper building concepts. This lead a lot of people to the false conclusion that domes are inherently leaky.

UNDERGROUND HOUSING DESIGNS

Underground housing proves low energy consumption and a low maintenance way to achieve the ultimate in privacy, safety, and security. Not very far underneath the surface of your own backyard, or any property you might buy, the temperature stays quite constant. This constant temperature will depend on your overall climate, but it will be around 50 degrees Fahrenheit in temperate climates and about 60 degrees in warmer climates. By "burying" your home in this stable, moderate temperature environment you can see how you can save on heating and cooling costs. Usually, a little passive solar heating is all that is necessary. And yes, you can use solar heating underground.

Underground homes are often lighter, brighter, and more sunlit than traditional homes because lighting must be carefully planned. Most underground houses are built around open atriums. They make use of conventional windows where green plants grow just outside the window at the bottom of a light well. One side can be open as when the house is burrowed into the side of a hill.

The Bordie residence in Austin, Texas is a good example of an underground home that is comfortable, light and cheery, costs little to maintain and, in spite of the fact that it is only halfway underground with only 18-inches of earth mounded over the top, still uses less than half the energy consumed by a similar house all above ground. Heating is solar with electric furnace back-up (almost never used) and hot water is 100 percent solar. Safety as well as economy was a major factor in going underground for the Bordies' because their property had twice been visited by tornadoes.

The floor plan of the Bordie house (Fig. 10-8) is dominated by a 30 foot-×-20-foot atrium that floods the entire house with daylight. The central circulation space of the atrium provides privacy between wings of the house. In the mild Austin, Texas climate, the atrium remains open, but in colder climates it could be covered with a small geodesic dome or perhaps even an inflatable dome to make it convertible.

Architect John Barnard, Jr., who has designed many underground homes, including the famous Ecology House (Fig. 10-9), maintains that an underground house costs 25 percent less to build than conventional construction because the construction is so simple most of the labor can be supplied by unskilled workers. Where you need experience and skill, according to Barnard, is in the pouring of the concrete and installation of the insulation and waterproofing.

In drawing plans for an underground house, the paramount thing to keep in mind is to design in adequate drainage. As an elevation of the Ecology House shows (Fig. 10-10), the house drains through the open courtyard and down the hill away from the house through drain tiles large enough to accept runoff from the heaviest rainfall Massachusetts has had in the last 100 years.

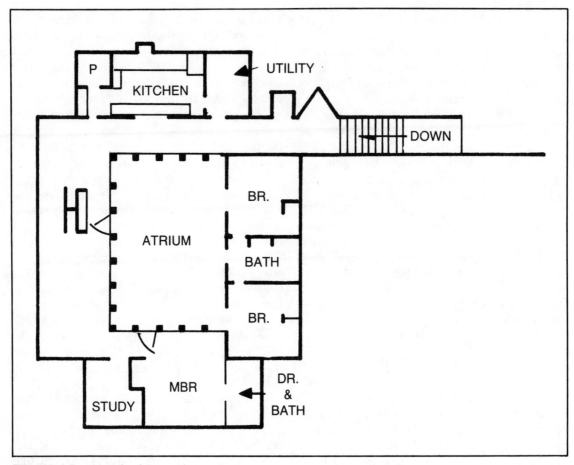

Fig. 10-8. A floor plan showing an atrium.

You would not, of course, design an underground house for a swampy area or for areas where there was nothing but rock under a few inches of topsoil. These areas could, however, lend themselves to above ground construction and then be buried under a few feet of earth carried to the building site. Such a design would need to be built on a slight rise in the ground (as would any other type of structure) with good drainage provided away from all sides of the house.

Other considerations in underground design include roof loading and insulation. Roofs covered with anywhere from 6 inches to 6 feet of dirt need to be designed with strong supporting systems. Insulation on underground houses is on the *outside* not on the inside of the house. Careful waterproofing is essential. You must know exactly where the water table is on the site you are designing for so as not to build below it.

Foresight is helpful in underground design. Design in your future expansion space and put it there when the structure is built. It will not cost

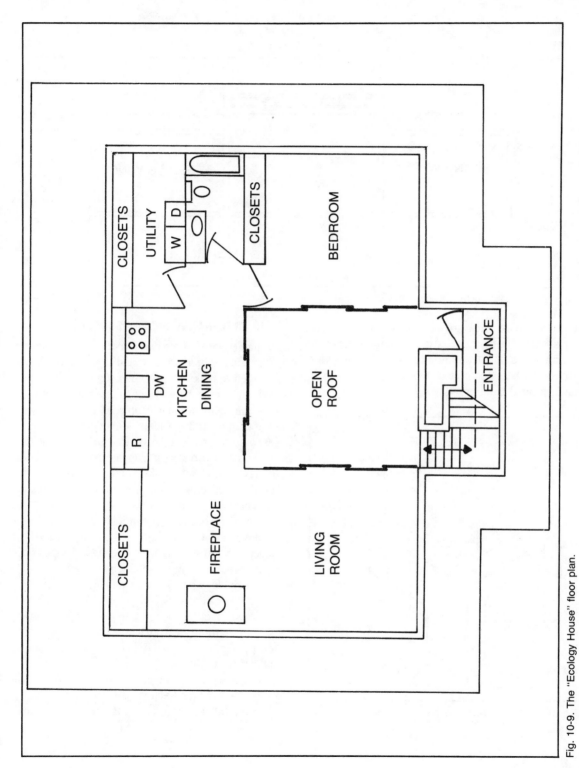

Fig. 10-9. The "Ecology House" floor plan.

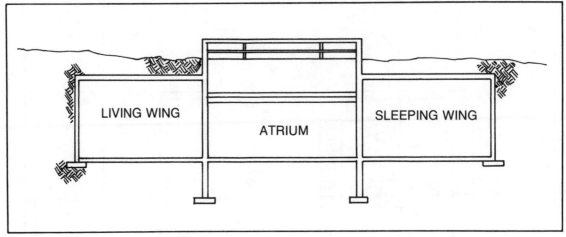

Fig. 10-10. Elevation of the Ecology House.

much more to excavate an additional 500 or so square feet and pour the extra concrete. Then leave it unfinished until you need to expand your living space. Afterthoughts tend to come expensive in underground building.

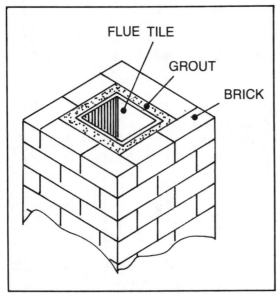

Fig. 10-11. A cross section of a brick chimney.

ALTERNATIVE ENERGY SOURCES

Most underground home dwellers find that wood is an excellent source of any additional heat they might need to make their homes comfortable. The main thing to keep in mind when designing for wood heat is that conventional fireplaces can be better cooling than heating devices. A good fireplace flue is designed to create a lively draft to carry smoke and combustion products up, up, up and away. It will also carry away about one-fifth of the already heated air in your house and about four-fifths of the heat from every log you burn!

There are things you can include in your design, however, that will insure a more efficient fireplace. The first thing is to specify a damper on the fireplace. The damper should be closed down as far as possible when heating and wide open for cooling. You can also design a closed-in fireplace with a cover over the opening to keep your expensively heated room air from sailing up the flue. The best type of cover to specify is one, made by many manufacturers, that uses fire-resistant glass in conjunction with a steel grate. You receive heat through the glass (and enjoy the fire), but you lose little of the heated room air up the chimney. Your

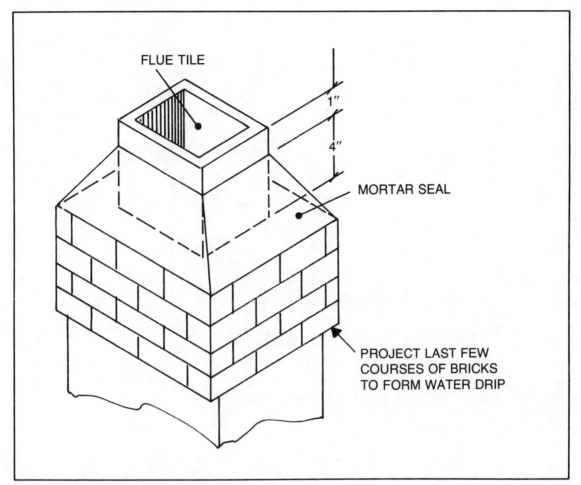

FLUE TILE

1"

4"

MORTAR SEAL

PROJECT LAST FEW
COURSES OF BRICKS
TO FORM WATER DRIP

Fig. 10-12. Topping off the brick chimney.

fireplace heats by radiation only so you do not block your heat by using a transparent cover.

Far more efficient than a fireplace is a wood-burning stove that heats by convection and conduction in addition to also heating by radiation. Designing in flues for use by wood-burning stoves will also accommodate free-standing fireplaces. Figures 10-11 through 10-17 illustrate a variety of designs for flue and chimney packages in different types of structures. It is always recommended that chim-neys be directed to the outside through the ceiling, but Fig. 10-12 shows a safe way to direct a stove pipe out through a wall and then up the side of the structure.

Solar energy systems are becoming more and more popular as both primary and complementary sources for economically heating (and sometimes cooling, too) living structures. The easiest way to use solar energy is to complement another heat source. This way the intermittent and variable na-

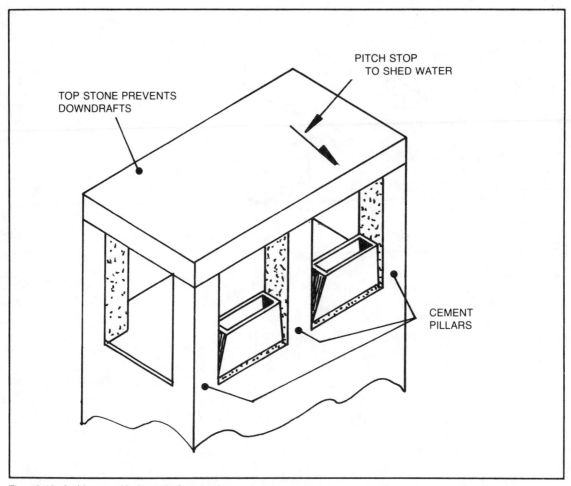

PITCH STOP
TO SHED WATER

TOP STONE PREVENTS
DOWNDRAFTS

CEMENT
PILLARS

Fig. 10-13. A chimney with down-draft protection.

ture of the sun as an energy source will give you no problem. If you design for solar energy as the primary heat source, you must take into consideration the necessity for storage of the energy for use when the sunlight is not available for direct use.

Keep in mind that the sun heats by radiation, just like a fireplace does. Whatever surface the sun's rays fall on will heat up. When the surface has heated to a temperature higher than the surrounding air or objects, that surface will begin to put out heat by radiation, convection, and conduction. If the sun heats a surface of masonry, for instance, a lot of heat energy can be stored and released slowly after the sun has set or disappears behind the clouds. More active systems will use collectors to take up the sun's heat for storage.

Solar collectors are heat traps making use of a transparent cover that allows the sun's heat to enter, but not leave, a black box containing a liquid such as water or alcohol that absorbs the trapped

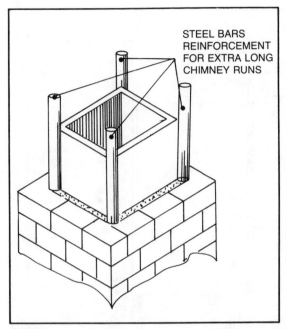

Fig. 10-14. Tall brick chimneys must be reinforced.

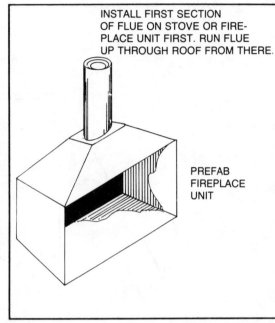

INSTALL FIRST SECTION OF FLUE ON STOVE OR FIRE-PLACE UNIT FIRST. RUN FLUE UP THROUGH ROOF FROM THERE.

PREFAB FIREPLACE UNIT

Fig. 10-16. Building a chimney from the ground up.

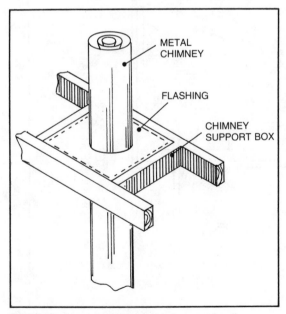

METAL CHIMNEY

FLASHING

CHIMNEY SUPPORT BOX

Fig. 10-15. A metal chimney through a wood wall.

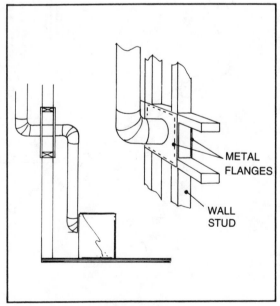

METAL FLANGES

WALL STUD

Fig. 10-17. Venting a chimney safely.

217

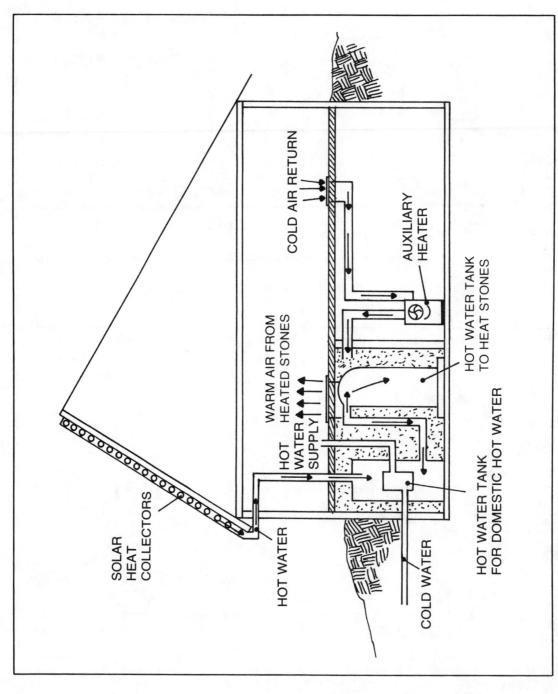

SOLAR HEAT COLLECTORS

HOT WATER

COLD AIR RETURN

AUXILIARY HEATER

WARM AIR FROM HEATED STONES

HOT WATER SUPPLY

HOT WATER TANK TO HEAT STONES

COLD WATER

HOT WATER TANK FOR DOMESTIC HOT WATER

Fig. 10-18. An active solar heating system.

heat and carries it through a piping system to a storage tank. The heat is then taken out of storage and used as needed. Figure 10-18 shows a typical active solar heating system.

The wind is another source of solar power (wind currents are a result of uneven solar heating of the Earth's atmosphere) that can be used as a primary or complementary energy source for heating , cooling, and other energy needs. Electric wind generators can be wired directly into the power lines coming into your house through a phasing unit and an out-metering circuit to supplement your electric service when there is sufficient wind blowing.

The local electric utility will even pay you the going wholesale rate for any excess electricity your generator feeds back into the power grid. For use as a primary energy source, batteries are needed to store the electricity and to dole it out as needed.

If a good, dependable source of running water is available at your building site, a small hydroelectric generator can supply energy needs. Methane generators are another energy source being used by some. Heat pumps buried in the ground to tap geothermal energy are undergoing experimental development. These systems might become important energy resources in the near future.

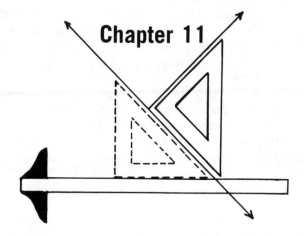

Chapter 11

Scale Floor Plans: Part 2

THE SITE PLAN YOU DEVELOPED IN CHAPTER 9 and the needs of you and your family will determine the kind of plans you finally draw. Don't try to design a house for yourself or for anyone else until you have gathered all the information you can about the site on which the house will be built. Put this information into a site plan. A house that works well for you when facing south might not work at all if it must face to the west. The three basic areas of a residential structure (working, living, and sleeping) must always relate to the site in a satisfying way.

You are probably approximately aware of what you want in the way of a house plan and that is always the starting point. To help you develop, refine, and express your ideas, it is best to keep in mind some basic ideas about architectural planning. Some obvious ideas follow.

☐ The amount of money you have available for building will affect the size of your house, and to some degree its quality.

☐ The size of your family will also be a determining factor in the size of your home.

☐ The age and sex of your children or other live-in dependents will probably determine the number of bedrooms.

☐ The number of vehicles you own will determine the size of your garage, in most cases.

Here are some other ideas that are not so obvious.

☐ If you own or have a liking for oversized furniture or antiques such as four-poster beds, be sure to make your rooms oversized. Such things as weaving looms require higher than standard-sized, 8-foot ceilings.

☐ Take into account the extra storage space that will be needed for any special hobbies or interests you have. Do they require a room of their own?

☐ Study the sociology of your family carefully. Do you really need such things as a game room or a family room? Do you need a special-purpose room to suit your own particular life-style? If you like to entertain often, consider the special needs of that activity (such as easy-to-clean floors and walls). Is your preference for formal or informal entertaining? Open plans are very good for informal entertainers, but closed plans and formal dining rooms are a must for formal entertaining. If guests often stay overnight, extra bathrooms with dressing space might be needed.

☐ Be sure to include all of your ideas in your planning. If you have to leave something out, be sure to give yourself a very good reason for it. Try alternate ways to get what you want. Don't give up easily.

GENERAL REQUIREMENTS

One big advantage of drawing your own house plans is that you can scale your plans for yourself and your family. This is something architects seldom do. They refer to tables called Architectural Graphic Standards for the sizes of working heights, furniture, appliances, etc., to get their scale. This is fine for people who are "average" height and weight. Check individual family members for a scale that suits them. Plan your house not just to accommodate the "average" person, but for the real persons who will inhabit the house.

Your basic floor plan will develop from the three basic areas of your house, living area, working area, and sleeping area, and how they are laid out on your site plan to take best advantage of the weather, the view, the access to the property, and any special energy considerations such as geothermal or solar.

Plan your walkways, driveways, garage, outdoor living areas, service areas and even your major landscaping before any detailed floor plans are drawn. Your three basic areas will include living room, dining room, and family room in the living area; kitchen, pantry, workshop, and tool-storage are with the furnace/air conditioner closet in the working area; and bedrooms, den, bath, storage, halls and, to save miles of walking, utility room are

in the sleeping area. You may also want to include a powder room in the living area and a half bath in the working area.

The three basic areas can have some overlapping. Try for efficient use of space and ease of traffic flow. But don't be too rigid or swayed by convention. Many house planners will tell you that hallways are wasted space. Don't you believe it. Hallways are efficient and beautiful traffic movers and the best sound insulators you can have.

We learned this lesson when we moved into an old house in Indianapolis that featured a big center hall downstairs and a huge central hall upstairs. All the rooms in the house opened into one of the hallways that were connected by a broad stairway. First we thought, what an elegant waste of space. Very soon, however, we discovered what all this space was for. We had three teenaged children who were always having overnight guests. We were at an easy-off, easy-on location near east-west U.S. Interstate 40 and all our friends who were traveling east-west those days stopped over for always most welcome visits. We had relatives attending the University of Indiana nearby who often came on weekends. The big old house took it all in stride without ever seeming crowded or noisy.

Those hallways (Fig. 11-1) kept everyone from tripping over everyone else, and served as sound barriers when the house was being used by lots of different-aged persons engaged in all kinds of varied activities. We have included the floor plan of that house because it is such a good one. We have used variations of it many times in remodeling and designing homes from scratch.

The problem of traffic flow is always the first consideration when you begin to design your floor plan. The traffic patterns made by the family members who do the housework and household chores should be studied and kept in mind during the formulation of a floor plan. If you do this, you will see that many of the conventions of residential architecture are not very logical. All architects should serve

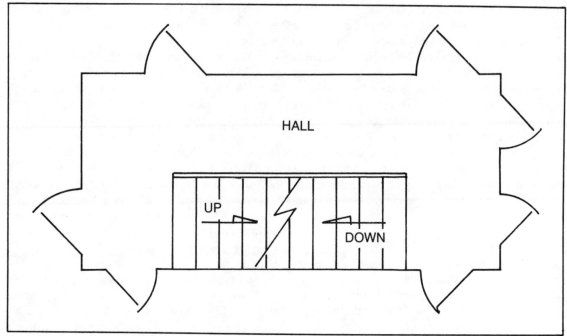

HALL

UP

DOWN

Fig. 11-1. A hallway and stairs.

an apprenticeship as housewives or househusbands before being allowed to draw their first residential floor plan!

Because the textbooks say that the utility room is part of the working area and not part of the sleeping area, your friendly neighborhood architect designs in a long, traffic trail to plague the person who does the laundry. Who ever heard of putting in washer and dryer outlets in the master bedroom? Why not?

On the floor plan of our house in Indianapolis (Figs. 11-2A and 11-2B), notice that the washer and dryer are tucked away neatly in the bathroom, handy to all the bedrooms. We understand this was done at the insistence of the lady who had the house designed. The architect protested and, in a supreme act of defiance, also put washer-dryer outlets in the basement "laundry room." These outlets, of course, were never used, but the basement "laundry room"

did make a dandy tool-storage room and handyman workshop.

Among the general requirements of other rooms in your house might be as follows.

Entryway

No house should be without an entryway. The entryway can work almost like a center hallway in that all three main areas of the house should have access from the entry. It should be a minimum of 4 feet by 4 feet square and it should be walled off or set off by room dividers (not just an extension of the living room or dining room).

Living Room

Whatever else it is, the living room should not be a highway to other parts of the house. It needs to be dead ended, if possible, and isolated from the

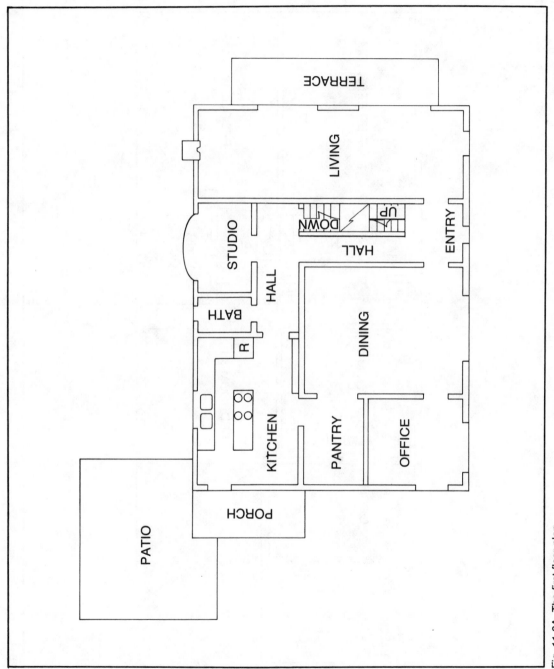

Fig. 11-2A. The first floor plan.

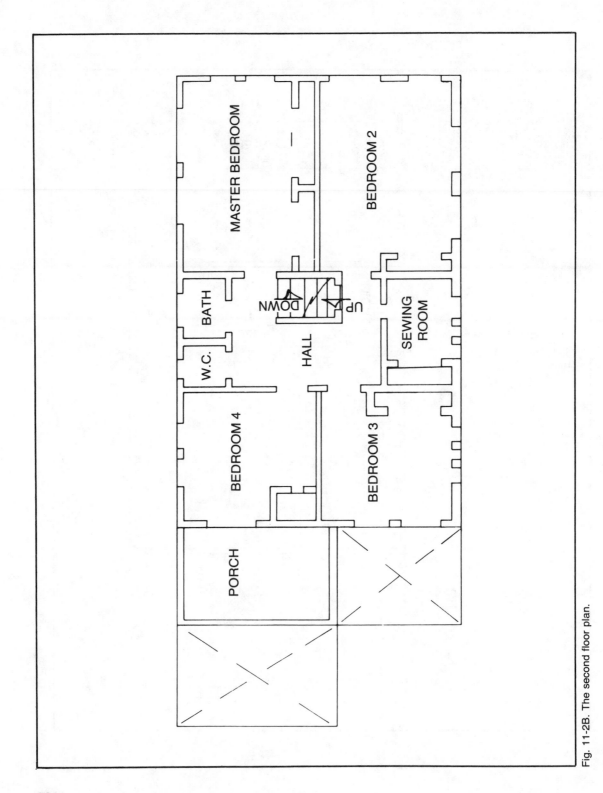

Fig. 11-2B. The second floor plan.

sleeping area. If a lot of dinner entertaining is done, it needs to be accessible to the dining room without guests having to trail through other parts of the house. About 300 square feet seems to work well as a living room size for most families.

Dining Room

For families that enjoy formal entertaining, a separate dining room is a necessity. It can also double as a music room and homework room. Don't plan it too small. About 120 square feet works if your dinner guest roster seldom exceeds a dozen. Scale up from there to suit your needs and family dinner habits.

Family Room

A family room (Fig. 11-3) is a logical extension of the kitchen. Viewing television is often accompanied by much eating and drinking. Be sure to give your family plenty of elbow room (at least 240 square feet).

Kitchen

The "working end" of the kitchen can be quite small. About 120 square feet will do nicely if everything is efficiently arranged. A large family kitchen should not require roller skates for the cook. The kitchen shown in Fig. 11-1 is the result of some remodeling. What we got when we moved in is shown in Fig. 11-4. You can see why roller skates were high on our grocery list the first time we shopped to stock the pantry.

Kitchens do not need to be near the front door, as some planners insist. Back door access to your service and trash disposal areas is a requirement along with handy access to the garage or driveway for short-haul grocery carrying. Whoever works most in the kitchen should design it. The general requirement is for a small triangle between the sink, the stove, and the refrigerator, as illustrated in Figs. 11-5A through 11-5D. You might want to make the triangle between a cook table, a warm box

(for raising yeast doughs), and an oven if you do a lot of baking.

You will also want to consider the height of the person who cooks. The height of work areas, storage cabinets, shelves, racks, and hooks should not be designed to some average or standard, but for the comfort of the person who does most of the work in the kitchen. If you design a corridor kitchen, don't make the isle too wide or you'll defeat the whole purpose of this useful design.

Bedrooms

Bedrooms need quiet, isolation, and bathrooms nearby. They need plenty of storage space and easy access to laundry facilities. About 130 square feet is a good size for a single-purpose bedroom. Scale up from there if you use it for sewing or writing the great American novel, etc.

Bathrooms

The most taken-for-granted room design in America, and the most in need of a redesign, is the bathroom. The Wolverton bathroom design separates bath and toilet facilities. The *bath* room ought to be big enough to accommodate a hot tub. Large potted plants and skylights are also included in our designs. See Figs. 11-6A through 11-6D. About 100 square feet is a good size, while the toilet cubicle can be as small as 15 square feet. If you insist on a conventional bathroom, give yourself about 50-square feet per bathroom.

Halls

We do not believe in saving space by skimping on hallways. Make them at least 3½ feet wide and use them to move traffic between areas and rooms.

Laundry Room

Remember to design in enough space in your laundry room for ironing. A large clothes hamper for soiled clothing is a basic requirement. You might

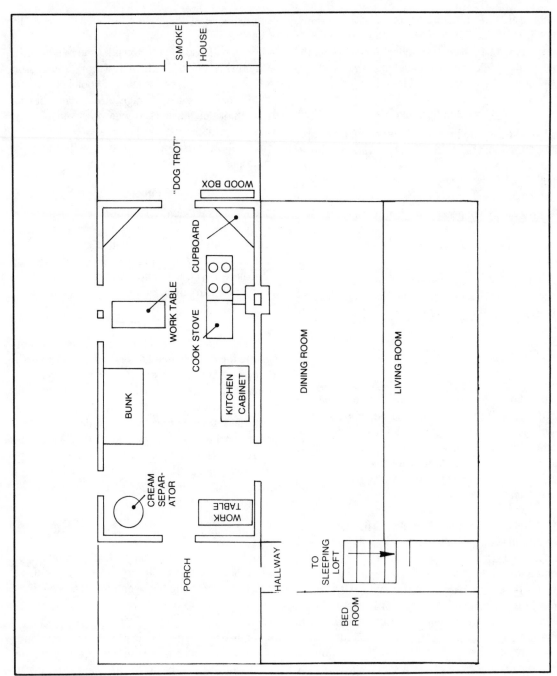

Fig. 11-3. Grandpa's great family room forerunner.

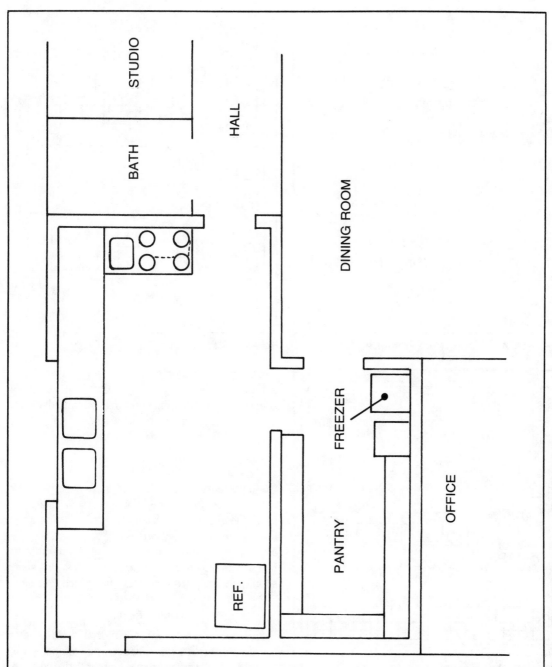

Fig. 11-4. The before plan for a roller-rink kitchen.

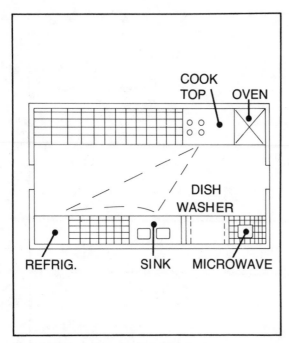

Fig. 11-5A. A corridor plan for a kitchen.

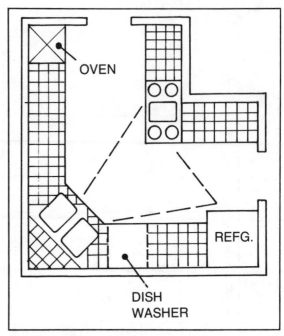

Fig. 11-5C. The L-shaped plan.

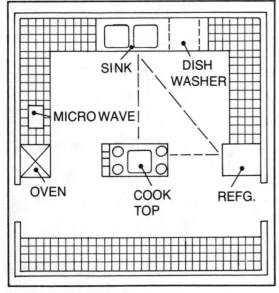

Fig. 11-5B. The island plan.

consider having a combination laundry sewing room if there are family members who sew. About 60 square feet is a starting point for your laundry room if it is to contain the basic washer-dryer-ironing board and hamper. Scale up from there.

Workshop

Good placement for your handyperson repair place and tool-storage room is where most designers place the utility room. That would be adjacent to the kitchen and back door with easy access to the garage. Depending on how much handyperson work you or one of your family members does, this space should scale up from at least 40 square feet.

Mud Room

Every house inhabited by children needs a mud room with full hot and cold running water wash-up facilities. Mud rooms are not just for little old ladies

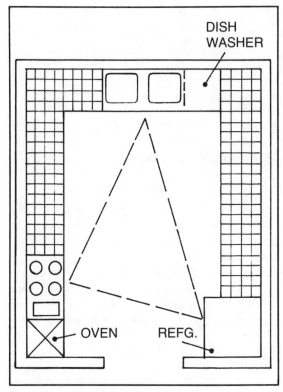

DISH WASHER

OVEN REFG.

Fig. 11-5D. The U-shaped plan.

and gentlemen to park their tennis shoes and rose bush trimming shears. Instead of having dirty footware and dripping snowsuits entering directly on living room rugs or newly scrubbed kitchen floors, a 30-square-foot-plus mud room is worth its space in kept tempers.

Garage or Carport

If you are serious about using your garage or carport for protection and storage of vehicles, your space requirements will depend on the number and type of vehicle stored. About 200 square feet for a single garage and 400 square feet for a double will accommodate most family vehicles. Other uses to consider are other types of storage, indoor play space, space for hobbies or a small business (if zoning laws allow), and expansion of living space for the future.

Basement

Basements are useful for future expansion of living space, play areas and hobby areas. A basement is the best place for heating and cooling equipment, water heaters, water softeners, solar hot water storage tanks, etc. Use of a full basement under the

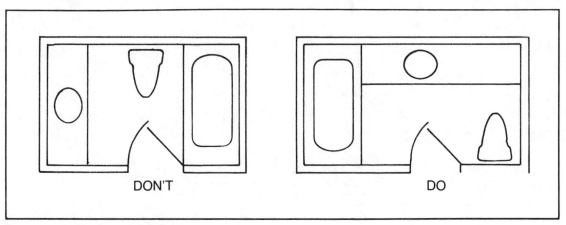

DON'T   DO

Fig. 11-6A. Bathroom dos and don'ts.

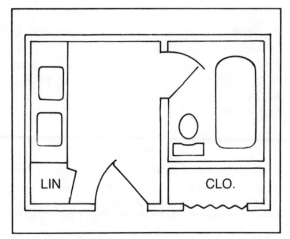

Fig. 11-6B. A divided bath plus closets.

entire house area is an economical way to have a lot of extra potential living space enclosed

Air Conditioner and Heater Room

With no basement, but with central heat and cooling

planned for a house, you will need 15 to 30 square feet for the equipment. This space should be as near to the center of the house as possible to avoid long runs on ductwork.

Other Room Needed

Other considerations will need to be made as you begin to make your first trial floor plans. Such items as coal or oil storage tanks, LP gas tanks, septic tanks, utility meters, hot water heaters, etc., will need space in, on or around your house.

SCHEMATIC PLANS TO SCALE PLANS

Your floor plan should not begin as a scale drawing with straight lines and squared-off corners. This tends to discourage changes that you should make easily in the early drawing stages. Use light sketchy lines that can be erased and drawn over with ease. Make your area or room boundaries schematic; they should be in the shape of "balloons" or ovals. Draw them on a sketch of your site plan in order to study

Fig. 11-6C. A square bathroom with a roomy corner tub.

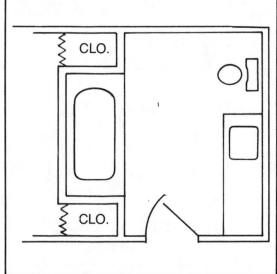

Fig. 11-6D. A tub flanked by closets.

the relationships between your environment and your living structure (Fig. 11-7).

While you are not drawing to scale, be very careful about proportions and make your ovals approximately the right size in relation to the lot and to one another. If you need some help getting started on placing the relative areas for your plan it will help to fill out a planning checklist. See Fig. 11-8.

From the detailed information you will generate by filling in the blank spaces in the checklist, you can make your first sketches showing the relationships of your living, working areas, and sleeping areas. You will probably develop more than one basic plan. Explore every possibility until you are happy with the way these areas relate to the site plan. Figure 11-9 suggests several studies of a possible floor plan schematic.

The next step is the really important one in developing a floor plan you can live with happily. Make a complete traffic diagram, room by room, as illustrated in Fig. 11-10. Access routes between all rooms and outside areas must be plotted out using different types of lines and even different colors for different family members, visitors, service people, and vehicles. Take plenty of time to draw and redraw and study these patterns. Once you decide on the one you like stay with it. Changes behind this stage are difficult to make without upsetting other relationships.

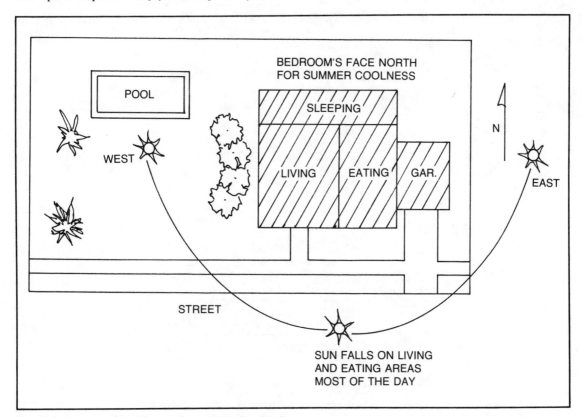

Fig. 11-7. An area schematic superimposed on the site plan.

I. Plot Plan
   A. Size & Shape of lot (describe) _____
   _____

   B. Direction faced by largest window areas _____
   C. Location of patio _____
   D. Location of utilities : gas _____ electricity _____
      sewer _____ water _____ TV cable _____
   E. Type of fences _____
   F. Swimming pool/size/shape/location _____

II. Structure
   A. Floor/concrete/wood other? _____
   B. Walls/stud/post & beam/brick veneer/concrete block/other _____
   _____
   C. Roof/one pitch/hip or gable/other _____
   D. Skylights? Clerestorys? _____

III. Finishing
   A. Walls/stucco/brick/wood/other _____
   B. Roof/shingle/shake/rock/other _____
   C. Doors/panel/slab _____
   D. Fascia board description _____
   E. Planters? Kind? Where? _____

IV. Rooms
   A. Living room
   Area _____ sq ft. Faces front or rear? _____
   Walls _____ floor _____ ceiling _____
   Describe special features such as fireplace, etc. _____
   _____

   B. Dining area or room
   Area _____ sq. ft. Walls _____ floor _____ ceiling
   _____ features _____
   C. Kitchen
   Area _____ sq. ft. Eating area? Size? _____
   Type of cabinets/counters _____
   Walls _____ floor _____ ceiling _____
   Special equipment & features _____
   _____

   D. Family room
   Area _____ sq. ft. Walls _____ floor _____ ceiling
   _____ special features _____

   E. Bedrooms, Dens

	Area	Walls	Floors	Ceiling	Closet
BR #1	____	____	____	____	____
BR #2	____	____	____	____	____
BR #3	____	____	____	____	____
BR #4	____	____	____	____	____

   F. Bathrooms

	Area	Walls	Floors	Ceilings	List Fixtures
B #1	____	____	____	____	____
B #2	____	____	____	____	____
B #3	____	____	____	____	____
B #4	____	____	____	____	____

   G. Entry & Halls
   Area, total _____ sq. ft. Opens to following rooms _____
   _____

   H. Workroom, Shop or Studio
   Area _____ sq. ft. Special equipment or features _____
   _____

   I. Storage & services
   Linen closet, linear ft. _____ Other closets total
   linear ft. _____ special features _____
   Area of heater/air conditioner space used _____
   Space for hot water heater _____ space for solar
   or other alternate energy storage _____
   Tanks & bins _____ Other _____
   J. Car port/garage
   Area _____ sq. ft. Features _____
   K. Total area of house excluding garage, approx. _____ sq ft.

Fig. 11-8. A house-plan checklist.

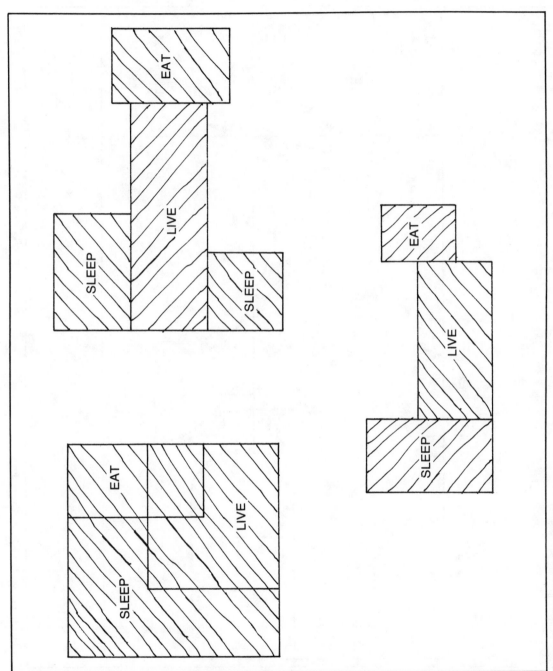

Fig. 11-9. A floor-plan schematic.

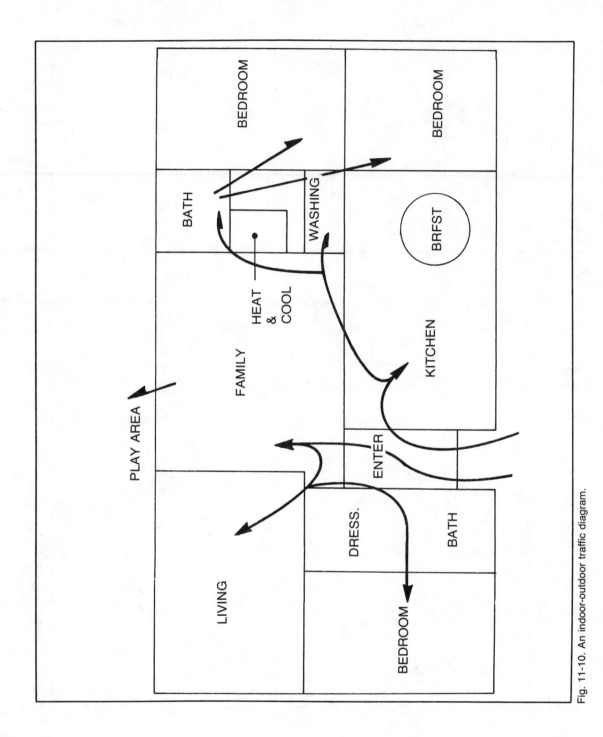

Fig. 11-10. An indoor-outdoor traffic diagram.

234

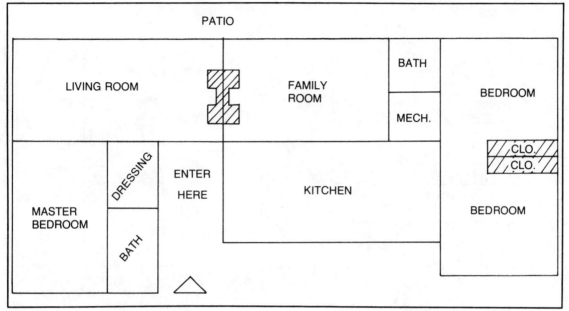

Fig. 11-11. A rough sketch of a floor plan.

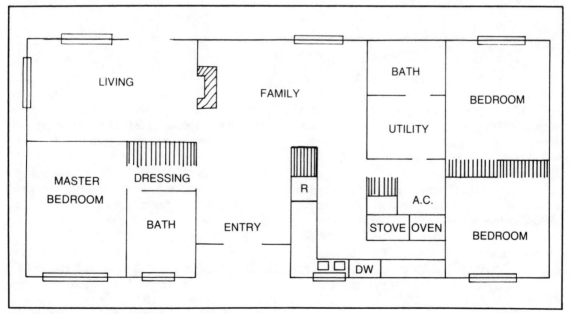

Fig. 11-12. A one-line floor plan.

235

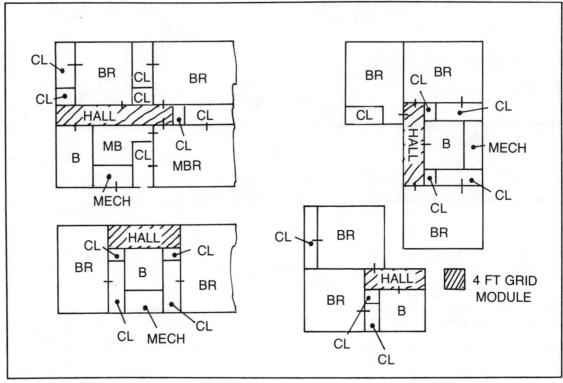

Fig. 11-13. Sleeping wing ideas.

Now develop your preliminary schematic into a more detailed sketch like the one shown in Fig. 11-11. Check on the space requirements of certain important items such as fireplaces, kitchen equipment, etc., and put them in fairly close to scale. This will help you stay out of trouble later when you are drawing to exact size.

From your detailed sketch, it is an easy step to a one-line floor plan like the one shown in Fig. 11-12. We like to do these one-liners (thickness of walls not shown) on graph paper or on 4-×4 quad ruled paper with each square equal to one foot. You can still sketch, without a straightedge, but get everything down to scale and begin to see how it will all work together. Your finished floor plan can be drawn from this rough copy.

Once your floor plan has been developed in the one-line stage, you can make any final adjustments necessary to satisfy such requirements as the direction of view or the shape of the lot without any basic changes by revolving the floor plan on the site plan or tracing it from the back.

Try to keep the outline of your plan clean and simple without many breaks. Jogs in walls cost a lot of money to build and seldom contribute much to the function or beauty of a building.

You will probably find that the design of the sleeping areas is the most difficult. They will need storage places and access to several rooms from small hallways. Figure 11-13 shows some suggestions we have found useful in solving bedroom wing design dilemmas.

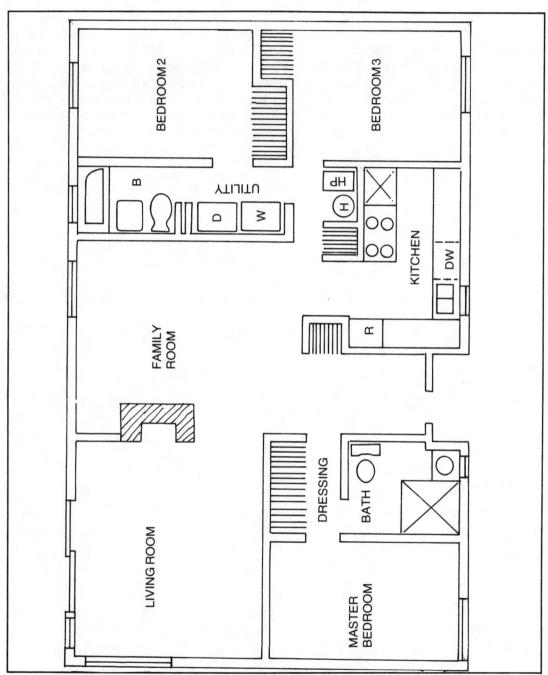

Fig. 11-14. A double-line floor plan.

Don't overlook the delights and economies of multistory and split-level houses in your planning. Two-story buildings give you more space for less money than one-story ranch style houses. A big house can be built on a small lot by going multistory. If your land is sloping, a split-level plan will usually work better and varying floor and ceiling heights are very pleasing esthetically.

After all strategies have been tried and all considerations have been met, you will want to trace or copy your final one-line floor plan into finished form such as the plan shown in Fig. 11-14. Everything should now be drawn to a scale of ¼ inch = 1 foot. Draw straight lines and square corners. Wall thickness and other essential construction details will be drawn in on your final floor plan.

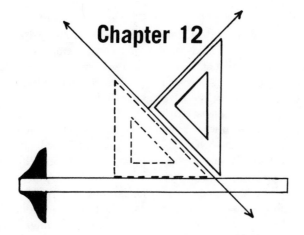

Chapter 12

Drawing in the Extras

THE SITE PLAN YOU DREW IN CHAPTER 9 IS THE starting place for drawing for your own landscaping plan. You might also want to draw plans for gardens (vegetable, flower, rock, etc.), swimming pools, decorative pools, and fountains. Your landscaping plan should show everything you want on your property.

MAKING A LANDSCAPING PLAN

Trace your site plan while omitting utilities and dimensioning. Trace in all large trees and shrubs you had on your site plan. Be sure to draw them as mature plants even though you plan to plant small plants. Mark the location of all tree trunks as small circles. Be sure to outline all planters and areas of lawn and ground cover. Don't overlook your small plants and hedges. Make notes to identify all plants and planting areas. Use the common names for trees and shrubs unless there might be some confusion about the plant.

If you plan to install a sprinkler system, it should go on your landscape plan. The manufacturer of your sprinkler system will furnish you with a catalog that will give you the information about areas covered by various sprinkler heads, pipes, valves. You will need this information to design the system. Be sure to start from the water source where you place the valves or automatic timing device that activates the system. Identify all sprinkler heads and run your water lines where they are needed to give you the coverage you desire with the type of sprinkler heads you choose.

The major secret to drawing successful landscape plans is to put in complete information. Even professionals often draw landscape plans that are too sketchy. Keep in mind that the plans you draw are carriers of information. Get your message across loud and clear. So never fear to put too much information into your landscape plans. Err on that side rather than leave something out. You might even want to put your utilities and dimensioning back in if you feel that is needed to clarify the fact that you want all power lines underground.

Most plans are drawn to a scale of 1/16 inch=1 foot; that is not really a good scale for a landscape plan. If you use a combination site plan and landscape plan, draw your site plan to a larger scale such as 1/8 inch=1 foot. This is a job for an inexpensive pantograph. Most of the site plans, plot plans, earth section, and contour maps you need to work from will have to be copied at a larger scale than the original. You might also want to blow up certain sections of your own landscape plans from ⅛-inch scale to ¼-inch scale or larger to show and clarify certain details. A pantograph is essential for that kind of duty.

Another bit of information often left off of landscape plans that really needs to be there is an indication of the structural members of the roof of any building shown on the plan. This will not be a roof framing plan, but one with lines to show the direction and location of the main roof members. Figure 12-1 shows such a roof plan as well as details of the sprinkler system and other information that needs to go on a good landscape plan drawing. This plan shows the roof lines as object lines, the wall lines as hidden lines, and even dimension lines that are drawn the same weight as the lines indicating landscape materials. These lines, by the way, can overlap anything else. The drawings are more readable if drawn this way because of the relative importance of the concrete areas, the house, etc., compared to less distinct items such as shrubs and trees.

After looking at hundreds of professional and amateur landscape drawings it became obvious to us that there is no standard method for drawing ground cover, trees, shrubs, but the pros seem to consistantly make their lines delineating these objects the same weight as dimension lines.

Those who drew their trees and foliage in great detail seem to be doing so primarily to create an artistic effect. You can take plenty of artistic license if you want to make your foliage fancy. For purposes of working drawings, circles drawn with a compass or a template will do nicely for all trees and shrubs. Landscape templates are available at a reasonable price and they will help you save time in your drafting work.

If a professional architect is making a drawing to be used as a presentation drawing (not the working drawing), he will make the foliage quite artistic to impress the client. If you have a problem getting your spouse to agree to an expenditure for some landscaping flourishes, you might resort to the same tactics and pull out all your artistic stops on a presentation drawing. It is a matter of taste and wiles when you get right down to the bottom line.

Do include on your drawings, plain or fancy, a schedule of plant materials. Describe the size, quantity, and names of all trees and shrubs. Always be sure to check all maps. such as official ones that come from your accessor's building-tract office, against the land itself before using it as the basis for a landscape plan. Correct any discrepancies you find when you copy the map. Be especially aware of the accuracy of contours, the locations of curbs and gutters, easements, utilities, etc.

When starting what you consider to be your final landscape plan, be sure to leave space on the right side of the drawing for an index (as shown in Fig. 12-2). Include more than enough information so that any landscape contractor can pick up the plan and do what you want done even if you are away skiing in Colorado at the time. Even if you do your own landscaping from your own plan, include everything in the plan so that nothing can be forgotten in the heat of mixing concrete or planting that New Zealand Flax.

Now that you know how to make a landscape plan, the real challenge becomes how to plan your landscape!

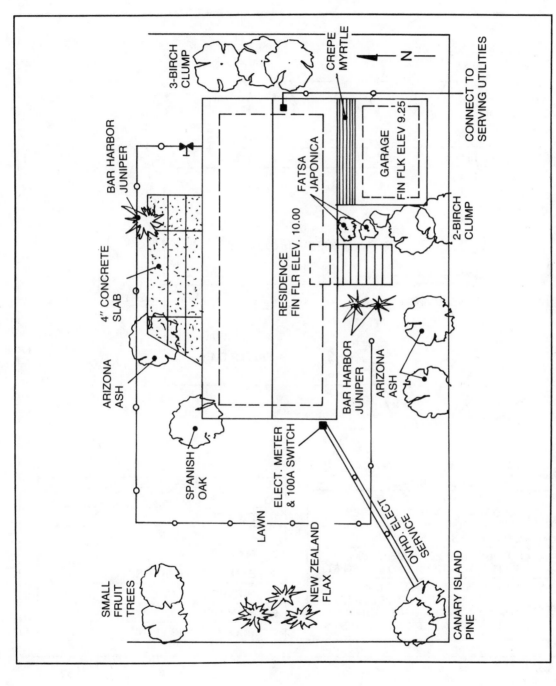

Fig. 12-1. A landscape plan that includes roof lines (shade), overhang, and the location of a sprinkler system.

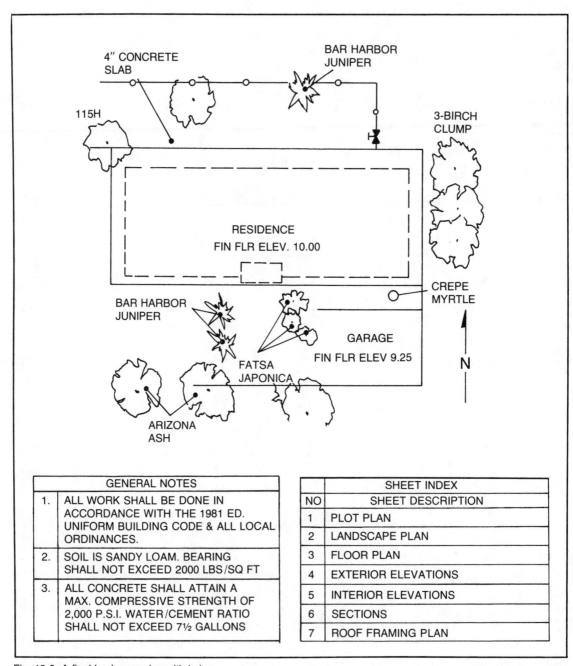

4" CONCRETE SLAB

BAR HARBOR JUNIPER

115H

3-BIRCH CLUMP

RESIDENCE
FIN FLR ELEV. 10.00

CREPE MYRTLE

BAR HARBOR JUNIPER

GARAGE
FIN FLR ELEV 9.25

N

FATSA JAPONICA

ARIZONA ASH

GENERAL NOTES	
1.	ALL WORK SHALL BE DONE IN ACCORDANCE WITH THE 1981 ED. UNIFORM BUILDING CODE & ALL LOCAL ORDINANCES.
2.	SOIL IS SANDY LOAM. BEARING SHALL NOT EXCEED 2000 LBS/SQ FT
3.	ALL CONCRETE SHALL ATTAIN A MAX. COMPRESSIVE STRENGTH OF 2,000 P.S.I. WATER/CEMENT RATIO SHALL NOT EXCEED 7½ GALLONS

SHEET INDEX	
NO	SHEET DESCRIPTION
1	PLOT PLAN
2	LANDSCAPE PLAN
3	FLOOR PLAN
4	EXTERIOR ELEVATIONS
5	INTERIOR ELEVATIONS
6	SECTIONS
7	ROOF FRAMING PLAN

Fig. 12-2. A final landscape plan with index.

DON'T FORGET THE LITTLE TOUCHES

Attracting birds is one of the best parts of any landscape plan. This is especially true in the city. Bird feeders, birdhouses, and shelters are inexpensive and easy to build for the do-it-yourself landscaper. The pay back is more than esthetic. Birds will eat insects that tend to destroy plants, shrubs and trees. A small flock of Martins will keep a small garden nearly free of mosquitoes because they devour them by the hundreds of thousands. But don't plan just for housing your winged garden exterminators, you'll need feeding stations for when insects are out of season.

Placement of bird houses, feeders, and shelters should be on metal poles that cannot be climbed by cats or squirrels. They should face away from prevailing winds and be tilted slightly downward to avoid flooding.

A summer vacation spot for your house plants is a fine little touch to your landscaping. You could have a built-in plant stand or a special terrace. A northern exposure is ideal for summering house plants.

Built-in wind and sun screens, properly planned and placed, will improve your landscaping over the old wrap-it-with-burlap method of protecting plants and shrubs. Every garden area can use a permanent cold frame for winter vacationing of tender plants and getting a head start on spring.

TRELLISES AND ARBORS

A trellis is a frame of light wood strips crossing one another with open spaces to make a frame for supporting vines. Arbors are built of heavier wood in multiple units set at angles to create three-dimensional structures that deserve notation on landscape plans. The whole approach to your front door can be enhanced with a trellis and your back door area can become a charming entryway with an arbor arching over it.

If you are going to build a privacy fence, consider planning a trellis as a gateway or as a fence topper. You could use a trellis-type structure to tie the fence with the house. Such uses seem to make fences more friendly and they come alive with greenery during the growing season. Even in the dead of winter, your fence will be attractive if it is combined with trellises and arbors.

FRIENDLY FENCES

Fences can be friendly or unfriendly depending on what you are fencing in or out. If you are just fencing things out, your fence can do it in a friendly way if you give some thought to fence planning. Fencing out your neighbor's view to achieve visual privacy is one of the main functions of fencing in the city and suburbs. It can also double as a definer of property lines.

When designing your fences for privacy, don't assume you must have a high, tightly constructed fence around the entire area to be screened. These kinds of fences often create more problems than they solve. Problems of air circulation in living areas and drafty wind traps do not have to be traded for privacy. Baffle or louvered fences might be a good solution to consider. Baffle fences have the advantages of directing foot traffic away from flower beds and planted areas, while permitting free circulation of air and serving as a windbreak.

Fences for protection (keeping out unwanted animals and people and keeping in children and pets) need to be designed and placed with the size of animals being excluded or included in mind. Low, wire fences with posts painted green to blend in with the shrubbery might be a better answer than the more conventional post-and-rail fence with it's widely spaced louvers that admit small animals and permit small pets to stray.

If you live in a windy area and the only logical place for your outdoor sitting room or terrace is on the windward side of the house, a wind deflection fence might solve your problem. Use a baffle fence or bore a few holes in a solid fence to ensure ventilation of the area without the fence being blown away by the wind. You might also want to look at the possibilities of curving the fence, angling it, or stepping it up or down to fit the contours of the area.

Some things need to be hidden from view by fences. Some examples are garbage and trash cans, compost heaps, tool sheds, and incinerators. If possible, make these consealment fences as unobtrusive as possible. Try to design them to blend in with the general scheme of your landscaping plan. If that is not possible, then go all out and make the concealment fence into a feature attraction with some kind of unusual, interesting design.

Fences can become the walls of outdoor rooms, but try not to make them like interior rooms—boxy and squared off. Remember that fences can angle, curve, zigzag or snake. Fences can make your house look quite different: higher, lower, more important, or less aggressive.

Before you finalize your plans for fencing, be sure to check with your local zoning officials for any regulations concerning setback, height, or materials to be used in fences. Your city planning department can give you this information. Be sure that you know exactly where your property lines are before you design that fence into your final landscaping design.

GAZEBOS AND OTHER OPEN-AIR SHELTERS

The possibilities of outdoor living should not be overlooked when you are planning your landscape designs. Gazebos and other open-air shelters add a lot of comfort to outdoor living. Garden shelters are nice for escaping from sudden rain showers and we welcome the shade they provide. You will find that a place to sit and enjoy the great outdoors is a most enjoyable feature if some protection from the tricks of your climate is provided.

Open-air shelters should be placed where they are needed instead of where they will impress your neighbors the most. These shelters need not be formal or surrounded by formal plantings. They need to be practical and solidly roofed if they are to carry snow loads in winter. Roll-up bamboo shades might be a good idea in some climates. You could build a half-and-half structure that provides a roofed and nonroofed area to be used according to the season and the weather.

Old-fashioned gazebos seem to be in for a revival and A-frame and geodesic dome structures are beccoming more and more popular. The roofing of terraces is also becoming a thing to do. Perhaps you will want to consider that along with the traditional paved, but unroofed terrace.

There are five main questions you will need to answer about your design.

☐ What is your climate like?

☐ What will your budget stand?

☐ Will it be used for few or many years?

☐ How large is the family that will be using the shelter?

☐ What are their ages, interests, and inclinations?

There are several other factors to consider. Will it be used for entertaining, an eating area, or a playroom for the kids? Will it be used a lot at night and therefore need some kind of lighting? Be sure that the outdoor lighting will not disturb other members of the family who might need to be sleeping at the time.

The vagaries of weather and the path of the sun are important factors to always consider when placing your open-air shelters. Keep in mind that the afternoon sun is hottest at about 3 o'clock in the afternoon. A shelter placed on the southwest or west of the house will be quite hot then and on in to the early evening if it is paved. If you want passive solar heating of the area, this is fine. If you are looking for a cool summertime retreat, however, it won't work. You will find that around on the east or southeast side of your house. You can, of course, use trees or plantings to shade a westerly location.

You will also want to consider prevailing winds

and sudden showers. Consider putting at least part of the shelter under a good roof where you and your outdoor furniture can be protected during a brief downpour.

PAVED AREAS

Paving is a design element of landscaping that is often overlooked. Paving has a lot of landscape advantages that ought to be considered by any designer, amateur or professional. You might have noticed that children spend far more time playing on the driveway than they do playing in the yard. They often move out into the street even when they have a half an acre of grass. Could it be that they are telling us something? Roller skating, bike riding, basketball dribbling, and even hopscotch goes a lot better on a paved surface than on grass. Why not provide such a play area in the first place?

Paved walkways can look mighty good in any well-landscaped yard or garden. They deserve as much thought and planning as does the traffic patterns inside your house.

Try to provide dry passways from the car to the house. Think twice before you draw in that old convention of a walk across your front lawn. Why? Consider instead placing it beside the driveway where it really is needed and give yourself an unbroken expanse of front lawn that will look better and be easier to mow. And think of the edging you will save!

A semicircular drive-around or a T-shaped back-in, turn-around are worth considering to avoid the dangers of backing out into the street.

BUILT-IN PLANTERS

One idea that has caught on with landscape designers everywhere, even the designers of busy downtown city streets, is the decorative built-in planter. These structures often double as walls and seats. These planters "boxes" can become real show places for your favorite plants blazing with azaleas or afire with chrysanthemums. Think about placing some of these built-in planters beside entry doors, beneath a picture window, as part of a terrace or outdoor shelter, on the upper side of a retaining wall, flanking steps, or as a background for a flower bed. Design them in interesting geometrical shapes, such as French curves!

POOLS AND FOUNTAINS

You don't have to be wealthy to afford pools and fountains. There are many ways to include pools and cool running water into any landscape design for any kind of budget. You don't need to run up a large water bill now that small recirculating pumps are widely available. These little pumps take the water that drains from the pool and force it back up through a fountain jet or another pool inlet (waterfall, for instance). Only the little water lost through evaporation need be replaced. Once in a while you will need to drain and scrub your pools.

Pools need not be deep unless you are going to dive into them from a high diving board. For swimming, 3 feet of water gives you as much fun and exercise as 6 or 8 feet. If you want to grow water lilies, you can get by with a very shallow pool if you make a few plant pockets deep enough to hold soil for the roots. One small, deep pocket in the middle of a large, shallow pool works beautifully for all kinds of aquatic plant life.

Another neat trick we have learned is to paint shallow pools (4 to 6 inches deep) dark green, navy blue, or black. The pool will look as deep and mysterious as a pool that is 6 feet deep. And its a whole lot safer for any neighborhood kids that might wander in. Consider a shallow (say 3 or 4 inches deep) reflecting pool to mirror your favorite tree or to serve as the focal point for your entire landscape design.

If you design your shallow pools so that they taper outward and upward from the center like a saucer, you will have a pool that will not be damaged by freezing water in winter. When the water freezes in a saucer shaped pool, it expands upward and encounters no edges to push out and damage. This shape is duck soup to drain and scrub. You can siphon the water quite easily and scrub it with a brush or broom. No water source other than rain or your garden hose is necessary for filling these pools. A series of these pools can make a most attractive waterfall or cascade. Don't assume that a saucer-shaped pool has to be round. Make it square if you like with rounded corners or serpentine freeform.

Fountains, too, can be simple and inexpensive. Plastic pipe can be cut, drilled, glued, and painted to form fountainheads as plain or fanciful as your imagination dictates. A straight vertical pipe with a recirculating pump squirting water against gravity makes a classical fountain.

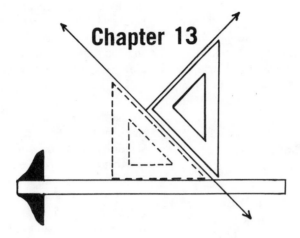

Chapter 13

Drawing in 3-D

M AKING MODELS OF BUILDINGS, BUILDING sites, and landscapes is part of the designer's art that is not often used for the benefit of individual homeowners. Designers of commercial buildings almost always build a model, usually in cardboard, of their proposed structure in order to be able to arrange and rearrange elements of the structure in three dimensions before settling on the final design. For the amateur architect who is drawing house plans, model making can be a real help in trying out ideas and space arrangements before committing the final design to a finished set of drawings.

There are three types of basic model making the do-it-yourself house designer needs to be familiar with: conventional, dome, and underground.

MATERIALS FOR MODEL MAKING

The basic material for model making is the same as the basic material for drawing—paper. Cardboard is actually the same thing as paper. It is made from groundup wood pulp. This wood pulp contains the cellulose fibers that are the main ingredient of cardboard and paper. The pulp is treated with various chemicals, after it is ground, then mixed with water, and rolled into sheets. The thickness of the sheet determines whether or not it will be called paper or cardboard. The thickness you use has a good deal to do with the kind of model work that can be done. It is a good idea to know about the different thicknesses of cardboard.

Shirt Cardboard

Buy a new shirt or send an old one to a good laundry and you will get a piece of shirt cardboard inside the shirt. It is stiff and strong and vary suitable for making architectural models of all kinds. We like this thickness of cardboard best of all

Package Cardboard

Buy a new pair of shoes and it comes in a box made

of package cardboard. It usually has one surface covered with a smooth paper on which information can be printed. Because you usually find package cardboard already made up into neat, right-angle boxes, you can often save time by using one of these whole or in part. We collect cardboard boxes of all sizes for our model-building projects. Often we find one we can cut a bit and come up with just the size we need.

Chip Board

This is the heaviest and stiffest of the cardboards. Buy a box of cigars and they will come in a chip-board box. We collect cigar boxes. We also save the backs of our large drawing pads as another source of chip board. As a last resort, you can always buy it at an art supply store. Be sure to get the lighter-weight chip board for general model building. The heavier kind is just too heavy to work well.

Other Boards and Papers

Once you start paying attention to cardboard and heavy papers, you will be amazed at the varieties in weight, texture and stiffness. In addition to chip board of several weights and finishes, you will find illustration board, bristol board, display board, mounting board, and mat board. As long as the board or heavy paper is not too thin or too flexible and can be cut easily, you can use it for making architectural models.

We recommend that you stay away from corrugated board; it is something quite different from cardboard. It is actually two layers of brown paper with a midsection of heavy-ribbed paper and is great for making great big boxes to ship stuff in. We do not find it a very pleasant material and down right frustrating to work with most of the time. Edges always look ragged and unfinished no matter how careful you try to be and it is hard to bend and fasten together. If you are constructing very large-scale, yard-sized models or childrens' play houses, corru-

gated board works well and you can tape and trim its rough edges. For small scale houses, buildings and landscapes, we recommend just plain cardboard.

Cardboard does retain the grain of the wood, and you can do neater work if you take the grain of the cardboard into consideration. If you have never noticed grain in cardboard, take a small square of cardboard and fold it once up and down, and then once across from side to side. Now you know why cardboard sometimes folds irregular and bumpy and sometimes neat and straight. The neat crease is the one that runs with the grain of the wood from which the cardboard was made. Rounded shapes are easier to bend if you bend with the grain. Structures will be stiffer if you keep the grain running the long way. This is a small point, but one that will make your models look more professional.

TOOLS

A pair of sturdy, sharp scissors, a sharp utility knife or a single-edge razor blade, a dull knife or large paper clip, a metal ruler, a roll of masking tape, a roll of cellophane tape, and a bottle of white glue should be regular inhabitants of your model-making tool box. See Figs. 13-1, 13-2, and 13-3.

CUTTING, BENDING, AND JOINING

You can easily cut the lighter-weight cardboards, such as shirt and package cardboard, with your scissors. Anything heavier than a shoe box, however, needs to be cut with a knife. A knife will also make a neater cut for such things as windows and

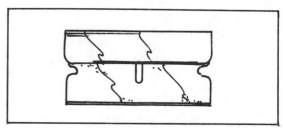

Fig. 13-1. A single-edge razor blade for scoring cardboard.

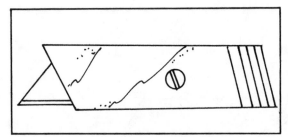

Fig. 13-2. A utility knife with a straight-edge blade.

doors. Always use a ruled line as a guide when cutting with scissors.

You can make an accurate cut using a ruled line with a knife, but it is difficult and fingers tend to get in front of the blade. Use a metal ruler and you will get a straighter cut and it is easy to keep fingers well behind the blade. Don't try to use a wooden ruler because the blade will cut into it. Hold the ruler down firmly with one hand so that it does not slip around. Don't try to go too fast or get careless or the knife is likely to hop off the cardboard.

Don't press too hard and try to cut all the way through the cardboard with one pass of the knife. Go back several times until the knife goes through the cardboard. Go slow and take it easy (Fig. 13-4). If you try to pull the knife too rapidly, it can get out of control and start hopping around and land on the hand that holds the ruler. Always work on a steady, flat surface with a good light. Work with a piece of scrap cardboard underneath your work. Be sure your knife is sharp.

Don't think because you are cutting cardboard you can get by with dull tools. A dull blade tends to slip around instead of cutting and it is far more dangerous than a really sharp blade. Be sure to keep your fingers as far away from the edges of the ruler as possible. If you find your knife wanders away from the straightedge, don't worry about it. Just

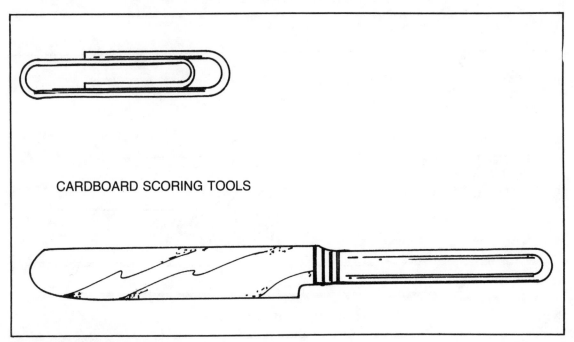

CARDBOARD SCORING TOOLS

Fig. 13-3. Scoring tools.

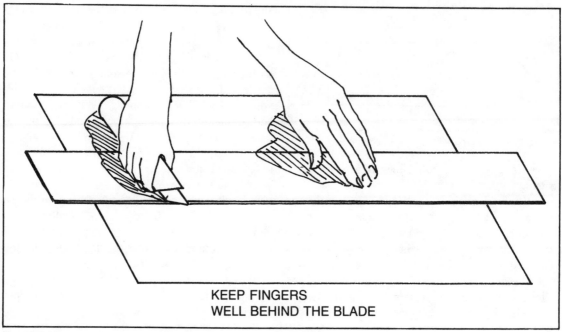

**KEEP FINGERS
WELL BEHIND THE BLADE**

Fig. 13-4. Keep your fingers well behind the blade when you are cutting.

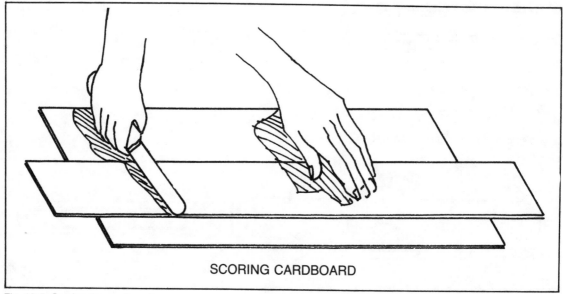

SCORING CARDBOARD

Fig. 13-5. Scoring the cardboard.

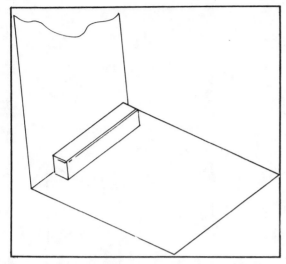

Fig. 13-6. Reinforcing cardboard joints with wood blocks.

practice a little more. With some good practice you will find it easy to keep the knife blade against the ruler and your fingers off its edges.

That dull knife in your tool kit is not for cutting; it is for scoring which you must do in order to get a neat bend. A butter knife or an old table knife works well. We use a large paper clip for scoring cardboard (using a ruler as a guide). Score and bend with the grain when possible (Fig. 13-5).

If you are working with chip board or other heavy cardboard, you might have to go back to your sharp knife for scoring. In this case, make your score along the *outside* of the bend and be sure not to cut all the way through the cardboard. Press down just hard enough to cut through the surface.

It sometimes helps to dampen your cardboard slightly when making gentle, curved bends. Always make these with the grain. If the cardboard is stubborn about bending and tends to crack instead, you will have no choice but to score it in many lines, close together, and do a series of sharp bends to get the curve you need.

Once you have cut and bent your cardboard into the pieces and shapes you need, you will want to assemble the pieces into one unit. There is no problem if one surface is to be placed on top of another; just a dab of glue will do the job. Joining cardboard by the edges is another thing entirely. Our favorite method, especially when building architectural models, is to glue a small block of wood into the corner where the two pieces of cardboard join (as shown in Fig. 13-6). This is one of the strongest joints you can make when putting cardboard edge to edge. Figures 13-7 through 13-12 show other methods for joining cardboard.

If you use narrow slits cut in two pieces of cardboard, make the slits by using two cuts very close together. Then remove the little sliver of cardboard between the cuts. The board will fit together neatly and make a rigid connection.

Corners can be strengthened with a small tab of cardboard. You can create a large surface for gluing by scoring the end of a piece of cardboard. The strongest joint is made when you are able to glue one flat surface to another. The weakest joint is made by gluing the edge of the cardboard to a flat surface. This can sometimes be done successfully and it makes a neat joint if the edge is perfectly straight and the strength requirements of the joint quite low. Staples can be used where they will now show. They are, however, rather unsightly to look at.

MAKING CONVENTIONAL MODELS

What the skilled subcontractor can do with his wood, bricks, concrete and steel, you can do with your scissors, knife and glue (on a small scale). But don't make the scale too small. We like to work with a 1 inch=1 foot scale if at all possible. This results in a rather large model if your dream house is a big one. Don't go below ½ inch=1 foot, or details you will want to clarify with your model will get too small.

Your house will look a lot different in three dimensions than in your drawings, and you might want to make some changes when you see it come

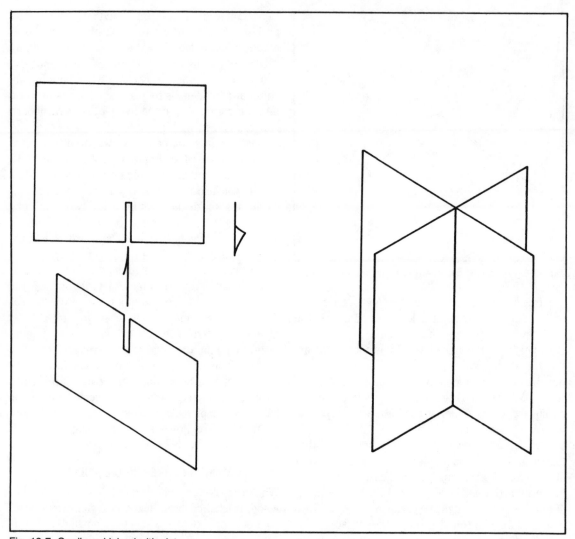

Fig. 13-7. Cardboard joined with slots.

to life in scale. If so, make the changes on your model and get them all just right. Then make the corrections in your drawings before you finalize them for financing and construction.

Even if you are planning nothing more than a one-room addition to your present home, it is a good idea to construct a three-dimensional model, in scale, to check on all those final details. You might notice something you might have overlooked in your drawings.

If this is your first model, follow the step-by-step instructions that follow for any kind of building that has four walls and a roof.

☐ Using elevation drawings and a pantograph,

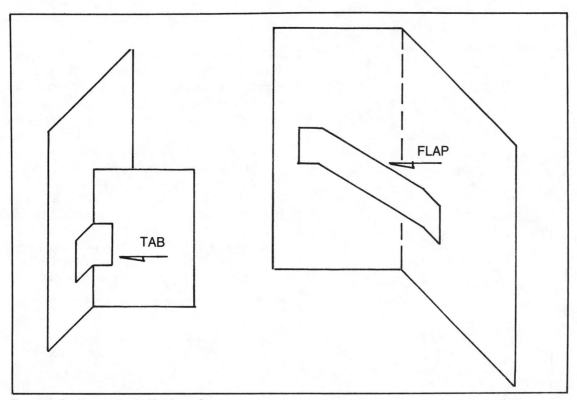

Fig. 13-8. Cardboard joined with tabs or flaps.

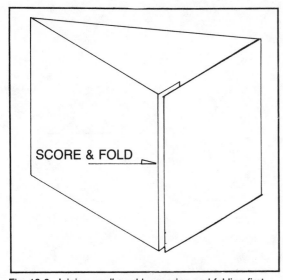

Fig. 13-9. Joining cardboard by scoring and folding first.

trace four walls out to a larger scale on sheets of cardboard. If you have no elevation drawings as yet, you can make them directly on the cardboard. Do this with your T-square and triangle. Never trust your eyes to make one line parallel with another (especially when making models). Try to draw or trace your elevations so that they join one another (as shown in Fig. 13-13). Draw dotted lines where the corners of your structure will be.

☐ Cut out the walls and score along all dotted lines. See Fig. 13-14.

☐ While you can still lay your walls down flat, cut out all window openings and cut around three sides of the door openings. Score the hinged side of the door so that it will open and close. See Fig. 13-15.

☐ Put masking tape along the edges of walls to be joined and apply glue to the edges. Press

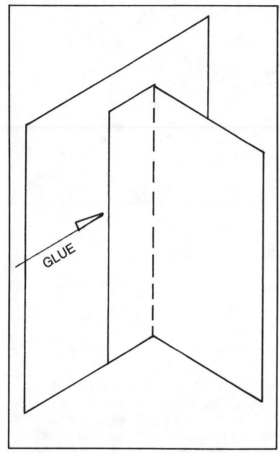

Fig. 13-10. Gluing the folded-over flap to the other wall.

they will fit accurately inside the four walls of your model. See Fig. 13-18. If your floor plan is at all complicated, trace it off to the scale of the model on a piece of thin paper and glue it down inside your four walls before you place any interior walls. Use the scale floor plan as a guide for placing your interior walls. Glue the walls in by their edges at first and assemble the whole model for study. Make any changes you want by stripping out walls and gluing them back in again. Only after you are satisfied that you have exactly what you want should you reinforce your walls with glued-in wooden blocks or tabs. You might even want to tape in some walls in some areas and try them out before gluing them in. Be sure to cut out all interior doors on your interior

together so that the masking tape will hold the joint while the glue is setting. See Fig. 13-16.

　□ Cut out a base for your house that is larger than the structure itself. See Fig. 13-17. Include any porch or patio or terrace that adjoins the house. Be sure to draw it out to proper scale before cutting it out. Stand the four walls on this base and make sure the bottoms of the walls are even all around. If not, even them up and glue them down, bottom edges to base.

　□ Draw your interior walls to scale on pieces of cardboard now and cut them out carefully so that

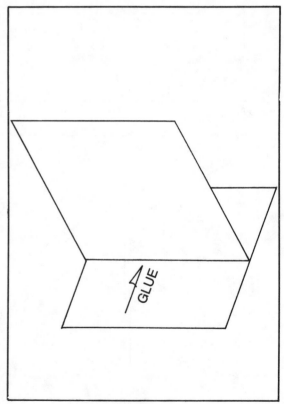

Fig. 13-11. A simple glued joint.

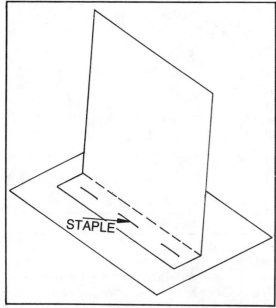
Fig. 13-12. A scored, folded, and stapled joint.

walls so that you can check your traffic patterns in three dimensions.

☐ The roof is usually made from one piece of cardboard, scored, and folded at the peak. Be sure your overhang is accurate and to scale so that you can check your model against the angle of the sun in a real or simulated setup. Do not glue the roof in place, however, just set it on so that it can be removed for inside inspections. See Fig. 13-19.

☐ Extra details can now be added to suit your artistic taste and to come up with some additional ideas for your house. These can be made from small boxes with portions cut away (as shown in Fig. 13-20). You can also give the exterior of your model a coat of paint and trim to make it look just the way you would like your finished house to look.

MAKING DOME MODELS

If you are serious about drawing plans for a geodesic dome home, it is often a good idea to start with a

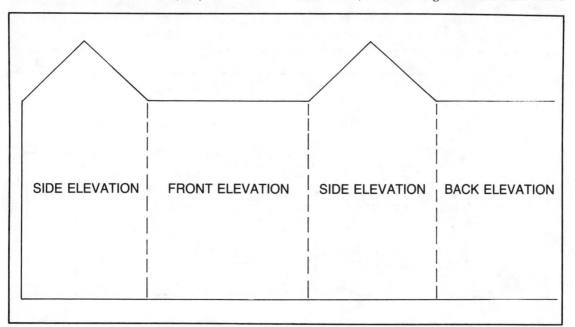

SIDE ELEVATION | FRONT ELEVATION | SIDE ELEVATION | BACK ELEVATION

Fig. 13-13. Elevations joined together on a strip.

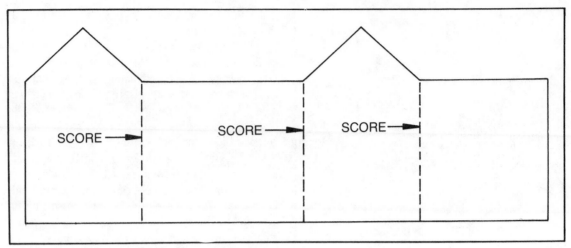

Fig. 13-14. Scoring along dotted lines on an elevation strip.

model before you try to put plans on paper. You can work out actual dimensions for curving walls in three dimensions and not have to go into higher mathematics.

A geodesic dome is basically a self-supporting structure consisting of triangles combining to form hexagons and pentagons. No interior supports are needed so you can arrange your interior to suit your needs without worrying about such things as bearing walls.

Figures 13-21 through 13-25 will give you the proper geometric forms to transfer to cardboard, cut out, and tape together to make a basic geodesic dome model around which you can design almost

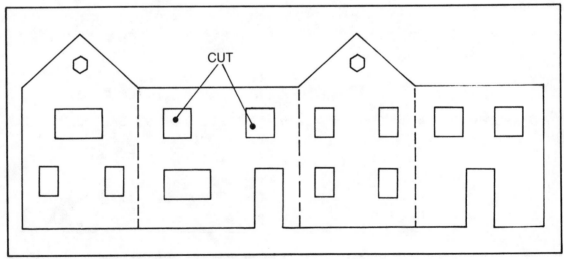

Fig. 13-15. Cut windows and score for opening doors.

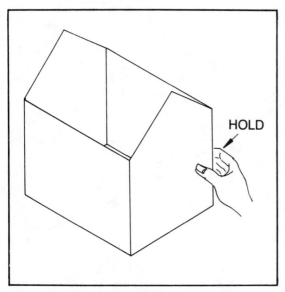

Fig. 13-16. Using masking tape as a clamp while gluing.

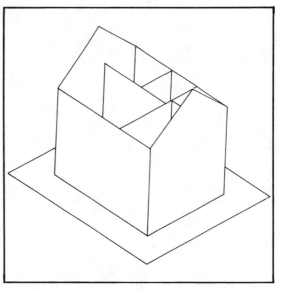

Fig. 13-18. Placing interior walls.

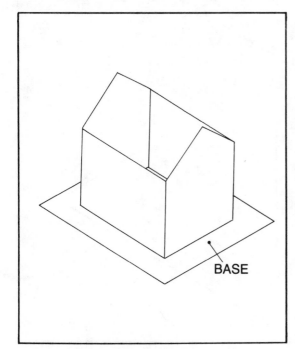

Fig. 13-17. Setting the house on a base.

any kind of domed structure you would like. Follow the plan step by step as follows.

☐ Place a tracing of the page of this book with the geometric forms over your cardboard and push pins through the illustrations at the corners of the figures as indicated.

☐ Connect the pin holes that outline the geometric shapes with solid lines and then draw dotted lines from the corners of hexagon and pentagon to the center. See Figs. 13-21 and 13-22.

☐ Cut out and score as indicated.

☐ Bend all shapes on score lines. Close gaps in hexagons and pentagons and tape underneath or on the concave side of the shape.

☐ Tape all shapes together using the plan and elevation drawings shown in Figs. 13-26 and 13-27 as your guide. Note that you begin with a pentagon; it is the very top of any geodesic dome. Tape one side of a hexagon to each of the five sides of the pentagon. The remaining pentagons are then taped onto two sides of a hexagon pair. The base pieces, entry, and picture window hoods are then taped

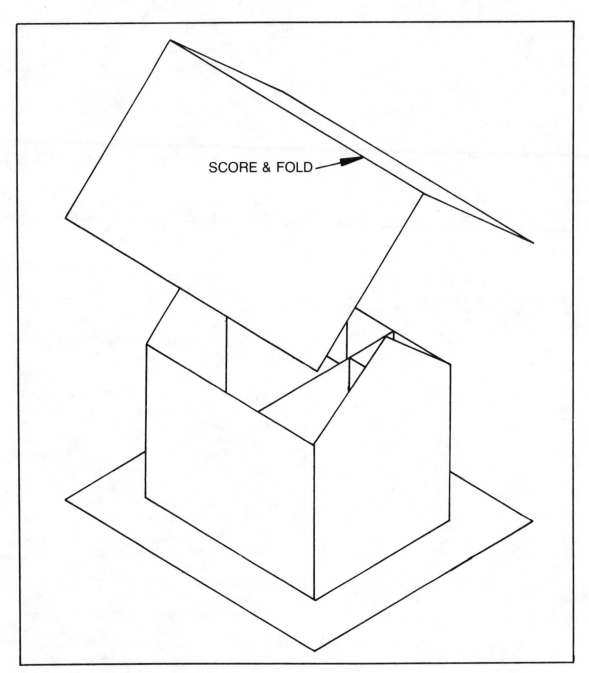

SCORE & FOLD

Fig. 13-19. Keep the roof removable.

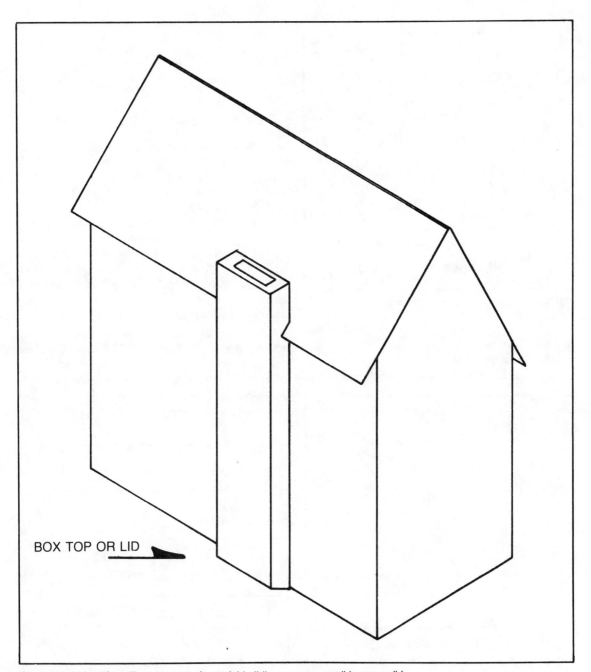

BOX TOP OR LID

Fig. 13-20. Using "found" components in model building such as small boxes or lids.

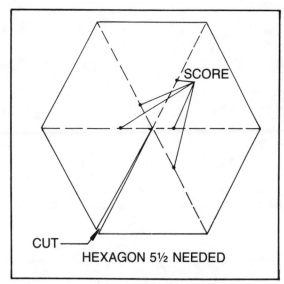

Fig. 13-21. Hexagon construction for a dome.

onto the bottom edges of the pentagons as illustrated.

☐ On a piece of cardboard larger than the diameter of the dome, draw a circle exactly the

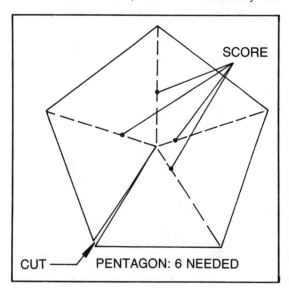

Fig. 13-22. Pentagon construction for a dome.

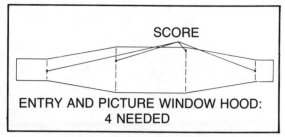

ENTRY AND PICTURE WINDOW HOOD:
4 NEEDED

Fig. 13-23. Entry and picture window hood (you'll need four).

diameter of the dome and set the dome in place on it (but do not fasten it down).

Now you are all set to start exploring the possibilities of space enclosed by a dome. You can sketch tentative floor plans and then erect interior walls on your floor plan to test your ideas. Replace the dome over your space arrangements and take a look in one of the openings to check your work. After you have evolved living spaces you like, then you can draw up a set of plans that can be used in actual construction. Figure 13-28 is a floor plan for a one-room dome addition we have planned for our home/office. It was drawn after we made a model of our house and then made a model of the addition and tied the two together.

UNDERGROUND HOUSES AND LANDSCAPES

When first we thought of making models of our

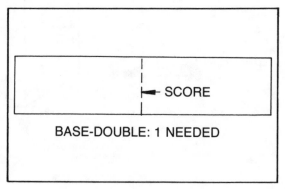

BASE-DOUBLE: 1 NEEDED

Fig. 13-24. Making the base.

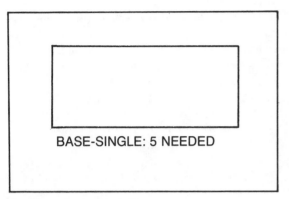

BASE-SINGLE: 5 NEEDED

Fig. 13-25. Another kind of base.

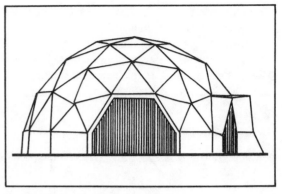

Fig. 13-27. An elevation view of a dome.

ideas for underground houses and underground additions to houses already constructed, we tried out all kinds of ways of making a model of the terrain into which these model houses would go. We made them of cardboard and papier-mache and even cloth and wood. Nothing was satisfactory until we got the bright idea of using just plain old dirt for our scale

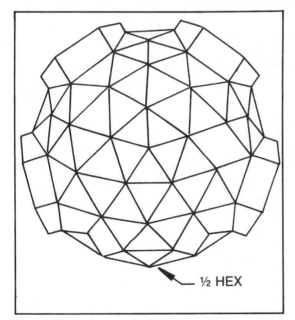

½ HEX

Fig. 13-26. A plan view of a dome.

model terrain. Later we cleaned up our act and made a sand table like the one illustrated in Fig. 13-29. This can be used to test underground models and to model landscaping for conventional homes and dome homes. With cardboard and sand, you can model any kind of buildings and landscaping your imagination prompts you to dream up.

When it comes to designing landscapes, our advice is the same as when designing dome homes. First model your ideas in dirt or sand and when you get what you like commit it to drawing. You might even want to include some instant photographs of your landscape modeling handiwork.

Models of houses that go underground should be constructed in accordance with the instructions for conventional or dome construction. If your model must bear a heavy load of sand or dirt, we recommend that it be built from the heavier cardboards such as chip board. We have found that geodesic dome structures will carry a lot of weight. This is one of the many great characteristics of geodesic domes.

TESTING SEASONAL CHANGES ON 3-D MODELS

You can do a lot of testing with your design in the area of energy efficiency. You can set the model in the sun and check out various orientations and different times of the year. You can make changes in the model to take better advantage of winter sun and get rid of summer heat.

If you do not have the time to test your model through a calendar year, you can make tests using photographic flood lights to simulate the sun. Work from sun angle tables for your latitude. Relative conditions of heat and cold can also be checked by charting differences in inside and outside temperatures produced by the heat from photographic lights.

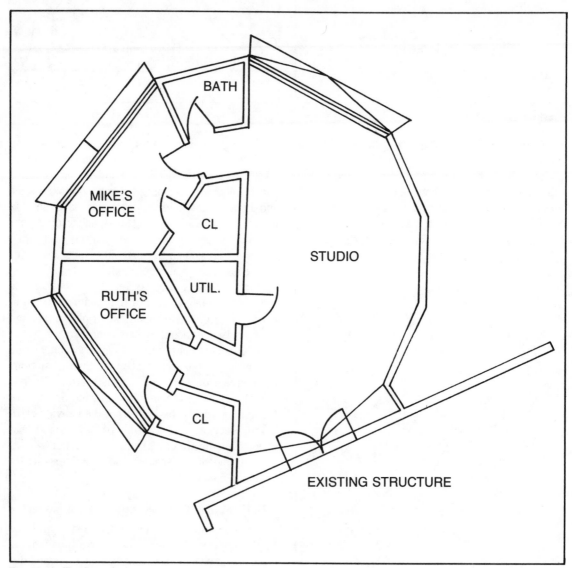

BATH

MIKE'S OFFICE

CL

STUDIO

RUTH'S OFFICE

UTIL.

CL

EXISTING STRUCTURE

Fig. 13-28. The floor plan.

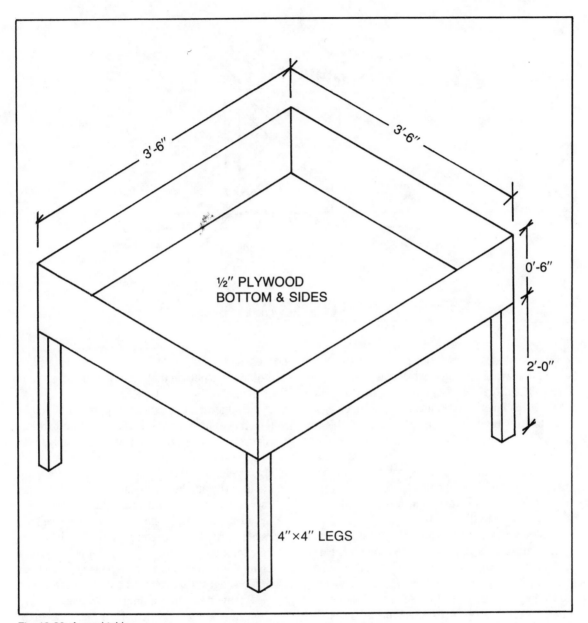

3'-6"

3'-6"

0'-6"

2'-0"

½" PLYWOOD
BOTTOM & SIDES

4"×4" LEGS

Fig. 13-29. A sand table.

Your model table can become a testing laboratory not only for your own ideas, but to test the opinions of others and especially those who write do-it-yourself books!

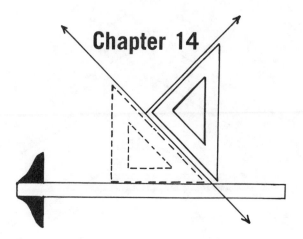

Chapter 14

Research

S O FAR WE HAVE STRESSED THAT YOU AND YOUR family will know best what you want in your house. The danger in this approach is that one tends to discover functional architecture all over again. This takes a lot of time. Furthermore, it is a learning process and, as with any learning process, there are bound to be mistakes. That is fine if you catch all your mistakes on paper. It is not so fine if your mistakes end up costing you quite a bit of extra money or make your new house less comfortable and liveable than it could be.

Research will teach you how to avoid the most obvious traps, show you ways to circumvent dangers and make you more aware of how other people have tried to solve the problem of building the ideal house for the ideal family for a reasonable amount of money. The reference to spending a reasonable amount of money is not necessarily valid in all cases.

There are two phases to house-plan research. One phase is to visit as many model homes, open houses, and homes under construction as possible. The other is to peruse the same course on paper via floor plans.

We suggest a two-pronged approach. If you've followed us thus far in the book and participated in the exercises we suggested, you are probably fairly good at reading floor plans. You have also most likely developed a good basic idea of what you want in a house: the number of rooms, the kind of rooms, the style, and the general size of the house.

You might still be having trouble visualizing sizes of rooms. Traffic patterns, while easily understandable in our examples, still present a mystery when met face to face in a model house or on a floor plan. We suggest that you visit as many new homes by as many different builders as possible. We suggest new homes, particularly in new developments, because as a rule you can get floor plans for the houses if you ask for them.

After you've walked through the house and admired each feature, take a moment to study the printed plan for the house. Now go swiftly through the entire house again. Make some notes on the back of your plan describing some feature that caught your eye, a special arrangement, or anything else that will jog your memory so you will remember the house when you look at the plan again later. Repeat this procedure with the next three or four houses. Then stop and spend the rest of the day doing something else.

At a later time, take out those plans again and study them closely. You'll be surprised at what you see. Without all the tried and true marketing and decorating tricks, you are suddenly faced with underlying basics.

For example, in one of the model houses we saw recently, we noticed a very attractive feature in the living room. The house was fairly small, but the single living area seemed nicely spacious. The dining area adjacent the kitchen was set off from the main living area by a waist-high partition topped with a foot-wide shelf. See Fig. 14-1. The result was quite attractive and both of us immediately visualized the shelf adorned with lush plants and tasteful objects d'art. We were so intrigued by this idea that we talked about incorporating it into a remodeling job we were designing.

When we got home and looked at the plan of the house, we noticed what had escaped us before. This same attractive eating area was the only place for a table in the whole house. It also was smack in the traffic pattern between the front hall and entrance and the kitchen. Furthermore, the kitchen was deadended so that carrying in all the groceries and taking out the garbage and so forth had to trail right through the same space. The space was part of the living room and it was covered with gorgeous off-white carpeting! It seemed to us, on second thought, that far from being a decorative way to designate special use areas, the low partition was a traffic snarl.

We even became disenchanted with the idea of a low partition because it proved to be much less functional than it seemed on first glance. If we put plants on the wide shelf, sooner or later water, fertilizer, or insecticide would drip on the off-white rug. If there were any children in the house (it had three bedrooms), any object d'art would be in constant danger from the exploring fingers, flying elbows and knees, and sweeping gestures.

Another model we looked at was a more expensive house. The special feature that caught our eye and was also drummed into us by the salesman, just in case we didn't notice, was that this two-story job had an upstairs playroom for the children. The builders offered this feature in two different models. A four-bedroom version is shown in Figs. 14-2 and a three-bedroom one is shown in Fig. 14-3.

A second look at the plans in the privacy of our own offices proved just as disillusioning as the waist-high partition. All packaging was with little thought of actual living as experienced by ordinary families.

As you can see from the plan (Fig. 14-2), the large space at the top of the stairs was designated as the playroom. It could double as a fifth bedroom. As far as play space was concerned, it was better than most. It measured about 10 by 18 feet, had a closet of its own, as well as adequate windows.

Look closely at the plans before you read on. See if you can find the joker in the deck. Don't feel bad if you didn't. This one is tricky. As you can see, there is an open area protected by a railing along one wall, next to the stairs. This playroom overlooks the living room. That is all right because you can keep an ear on the children if you're so inclined. Nevertheless, you can't watch TV, listen to the stereo, entertain, or read a book in peace at any time if the children are going to use the playroom. You'll hear every scream, every bang, every shove and each argument—word for word.

Sooner or later, your children will try walking that rail, using it as a balance beam, or hanging from it by their hands or teeth. Also, if your children are small, that railing makes an ideal ambush area from

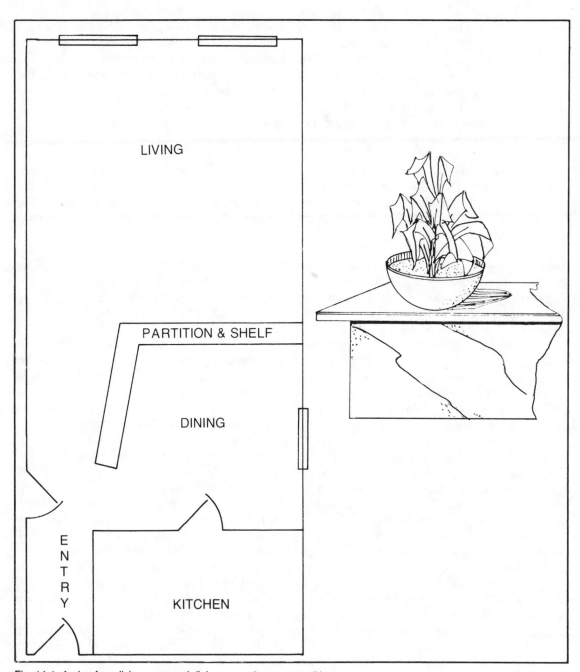

LIVING

PARTITION & SHELF

DINING

E
N
T
R
Y

KITCHEN

Fig. 14-1. A plan for a living room and dining area witn a low partition.

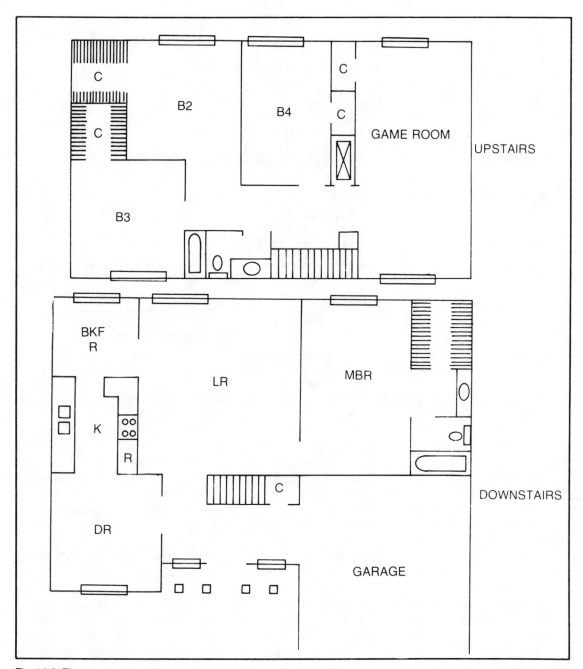

Fig. 14-2. The game room.

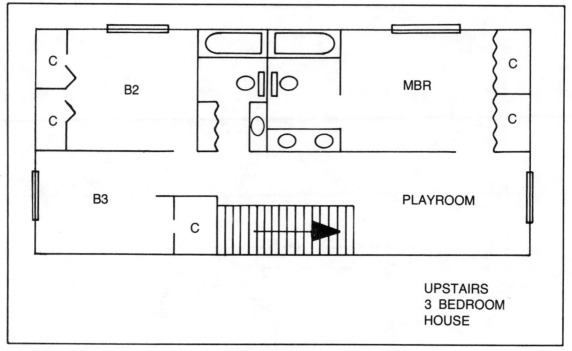

Fig. 14-3. The economy version game room.

which they can fire their ammunition of blocks, beads, puzzle pieces, and other such things at unprotected adults below.

Now if you think that is all that's wrong with the playroom take another good look. This time include the plan for the first story in your scrutiny. See what we mean? Yes, the playroom is directly above the master bedroom suite. The salesman was warbling about how nice it'll be to have all that privacy. "Just think of it, the whole first floor is yours. You can withdraw to your suite and the kids will play in the playroom undisturbed."

Sure, the little darlings will be undisturbed. They usually are unless you descend on them like a pillar of fire. But how about you? How undisturbed are you going to be if the patter of little feet is directly overhead? Ditto the crashing of toys, the jumping, rolling, running, and other activity and sounds created by active children's play? We're sure you see what we mean.

In the plan shown in Fig. 14-3, that of a smaller house, all three bedrooms are located on the second floor. All the same detriments apply to this one except that you have to cross this minefield every time you want to reach your room. As for the noise level, it has shifted to assault you frontally in your suite rather than from above. That is not much of a gain.

Now let's get a bit more advanced. Take a good look at Figs. 14-4, 14-5, and 14-6. The living area has a spacious feeling about it, yet boasts a separate dining room. The master bedroom is nicely buffered by a walk-in closet, another closet, and a short hall. The other two bedrooms are fair sized with nice, large closets. So what's wrong? What more do you want?

Fig. 14-4. The traditional version.

Fig. 14-5. The contemporary version.

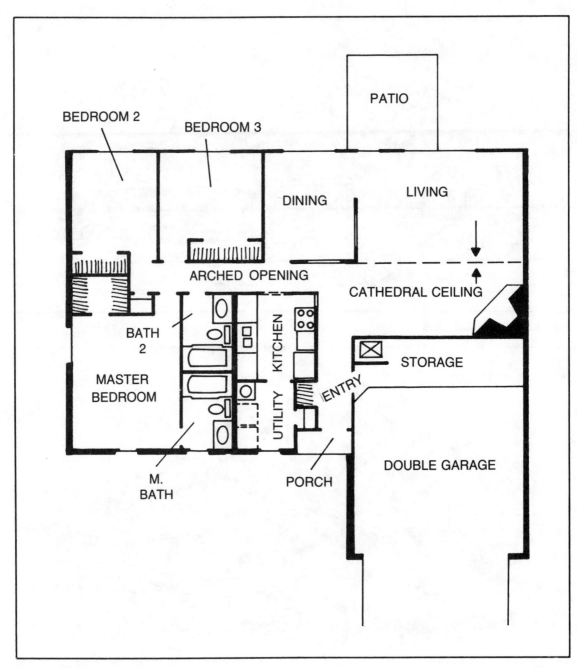

BEDROOM 2

BEDROOM 3

PATIO

DINING

LIVING

ARCHED OPENING

CATHEDRAL CEILING

BATH 2

MASTER BEDROOM

UTILITY KITCHEN

ENTRY

STORAGE

M. BATH

PORCH

DOUBLE GARAGE

Fig. 14-6. The floor plan.

270

Take another look. Imagine your children occupying these rear bedrooms. Imagine those same children wanting to go out to play in the yard. Better yet, sketch the way they would come in and out. Yes, right smack through your living room. It is the only place in the entire house that gives access to the backyard. If you have young children and keep the gate locked so they won't get out into the street the poor kids really don't have any other choice. The older children might also traipse in and out the front door and so make a secondary path to match the ones their siblings trod across the living room.

There is also a secondary problem, not quite as acute as the first, that concerns the kitchen and utility room located at the front of the house next to the entry. They can only be reached through the living room. That poor living room would require access ramps before very long.

Is there a solution? Take a pencil and trace the outline of the plan on another piece of paper. Now try to find solutions. Basically, what you need is more outside doors: one toward the backyard, and the other leading out somehow.

Our suggestions would be to open either Bedroom 2 or Bedroom 3 to the backyard via sliding glass doors set where the windows are. Another solution (a cinch at the paper-and-pencil stage) would be to offset the window in one room and include a narrow wooden door in one of the bedrooms. You could possibly get by with Dutch doors. They are quite costly though. Still another solution would be French doors. Made of wood, they are superior to the sliding glass variety in insulating qualities and they will take storm doors easily. See Figs. 14-7, 14-8, and 14-9.

Now about that kitchen utility room question. You can't cut a door into the outside where the window is because it would ruin your facade. Stumped? Give up? There is a simple solution. Notice that little utility room closet next to the entry closet? That's where your solution lies. Simply take out the entry closet wall and you have direct access to the kitchen and utility room from the front door and and the garage. Now change the door into the other closet, the one in the utility room, to open the other way into the entry and you are home free. See Fig. 14-19.

Want to try another? This one needs a bit more ingenuity, but it can be done. As you can see in Fig. 14-10, it is a 1½-story model. This is usually an economical way to build, because a second story or half a second story doesn't cost near as much as the same space would cost if you add it adjacent the main floor.

On first glance, the plan looks pretty good. It has a nice-sized living room, a separate dining room with those inevitable sliding doors to the patio, a fair-sized kitchen, and a nice private master bedroom suite. The childrens rooms are upstairs out of the way. They are located over the kitchen, the dining room, the utility room, and only partially over the master suite. Can you find any problems? See Fig. 14-11.

Notice that the door to the garage creates an interesting traffic triangle in your living room. You've also undoubtedly noticed that the kitchen again has no outside entrance. Most importantly, the full bath is hiding behind the utility room and it is only accessible to upstairs occupants by a quick run down the stairs and traversing the utility room. All of these little trips are clearly visible from the dining room and kitchen, and they will therefore necessitate innumerable drinks, trips to the refrigerator, and peeks into the living room to see what's going on.

Solutions anybody? Trace the outlines of the plans on a separate sheet of paper. With a pencil and an eraser handy, try out some options. Don't be bashful. Let your imagination soar. The most it will cost you is another piece of paper and a bit more tracing. We would advise you to make several tracings so you can see how the different solutions work. You can select the ones you like best.

Our solutions are shown in Fig. 14-12. Getting

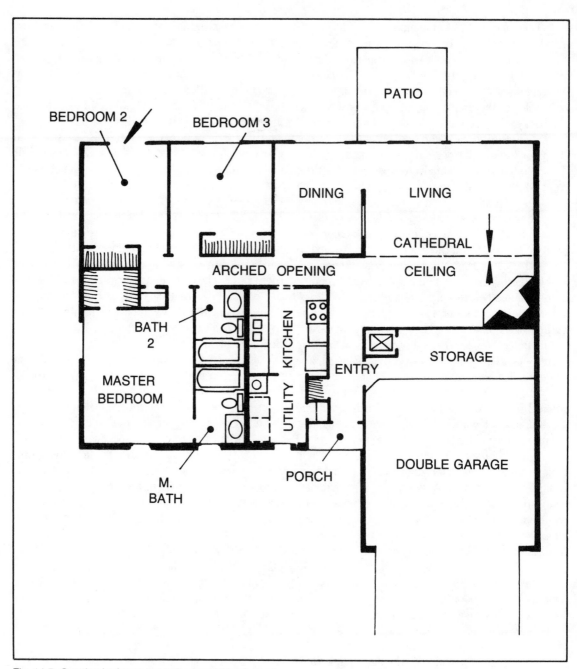

Fig. 14-7. Opening bedroom two to backyard (dutch-door).

272

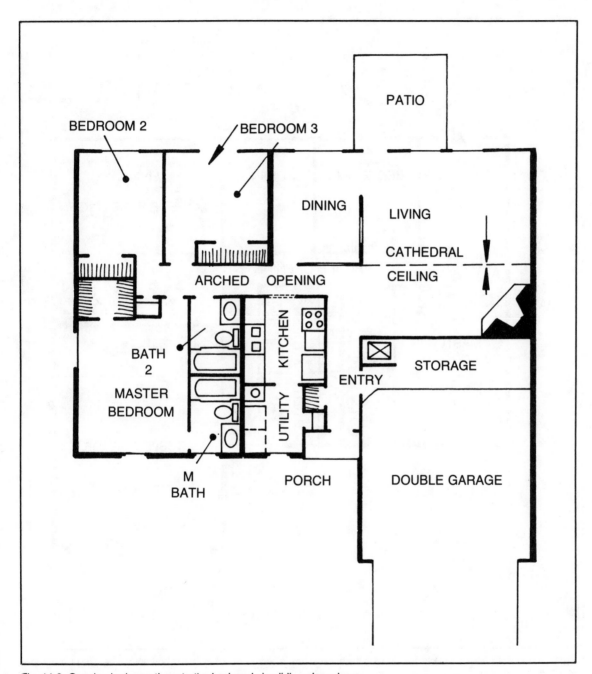

BEDROOM 2

BEDROOM 3

PATIO

DINING

LIVING

CATHEDRAL

ARCHED   OPENING

CEILING

BATH
2

KITCHEN

UTILITY

STORAGE

MASTER
BEDROOM

ENTRY

M
BATH

PORCH

DOUBLE GARAGE

Fig. 14-8. Opening bedroom three to the backyard via sliding glass doors.

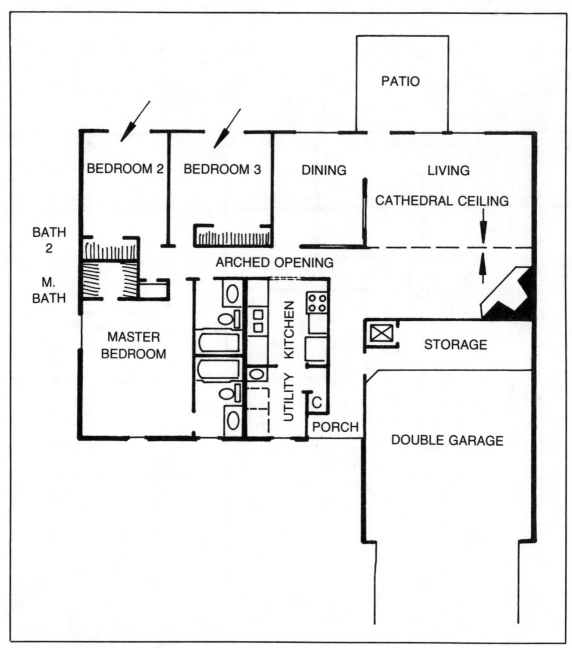

PATIO

BEDROOM 2 | BEDROOM 3 | DINING | LIVING

CATHEDRAL CEILING

BATH 2

ARCHED OPENING

M. BATH

MASTER BEDROOM

UTILITY KITCHEN

STORAGE

C

PORCH

DOUBLE GARAGE

Fig. 14-9. The revised floor plan with two doors to the outside, one in bedroom two and one in bedroom three. The utility room is now open to the entry.

Fig. 14-10. Exterior elevation.

the garage door out of the living room was easy enough. We solved the problem of outside access to the kitchen in the same maneuver. What we did was remove the pantry closet and cut a door into the garage at that spot. That took care of the door problem. We closed the door into the living room and included a new pantry closet that is shallower, but wider than the original, on the other side of the refrigerator. Alternately, we could have omitted the pantry all together or cut down the counter/ cabinet space next to the refrigerator. See Figs. 14-13 and 14-14. It occured to us that we still had a problem with the living room traffic pattern. It tended to go right down the center. There was a relatively simple solution on paper.

We changed the front door to the right side of the living room and moved the opening into the dining room from the center of the room to the right. In this way we gained a long unbroken wall and two good corners for furniture arrangement. In addition,

we had additional screening for the kitchen area. See Fig. 14-15. While we were working on the kitchen area, we added some counter space on each side and screened this from the dining area with a trellis.

We also decided that to invest a little extra money in a half bath upstairs would be more than worth it. We used the space of the closet along the stairs in the large bedroom, enlarged it so it would be adequate for a bath, and opened it into the hall-way between the rooms. In addition, we added a new closet and put in a linen closet (Fig. 14-16). Still another option would be to put in a shower or a complete bath with tub (Fig. 14-17).

Still another option for the upstairs would be to use the space under the eaves for closets and built-ins, including recessing the tub. This would be particularly helpful in the small bedroom and allow a little sitting area at the head of the stairs. (Fig. 14-18).

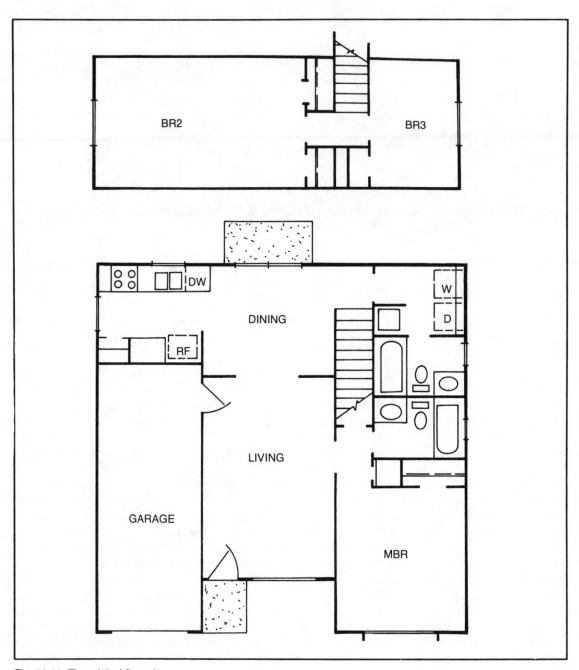

Fig. 14-11. The original floor plan.

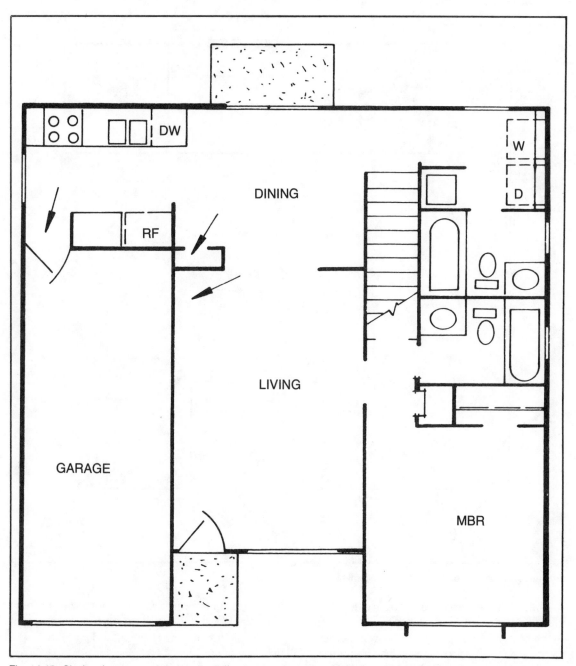

Fig. 14-12. Closing the garage door into the living room and opening the kitchen to the garage.

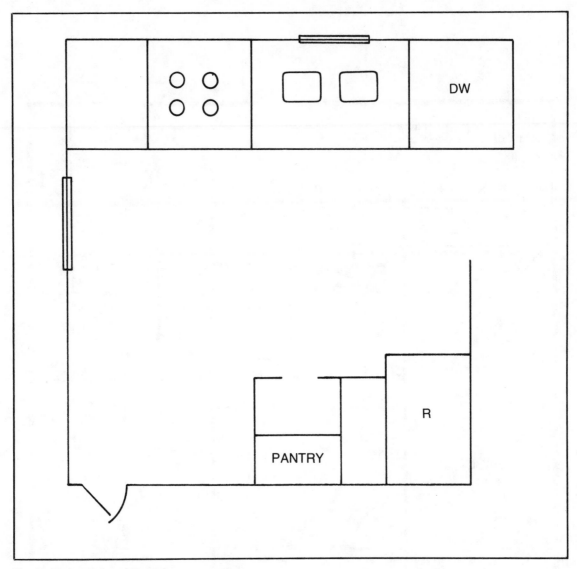

Fig. 14-13. A variation of the kitchen arrangement.

Two further improvements are easy to include. The one in front of the house consists of extending the front porch all the way across between the garage and the master bedroom wing. It is edged by a handsome railing and bordered by plantings. In the rear, we opened the utility room out into the yard. We used the existing window, but one could just as easily install a door next to the window (as in Figs. 14-18 and 14-19).

This allows the children to walk in and out of

the house and their rooms without trotting through the rest of the house. It also permits hanging out clothes without a hassle, airing blankets, and all those odd chores, like repotting plants, that are easily done if access to the outdoors is readily available.

Figure 14-20 is an example of one more of those development house plans. See what you can do to improve the design. Even a cursory glance should show you that there are several things wrong. Can you find them?

Of course you can. You saw right off that we have the same old deal where all traffic is routed directly through the great room of the house. Even to go to the bathroom from the kitchen one has to traipse all the way across the living room. The children must go through the living room when they go outside. The kitchen is a nightmare because it also is basically a passageway. It is also wide open to the great room so that every dirty dish and every spilled crum is clearly visible to anyone visiting or just trying to relax. The master bedroom, while buffered from noise from the kids, is badly chopped up.

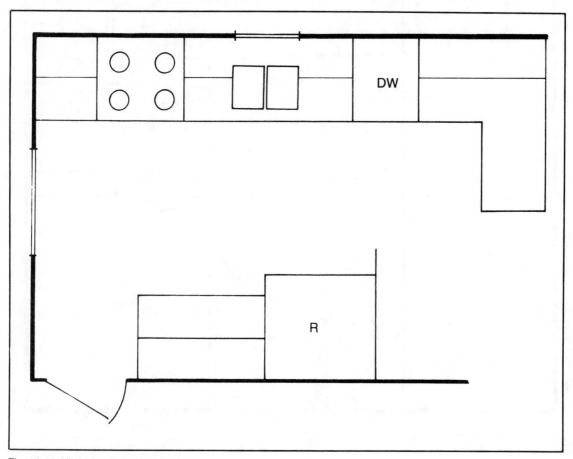

Fig. 14-14. Kitchen variation number two.

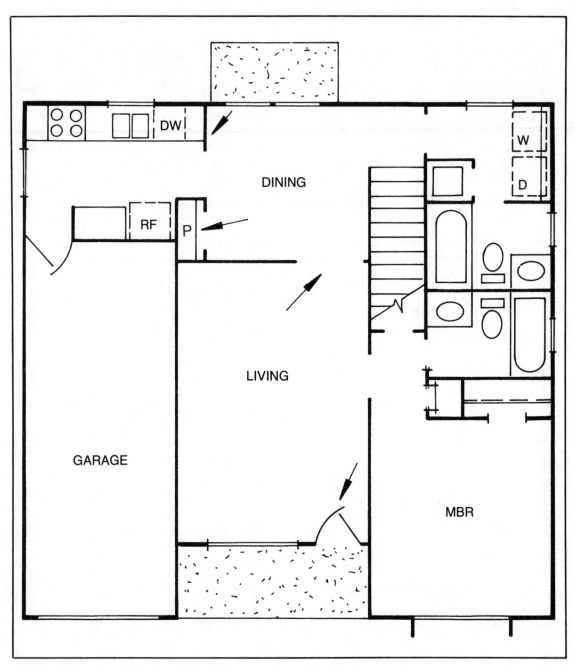

Fig. 14-15. Changes in living room and dining area to improve the traffic pattern.

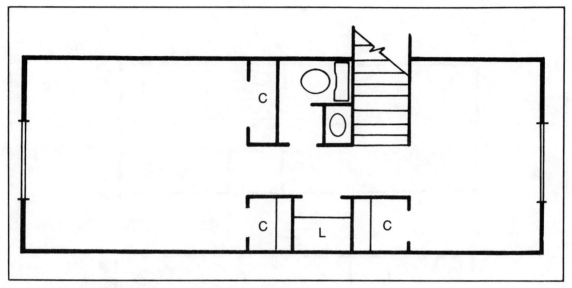

Fig. 14-16. The addition of a half bath and a new linen closet.

Don't be discouraged. We almost gave up on this plan while we were working out possibilities. It became such a challenge that we stuck it out.

We tackled the traffic problem first. The only way we could see to solve it (you might have better ideas), was to divide and conquer. In other words, we made some hallways. We took enough off the master bedroom to extend the hallway all the way to

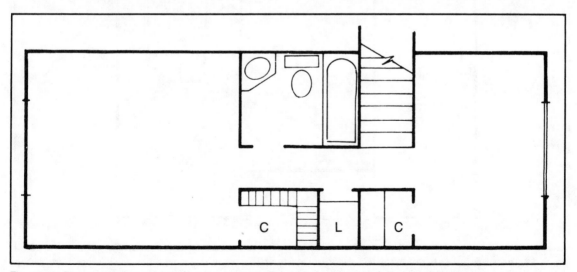

Fig. 14-17. The upstairs has a full bath, a new linen closet, and a new, enlarged closet in the bedroom.

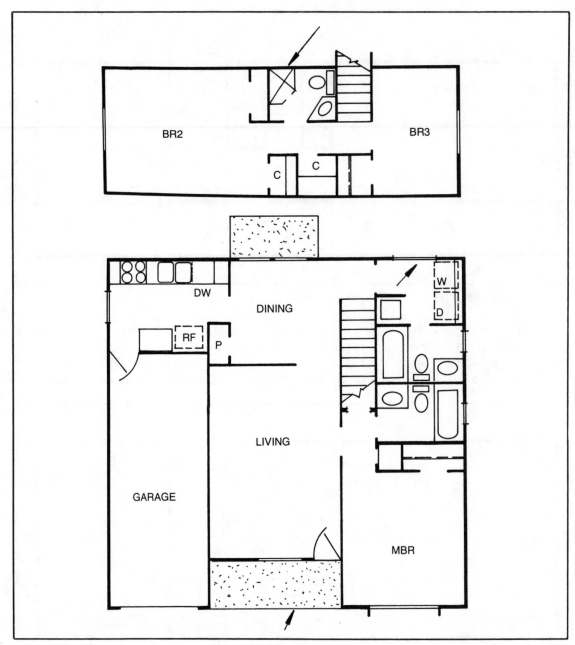

Fig. 14-18. The upstairs has a bath with shower, a linen closet and a closet in hall. Downstairs there is a new porch and sliding doors to the backyard from the utility room.

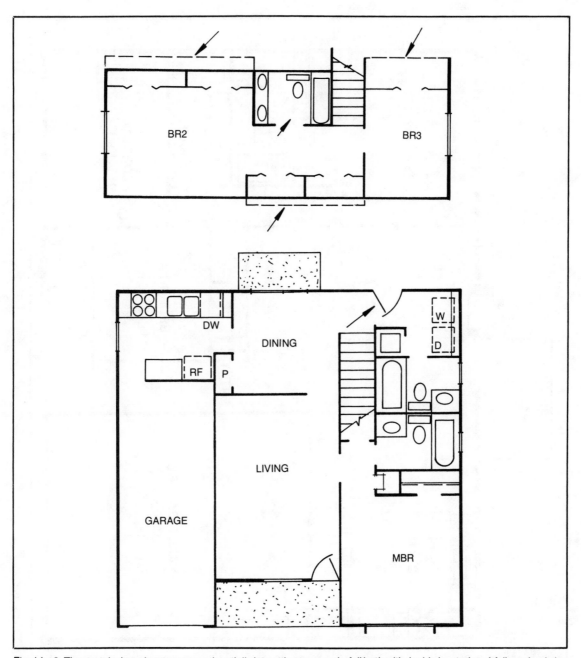

Fig. 14-19. The upstairs has closets recessed partially into attic space and a full bath with double lavatories. A fully revised plan of the downstairs.

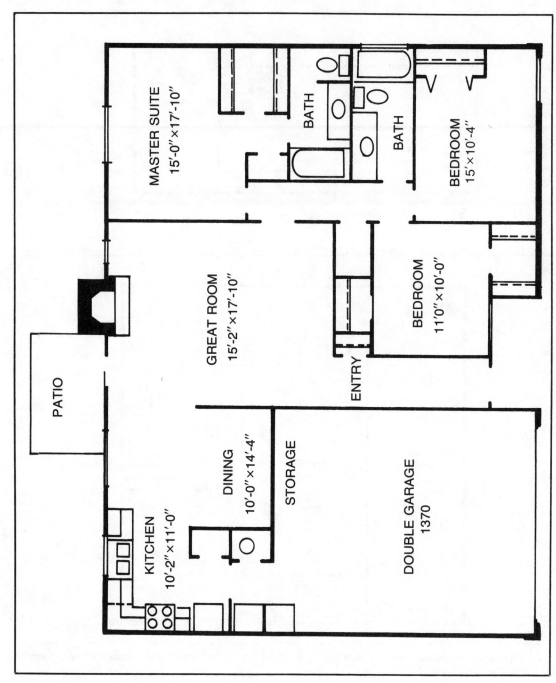

Fig. 14-20. The floor plan.

MASTER SUITE
15'-0"×17'-10"

BATH

BATH

BEDROOM
15'×10'-4"

GREAT ROOM
15'-2"×17'-10"

BEDROOM
11'0"×10'-0"

ENTRY

PATIO

DINING
10'-0"×14'-4"

STORAGE

KITCHEN
10'-2"×11'-0"

DOUBLE GARAGE
1370

the back wall of the house and to cut a door to give access to the backyard. This at least made it possible to go out without going through the great room (Fig. 14-21).

Next we eliminated three closets to create a second hall leading from the entry to the bedroom wing. This allowed us to close off the door into the great room from that side and put an end to the diagonal path on the rug (Fig. 14-22).

An additional measure to end traffic problems was to add a sink and toilet in the utility room area. Enclosing this area made a perfect mud room. See Fig. 14-23.

This still left the master bedroom and kitchen problems to be solved. There are no really good solutions other than tearing up the plan and starting all over. For practice, you might try to rearrange the closets in the master suite. By eliminating the walk-in closet, which basically is nothing but a status symbol and doesn't hold a whit more than two regulation 2-foot-deep closets that take a lot less room, we gained space. We put in those closets lined up against the new hall wall and so added to the noise buffering. We ended up with a long and narrow room. That is not the most ideal of choices, but all that was possible. See Fig. 14-24. Adding a coat closet to the entry helped the storage situation.

The kitchen and dining area needed complete reworking to make them functional. We took out the pantry closet and the bit of counter and cabinet directly opposite it. We needed that space for a refrigerator. Next, we turned a corner with the upper and lower cabinets at the outside wall by the sink and brought them all the way down to where the pantry closet used to start. The opening became the access to the kitchen from the dining area, and also made it easy to reach the new powder room without trailing through the kitchen proper (Fig. 14-25). That left putting in the powder room and the house was saved, at least on paper.

These exercises are great fun and very instructive indeed. We wager that now you can look at a set of house plans and tell their weak points quickly. To give you even more exposure to what other people have dreamed up in the way of abodes, we urge you to study the books put out by the Home Planners.

These books offer a wide variety of home plans and front elevation. You can get 250 one-level homes under 2000 square feet, 250 homes over 2000 square feet, 180 home plans of multi-level designs, 180 two-story ones, vacation homes, or whatever else you might like. The houses are both traditional and contemporary. The plans are quite detailed, but also quite small in scale. Each design is accompanied by a descriptive paragraph giving more details about the most salient features of the particular house.

These houses are actual designs for homes for which you can buy the blueprints, material lists, and specification outlines. These houses were designed by professionals and you can get some good ideas from them. Even here you will find things that wouldn't do for every day and that can be caught at the planning stage. It will sharpen your wit and ingenuity and your house plan drawing confidence to catch the experts.

Of particular interest is the section in the *250 Homes of One-Story Designs* on homes under 2000 square feet. This section deals with low cost homes. Study the plans carefully. They aren't that different from one another, but you can pick up a lot of know-how from the similarities. Notice, for instance, that the kitchen and bath, or baths, are all wall to wall. This saves on plumbing lines and should be taken into consideration when you design your own home or addition. While the glorious invention of plastic plumbing has helped those of us who love to design without being bound to having that plumbing core smack in the middle of the house, it is still wise to consider a central core or at least not to seperate the cores too widely.

Second on the list is the use of space. Space is generally eliminated as much as possible in hall-

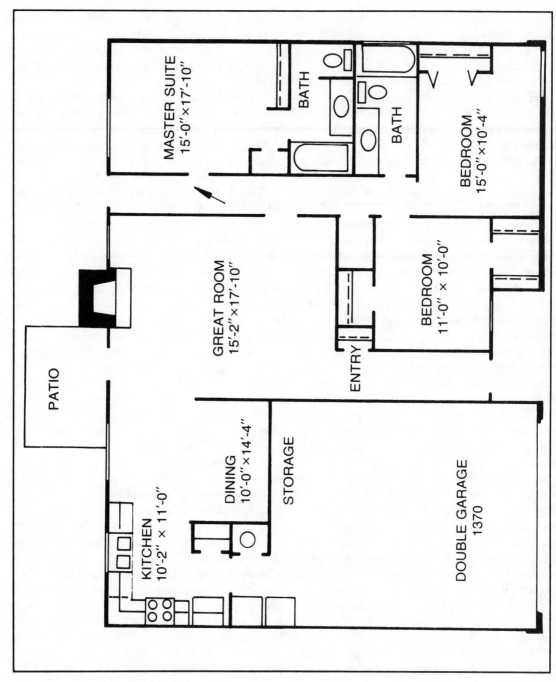

Fig. 14-21. Adding a hall to the bedroom wing and providing access to rear yard.

MASTER SUITE
15'-0"×17'-10"

BATH

BATH

BEDROOM
15'-0"×10'-4"

GREAT ROOM
15'-2"×17'-10"

BEDROOM
11'-0" × 10'-0"

ENTRY

PATIO

DINING
10'-0"×14'-4"

STORAGE

KITCHEN
10'-2" × 11'-0"

DOUBLE GARAGE
1370

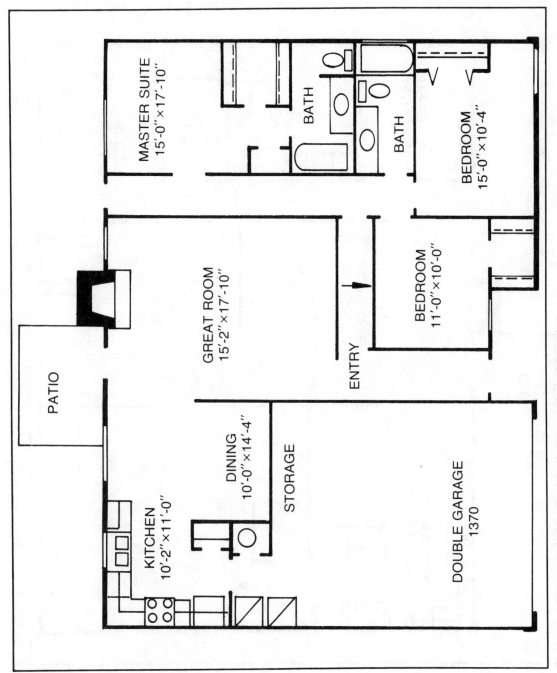

Fig. 14-22. Adding a new hall leading from the entry to the bedroom wing.

MASTER SUITE
15'-0" × 17'-10"

BATH

BATH

BEDROOM
15'-0" × 10'-4"

GREAT ROOM
15'-2" × 17'-10"

BEDROOM
11'-0" × 10'-0"

ENTRY

PATIO

DINING
10'-0" × 14'-4"

STORAGE

KITCHEN
10'-2" × 11'-0"

DOUBLE GARAGE
1370

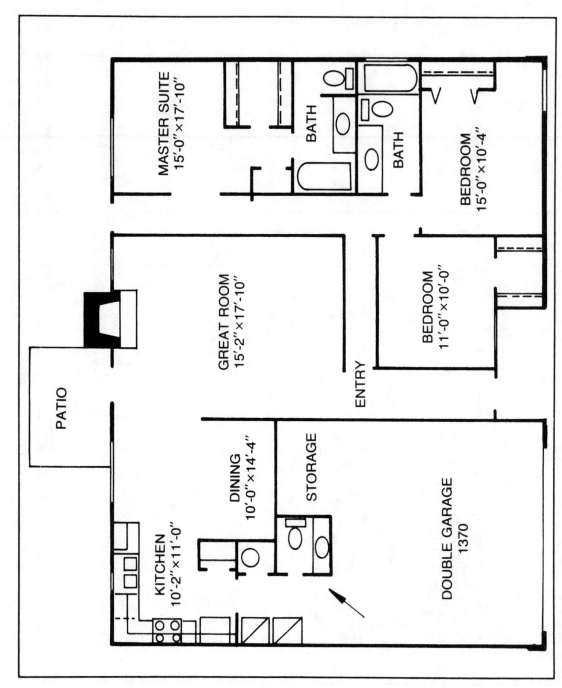

Fig. 14-23. Adding a mudroom/wash room.

MASTER SUITE
15'-0" × 17'-10"

BATH

BATH

BEDROOM
15'-0" × 10'-4"

BEDROOM
11'-0" × 10'-0"

GREAT ROOM
15'-2" × 17'-10"

PATIO

ENTRY

DINING
10'-0" × 14'-4"

STORAGE

KITCHEN
10'-2" × 11'-0"

DOUBLE GARAGE
1370

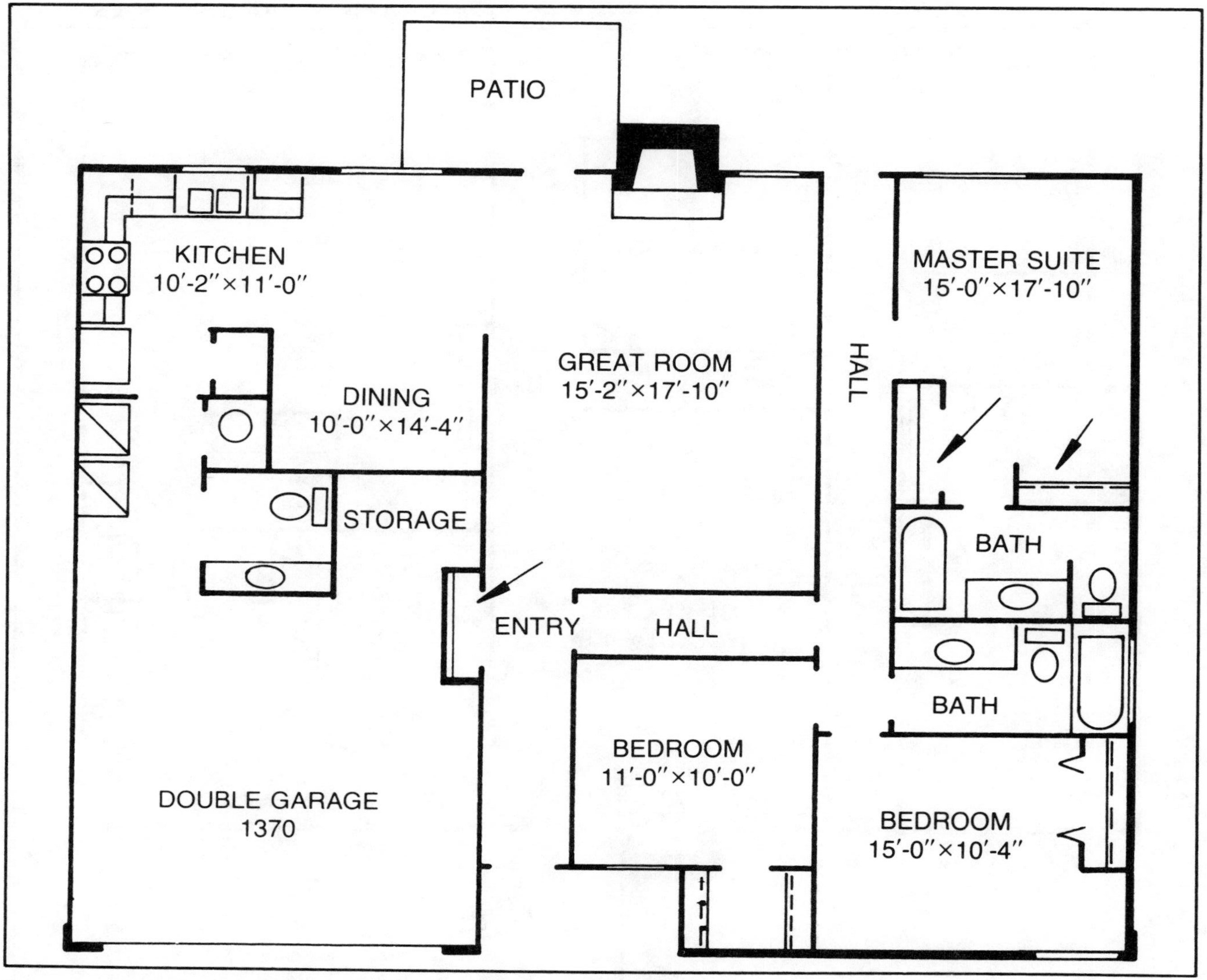
PATIO
KITCHEN
10'-2"×11'-0"
GREAT ROOM
15'-2"×17'-10"
MASTER SUITE
15'-0"×17'-10"
HALL
DINING
10'-0"×14'-4"
STORAGE
BATH
ENTRY
HALL
BATH
BEDROOM
11'-0"×10'-0"
BEDROOM
15'-0"×10'-4"
DOUBLE GARAGE
1370

Fig. 14-24. Adding a coat closet to the entry and redesigning the master bedroom.

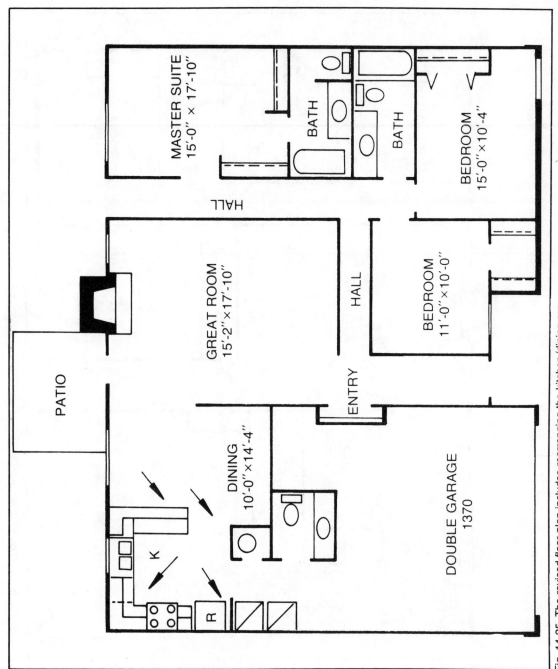

Fig. 14-25. The revised floor plan includes rearranging the kitchen/dining area.

ways. Why? To keep the rooms, that are tiny to begin with, from disappearing all together. If you study the plans, you will find that, while you have saved on walls, you are not really gaining space. It is simply an illusion. We will vote for hallways in spite of added costs and so-called wasted space.

You'll notice a skimpiness of closets and storage space. Again the reason is to save space. In these designs, space is at a premium. Yet you will find, if you look closely, that some of these designs have not sacrificed comfort after all. Instead they have used ingenuity to overcome obstacles. We are particularly fond of a design that has 1142 square feet. It boasts three bedrooms; the largest is 10×12 feet, but it has its own bath with shower. A family/dining room (13×10 feet) is adjacent a very functional U-shaped 8-$\times$-10-foot kitchen that is superior to many others in much more elaborate homes. There is plenty of extra storage space in the garage.

Give some attention to the large, expensive-looking homes that have halls stretching seemingly for miles, oddly shaped rooms, imaginative use of space, all kinds of build-ins, and some fancy baths and kitchens. When you have thoroughly familiarized yourself with these plans, go out and take a look at what the top builder has to offer for the top dollar in your part of the country. Don't be taken in by glossy paint or shiny chrome. Look at the features, the walls, the doors, the size and shape of the rooms, the traffic patterns, the comfort, and convenience of the houses. We bet you'll be surprised.

Research is almost done. What remains is to take your own plans, the ones you swore you'd never again change, and compare them with the designs you found had the most glaring faults. If you're a quick study and have lots of luck, you'll find only one or two of these glaring problems on your plans. If you are more like the rest of the thundering herd,

like yours truly, you'll be amazed at the now so obvious things you didn't notice at all before. Don't berate yourself. Don't feel foolish or incompetent. Instead, take your eraser and change what needs to be changed right then and there. It's so easy at this stage and doesn't cost a cent.

While you're at it, try two or more solutions to each problem. Again all it takes is paper, pencil and a little bit of your time. Put the solutions aside for a day or so before you narrow down your choice. Don't hurry at this stage. A little time spent now will save much time later on.

Other sources of research are magazines and soft-bound pamphlets that feature vacation homes. On the whole, these publications offer more genuinely interesting ideas and approaches than all the other garden and home variety of publications put together. It might be that people are less inhibited when it comes to designing their retreats in the woods or their beach houses. But whatever it is, you'll find some startlingly new designs.

Don't think that you'll be leafing through designs for log cabins, lean-tos or one-room structures. Study in particular any design that is not based on the old square or oblong shape. Take a good look at hexagonal structures. See what can be done with an octagon. And don't overlook the round structures. They are quite idea provoking, too.

Whether you want to incorporate an esoteric concept in your design is up to you. Studying them and reading the plans will stretch your imagination and your ability to recognize renderings.

Now you will be ready for that last look at your plans. Make a quality control check to ensure that your plans will result in the building you envision. Study your plans carefully once more. Check every feature and every detail. Take your time. Don't skip a thing. When you're done, go buy your materials.

Appendix

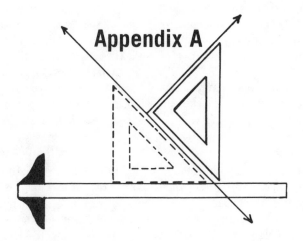

Appendix A

Easy-to-Make Drawing Boards

YOU'LL NEED A WORK SURFACE AND A FEW LITTLE items to do a professional job. We will show you how to accomplish all that with a minimum outlay of time, money, and space. For the first stages of your house planning—what we call the mobile stage— when you inspect things, measure, and sketch, a large clipboard will be ideal. We like to add to this a pad of squared paper (¼″) that is often called an executive pad. This kind of paper makes it easy to draw reasonably straight lines even without a ruler. To get the proportions approximately right, you can count off squares and set up your own squares-to-feet scale (such as two squares to a foot).

In addition to the clipboard, you'll need a metal tape measure and some nice, soft, well-sharpened pencils with eraser ends. You can add some regular drawing paper if you want. A sketch pad is fine and you can substitute the sketch pad for the squared paper pad.

When it is time for scale plans, you'll need to set up a work area. It can be anywhere as long as it has good light and a flat surface that won't be needed for any other activity for a while. Most of us have tables that work fine as long as the dinner and breakfast dishes, plus the kids homework, don't get hopelessly mixed up with your plans. If you are the proud owner of a desk, use it. If you can scrounge up a bit of space—say a drawer or two—for your paper, pencils and other accessories you have it made.

For those who do not have desks, we have designed a portable drawing board/storage setup that will see you through royally in any and all house planning activities. And it can be stored in the back of a closet. We have come up with two models of the drawing board so you can take your pick.

ECONOMY DRAWING BOARD

This board is quick and easy to make. You'll find it a joy to have and you will find lots of uses for it even after the house planning is completed.

Materials. One board, roughly 18×24 inches (but you can get by with one that is 14×20 inches) cut from ½-inch marine plywood. Two lengths of ¾-inch elastic twice the width of your board plus 1 inch. Wood sealer and clear plastic spray or adhesive-backed vinyl.

Tools. Sandpaper, a needle and heavy thread, a staple gun and staples, or tacks and a tack hammer.

Instructions

If the board is relatively smooth, sand it thoroughly on both sides, first with coarse, then medium, and finally with fine sandpaper.

Seal the wood with wood sealer. When dry, give it a coat of clear, plastic varnish as protection and for easy cleaning.

If the board is too rough for sanding, and you don't have a plane, cover the board with solid-color, adhesive-backed vinyl. See Fig. A-1.

For either board, sew or staple the ends of the elastic securely together.

Attach one elastic loop to each end of the board. Fasten it down on top and bottom as shown in Fig. A-2. There is your drawing board that can be wiped clean in an instant!

DELUXE DRAWING BOARD

Materials. A 1×10 (4 feet long), ¾ outside corner trim (3 feet long), a 2×2 (9 feet long), a 1×3 (37 inches long), 2d finishing nails, wood glue, sealer, small corrugated fasteners.

Tools. Saw, C-clamps, carpenters' square, ruler, hammer, plane protractor, sandpaper.

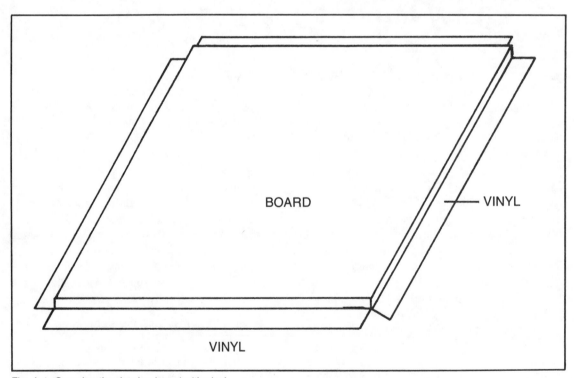

BOARD

VINYL

VINYL

Fig. A-1. Covering the drawing board with vinyl.

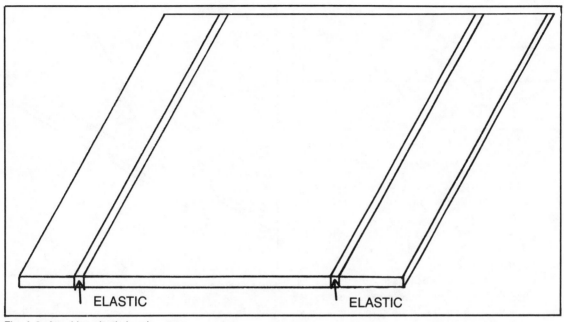

Fig. A-2. Attaching elastic bands.

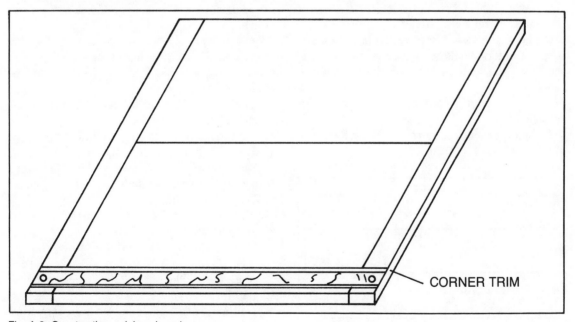

Fig. A-3. Constructing a deluxe board.

297

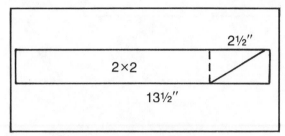

Fig. A-4. Cutting an angle on a 2 × 2 (13½ inches long).

Instructions

Cut the 1×10 into two 2-foot-long pieces.

Spread glue on one long edge of each of the boards.

Lay the boards on a flat surface, edge to glued edge, clamp with C-clamps (at least four clamps, but six is better) and let dry.

Cut two pieces of 1×3 (18½ inches long, each).

Spread glue on one long edge of each 1×3 piece and clamp to the board along the short sides. See Fig. A-3. Let dry.

Reverse the board and reinforce the seams with small corrugated fasteners.

Check corners and sides with your carpenters' square. Corners should be right angles (90 degrees) and sides should be straight. Plane and sand if necessary.

Sand the entire board smooth, and round corners slightly.

Cut the outside corner trim to fit one long edge of the board (about 29 inches).

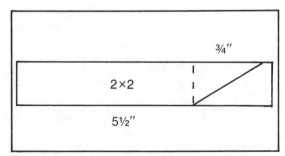

Fig. A-5. Cutting an angle on 2 × 2 (5½ inches long).

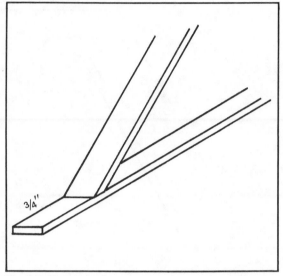

Fig. A-6. Frame details.

Glue and nail to the board forming a shallow well at bottom of the board.

Seal the board with a wood sealer or clear varnish.

For the stand, cut two pieces of 2×2 22 inches, two pieces 13½ inches, two pieces 14½ inches, two pieces 5½ inches and one piece 4¼ inches.

Mark off the 13½=inch pieces 2½ inches from one end.

Draw out a rectangle and mark the diagonal as shown in Fig. A-4. Cut along that line.

Mark the two 5½ inch pieces ¾ of an inch from the top. Again draw a rectangle and diagonal. Cut on the diagonal. See Fig. A-5.

Nail and glue the 14½-inch pieces to one of the 22-inch pieces forming a U shape.

Nail and glue the 5½-inch pieces to the corners of the U.

Mark the middle of the 22-inch piece and nail and glue the 4¼"=piece in place.

Nail and glue the other 22-inch piece across (as shown in Fig. A-6).

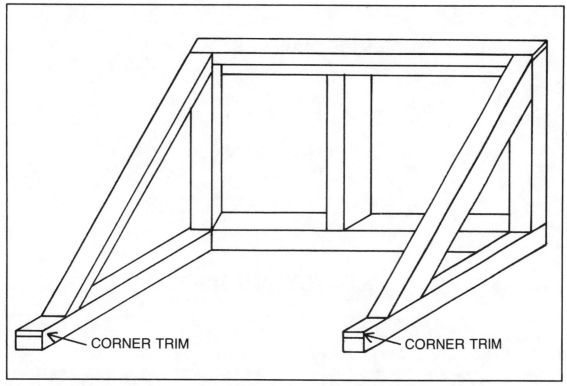

Fig. A-7. Constructing a frame.

Nail and glue the 13½-inch pieces to the frame, forming a triangle on each side. The cut end goes to the front ¾ inches in from edge of the base. See Fig. A-7.

Cut two pieces out of the scrap of the outside corner trim (each 1½ inches long).

Nail and glue to front of frame as shown in Fig. A-7.

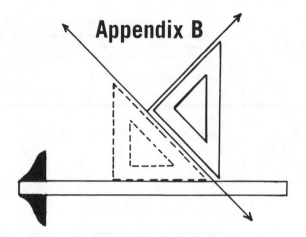

Appendix B

Abbreviations

ac—On houseplans, particularily when they appear on a box with a diagonal slash through it, these letters stand for air-conditioning unit. If these letters appear on a wiring diagram or plan, they most likely stand for alternating current. If the wiring plan is for an area that includes an air conditioner, it is a toss up and you better ask for more information.

asph—This means asphalt. Used as topping for driveways at times, but more often makes its appearance as a saturating substance as in asphalt paper or felt.

bldg—Stands for building and only that.

BR—Most commonly used on houseplans to designate bedrooms. Can also stand for brick, as in brick veneer, fireplace, or hearth.

BRM—Space set aside to house brooms, mops, and other such in a broom closet.

BS—On spec. sheets, B.S. means bevel siding.

casmt—Stands for those nifty windows that open outward or inward, but not up and down as most others.

cem—Cement out of which you can make concrete.

CI—Cast iron as in railings or bannisters.

cl—These letters stand for closets.

clg—This means ceiling. It usually appears when a specific finishing material is indicated, as in a sound proof ceiling, or if there is a particular feature to the ceiling, as in a suspended ceiling.

clr—It means clear, as in clear glass or plastic.

CO—A cased opening.

conc—Here is the concrete.

cond—This can have three separate meanings: mean conductor, conduit, or condenser. When in doubt ask.

cop—Means copper and usually is used to indicate copper pipes.

corn—Hold the butter, this refers to a cornice.

crys—This refers to crystal (likely a chandelier).

CT—Crock tile is what it means, but the designation of crock tile itself is something of conversation stopper. Crock means pottery vessel in one definition in another it stands for broken pieces of same. So a crock tile floor could be a ceramic tile floor (possibly you have relatively low-fired tiles), or it could be a floor made out of broken pieces of tile in a mosaic sort of way. If you want to be sure, ask.

D—Designates a wonderful appliance—the dryer.

d—Originally it stood for price-per-hundred of nails. It has nothing to do with the price of nails today, but the hardware stores still have 2d nails, 4d nails, and so on. It now refers to size.

dc—On a wiring diagram, it will mean direct current. On an elevation, it most likely refers to drip cap.

DG—Drawn glass. Glass that has been heated and stretched.

diag—Diagonal either in measurement or the way something is applied to something else, as in wood trim applied diagonally.

diam—This is for diameter and refers to something circular.

dim—Dimensions.

div—Divided as in a divided bath.

dn—Down, as in stairs, usually accompanied by an arrow pointing in the right direction and by the word up, plus an arrow going the opposite way.

DR—Dining room.

dr—A door

dr c—Drop cord. Usually seen on electrical diagrams.

drg—This abbreviation you mostly come across in those cryptical communications from your contractor or builder, the kind that goes like this: inld. 2 drgs for kit. cabnts. installation. Meaning two drawings, etc.

DRR—Usually means that little left over space between the closet and the bathroom that is grandly called the dressing room.

DS—Refers to downspout.

DW—The dishwasher.

ea—Each.

el—Refers to elevation.

ent—Entrance.

ext—Exterior, as in ext. trim.

fin—Finished.

fin ceil—Finished ceiling.

fl—The floor under feet.

flash—The flashing on your roof.

fl—The floor under your feet.

FMR—The family room.

FP—Santa's entrance—the fireplace.

FT—Foot or feet.

ftg—The footing.

gar—The place where you park your car, theoretically, but which is usually filled up with all kinds of things.

GI—Galvanized iron.

gl—Glass, as in sliding glass doors.

gr—Grade.

gup bd—Gypsum board (also called plasterboard).

HP—High point. Usually refers to the roof.

ht—It means height.

kit—The kitchen.

L—Center line.

lav—Lavatory.

lin—Linen closet.

lndy—The laundry.

LP—This means low point.

LR—The living room.

lt—Light.

MBR—The master bedroom. Part of the master suite (as they say in the ads).

mldg—Refers to molding.

mull—Refers to mullion; the name given to the slender strips of wood or metal that divide the panes of glass in windows.

O—The letter o stands for build-in oven.

obs—Obscure.

OC—On center. Measured from center of one stud to the center of the next stud. Another of those strange but wonderful rites. Can also stand for outside casing, as in a door or window.

OD—Outside dimensions; as in the outside dimensions of a house. In contrast to the inside dimensions which are, of course, smaller.

OS—Outside.

pl—May stand for plaster or plate (part of your building components inside walls).

pl ht—It stands for plate height.

PWR—This a quaint euphimism for half bath, meaning powder room.

R—If there's a circle anywhere near it means radius. On a floor plan in a kitchen, it stands for range.

ref'g—Usually found next to the R in the Kit. In case you're still not with us, the refrigerator.

rm—Rooms.

RO—This indicates a rough opening big enough to set in a whole door or window assembly.

RW—Redwood.

S—Sink.

scr—Means screen, as in scr. porch.

sdg—Siding.

specs—The specifications; plans and materials to build your house.

stor—Storage.

T & G—Tongue and groove (as in boards).

TC—Terra-cotta. Usually refers to a special kind of tile, low fired and red in color.

th—The threshold.

typ—Stands for typical (as in typical opening).

ven—Veneer. Like in brick veneer: BR Ven.

VT & G—Vertically grooved and tongued.

W—On a plan usually accompanied by D, it means washer. It can also stand for wide.

wc—Sometimes means wood casing.

WC—Water Closet.

wd—Wood.

WG—Wire glass (glass reinforced with wire).

WI—This stands for wrought iron. Like in a wrought iron railing.

wp—Waterproof.

WR—Wash room.

X—Marks the spot, usually on the plate, where the next stud goes.

yd—Yard. The measurement though it is sometimes used to designate the yard in which grass and flowers grow.

Glossary

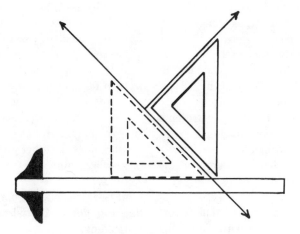

Glossary

across the grain—Perpendicular or at right angle to the grain of the wood.

adhesive—Any of a number of substances used to adhere objects. They come in various types and under many names. Some of the common ones are: glue, (white and otherwise), mastic, contact cement, panel adhesive, ceramic tile adhesive, and resilient tile adhesive.

AIA—The American Institute of Architects (1735 New York Avenue, N.W. Washington D.C. 20006).

airway—A space left between the insulation of the roof and the boards to allow air to move through.

alligatoring—A cracking pattern in paint that resembles the expensive reptile hide (considered undesirable by most people). *See* checking.

anchor bolts—Steel bolts embedded in fresh concrete and protruding through holes in the sill. When the concrete is cured, the framing material is fastened to these anchor bolts and held down by nuts

antihammer—A piece of water pipe installed in the line, about 1 foot long, one size larger than the line. The antihammer is capped at one end. The purpose of this bit of plumbing is to prevent hammering noises in the line.

apron—A piece of finish board. One type is a board located under a window that covers the joint between wall and sill. The other is as trim below a stool. *See* stool cap.

architect—Commonly used to describe a person who designs buildings and draws plans. It is also a legal term referring to a person who has been professionally licensed by one or more states to practice architecture.

asbestos joint runner—An asbestos jig with a metal clamp that is used to keep molten lead in place while caulking soil pipes in a horizontal position.

asbestos mastic—Sounds like an adhesive but it isn't. It is used to waterproof surfaces such as outside basement walls and such.

ash-pit cleanout—An opening with a metal door somewhere near the base of the chimney and used for removing ashes.

ash-pit dump—A metal trap door on the fireplace floor that allows ashes to fall into a container in the basement or through a pipe to the ash-pit cleanout outside the building.

asphalt—Technically, it is a residue of petroleum evaporation. It is used in roof shingles, in backing for exterior siding, and under finished floors.

asphalt roofing paper—Heavy paper used for insulating and waterproofing.

backer boards—The boards that partially overhang the plate and run parallel with the ceiling joists. The boards provide the nailers for ceiling boards at opposite sides of the room.

backfill—Replacing earth in an excavated area.

backfilling—Filling in the space between the foundation and the sides of the excavation with earth.

balustade—A porch, roof, or stairway railing that is made of a top rail balusters and often a bottom rail.

balusters—Vertical parts, often turned, or 1¼-×-1¼-inch connecting top and bottom rails of banister.

band—A fancy piece of millwork that is usually used as molding.

bargeboard—A finish board on the face side of the gable framing.

baseboard—Finish board nailed onto the wall at floor level to hide the joint between the two. Also called simply *base*.

basement—An area that is below grade level. Usually below the entire first floor of a building and accessible from inside the house.

base molding—The fancy band that goes on some baseboards as decoration or potential dust catcher (it depends on your viewpoint).

base shoe—Quarter-round or other molding nailed to the baseboard at rug or floor level.

batten—Narrow strips of finish or hardboard used to cover panel joints on exterior walls to get a finished appearance.

batten boards—A rough pair of boards nailed to stakes at right angles to each other. Set at the corners of excavations to show the first floor level and also to serve as supports for different guidelines used before framing in a building.

bay—The distance between two principal column lines.

beam—Horizontal supporting timber.

bearing posts—Partial supports of the girders of a building.

bearing seats—Recesses in the foundation walls for partial support of girders.

bearing walls—A wall or partition that supports another load in addition to its own weight. That includes ceiling joists, floors, and roof.

bed molding—Applied between any vertical and horizontal surface. For example, between eaves and an exterior wall. *See also* Cornice trim.

bell tile—The sectional tile with one bell-shaped end is used to lay ditches that carry waste water to a lower level or to the sewer.

bell wire—Small-gauge copper wire you use in wiring your doorbells or chimes.

benchmark—A surveyors' term meaning a known point of elevation above sea level. From this, the meaning has been expanded to include any known or given measure on which one can base other measures. A certain level of performance or excellence which has to be met or duplicated.

bevel cut—A board or timber cut or shaped to a desired angle.

beveled siding—A special type of siding that is made by sawing boards on the diagonal and so producing two wedge-shaped boards.

bird's moutn—Carpenterese for the notch sawn

into rafters to allow full seating on the plate of the wall.

blind nailing—Nailing through wood in such a way that the nail head won't show. You can do that with tongue and groove boards, for instance.

blueprint—Originally the copy of a drawing. Usually a tracing of the working plans which are drawn in pen or pencil. Now used synonymously with plans or working drawings.

board and batten—Vertical siding made of boards with batten covering the joints.

board foot—The waterloo of many a do-it-yourselfer. Actually a measurement that denotes a given size of a piece of lumber that is a board 1 inch thick, 12 inches long and 12 inches wide is said to be a board foot. A 1×12 a foot long contains one board foot. A 2×12 6 inches long also contains a board foot.

boot—A sheet-metal receptacle that makes a connection between some ductwork and a register. An example is between the air-supply duct and the register in your air-conditioning system.

Boston ridge—Overlaying and blind-nailing shingles on the ridge of a roof.

boxed cornice—A decorative boxy overhang on a building.

box gutter—A box-shaped gutter.

box sill—A built-up sill on the foundation that has the sole plate resting on the floor joists and not the sill.

brace—A board or a stud set at an angle to add support and strength.

brad—A small, thin nail with a deep head. It is used when a finishing nail or a casing nail would be too large.

branch circuit—Any of the electrical circuits that are connected to the service panel.

branch drain—A piece of pipe that is the drain line for only one fixture.

branch water line—A water line that serves only one fixture.

bridging—A technique for stiffening floor joists, ceiling joists, and partitions in which small wooden braces are put between the larger wooden pieces on the diagonal. Sometimes wood of the same size is used and is placed at right angles. It must fit tightly between joists or partitions.

building code—That body of rules and regulation covering the various phases of building and construction work you better know about before you make your final plans.

building drain—The piece of drain line from the foot of the stack to the sanitary sewer.

building lines—Refers to the outside and inside edges of the foundation. Usually put in solid on building plans.

building paper—Heavy asphalt-saturated paper that is put over sheathing or over subflooring.

bushing—A cylindrical lining that you screw tightly against the end of a conduit to protect insulated wires.

butt—To put boards together in such a way that all points of the edges, or ends, touch.

butt hinge—Usually a door hinge that has a loose pin that holds two metal leaves together. One leaf is fastened to the jamb and the other to the edge of the door.

butt joint—When two pieces of wood butt together, end to end or at right angles. The edges of each piece are square.

cantilever—A beam, slab, or portion of a building that projects out or overhangs beyond a vertical support.

cap—Anything that tops another piece, as in a column or a molding.

capillary attraction—The inside of a copper fitting that attracts melted solder and so makes a sealed joint between pipe and fitting.

casement windows—Windows hinged on one side that open either in or out (usually out).

casing—Trim for a door, window, or other framed opening attached to both the jamb and the wall.

casing nail—Similar to a finishing nail, but slightly smaller in gauge and with a slightly tapered head.

cat—Reinforcing or blocking between joists, studs, or rafters to assure a solid backing for nails or screws. Usually 2×4s nailed horizontally between studs to act as nailers for wood-board paneling.

caulking—Using soft, pliable material to seal seams, joints, and cracks for waterproofing and weatherproofing.

caulking compound—Used to make seams, cracks or joints watertight.

caulking gun—A metal frame for holding and applying tubes of caulking compound.

ceiling joists—These members are fastened to the top plates and run across the narrow span of a house. They are called the main ceiling joists. Short joists running at right angles from the last ceiling joist to a top plate are referred to as stub ceiling joists.

ceiling nailer—Usually a 2-inch strip of wood nailed-to the top plate with an overhang for ceiling material to be nailed to eventually.

ceiling tile—Square or rectangular blocks. Usually interlocking with a tongue and groove edge and some sound-deadening characteristics.

cement—A power of calcined rock or stone used in mixing concrete.

central vacuum system—The system has the tank (and noise) located in the basement along with the electric power unit. There are outlets in each room for a plug-in hose that uses the normal array of attachments. If your house doesn't have a basement, the power unit and tank can be located in a garage or utility room.

chalk line—This is an important gadget in the building trade to make sure things are plumb and true. Actually all it is is a piece of cord covered with chalk that is napped against a wall or over lumber to form a line. Incidentally that's where the expression of walking the chalk line originates.

checking—Cracks in a paint job that look like small squares. *See* alligatoring.

checkrails—The joint of the bottom of the top window sash and the top of the bottom window sash beveled to make an airtight joint.

cheek cut—A side cut at the end on both sides of rafters.

chimney—A vertical tube with a flue that carries the smoke and gases away from an open flame or fire.

clapboards—As on New England houses, a siding made out of beveled boards that overlap horizontally.

cleanout—A removable piece of pipe in a line, usually right by a drain, that allows cleaning out a stopped-up drain pipe.

cleat—A wedge of wood that's nailed on to serve as a check (as at the end of a drawer) or support.

cold chisel—A wedge-shaped steel tool with a cutting edge used for cutting or shaping metal without heating the metal to soften it.

collar beam—Boards, usually 1 or 2 inches thick, that connect opposite roof rafters. They are used to keep the rafters from spreading apart and to keep the roof from sagging under extra heavy weights such as snow.

column—A vertical support piece. Also called a pillar or post.

common rafter—A rafter that goes at a right angle from the ridge to the plate.

concrete—A mix of cement, sand, water and rocks (aggregate) that hardens to rock-like consistency.

concrete blocks—Blocks made out of concrete and used for building purposes.

concrete nail—A nail made to fasten wood to concrete (all others won't do).

conduit—A tube that carries electrical wires.

contemporary—Any modern house which doesn't follow any special traditional or special style, but sets its own character through the juxtaposition of materials and structural features.

coped joint—A joint in which the end of one piece is cut to fit the surface of another. For instance, a piece of molding cut to fit against the face of a second piece of such molding.

corner post—Three full-length studs and three spacer blocks (12 to 16 inches long) situated at the corners of wall or partition frames.

cornice—The top of a wall directly under the eaves. Also used more loosely for a board or molding that runs along the top of the wall at ceiling level.

counterflashing—Metal set into brick covering shingles and brickwork, usually used around chimneys.

coupling—A pipe fitting which joins two pipes.

cove—A wood molding that is used in interior corners or a plastic or ceramic piece. Also concave piece that fits between a countertop and the backsplash. Also used to top a ceramic tile wall that doesn't reach all the way to the ceiling.

crawl space—The area under the floor joists and the ground in a house that has no basement and isn't built on a slab.

cricket—A small gable roof which is used to divert drainage. Also called saddle.

crimped pipe end—A pipe with small, regular creases pressed into one end.

cripple jack rafter—A rafter that extends from a hip to a valley.

cripple studs—Short studs under or over openings.

cross cutting—Cutting lumber across the grain. The opposite of ripping boards.

cross members—Framing material fastened at right angles to other framing material (like 2-×-4 pieces nailed between studs).

crown—The highest point or the top of a building.

crushed stone—Bits of rock that are too big to go through a ¼-inch screen.

curing concrete—A way to treat fresh concrete. It is done by sprinkling with water at regular intervals.

dad—A groove cut across a board.

deep-seal trap—A neat little device in the main drain pipe designed to prevent sewage from backing up and flooding the basement.

diagonal thickness—Measuring lumber diagonally instead of the usual vertical or horizontal way.

dimension lumber—Lumber that is 2 to 5 inches thick and from 2 to 12 inches wide, in 2-inch increments.

direct nailing—What you do when you pound in a nail with your hammer and the nail head shows. Also called face nailing.

disconnect switch—A special switch wired into a circuit so that the circuit and the appliance or device connected to it can be disconnected when needed.

dormer—A window set in the framework of a gable-type intersecting roof.

double framing—Used to add strength such as around a stairway.

double-hung windows—Two-window sash where each window can slide up and down in the window frame, passing each other in their separate grooves.

downspout—The tube or pipe that drains the water from the gutter to the ground.

dressed lumber—No coverings added. Actually, the rough lumber is planed down, exposed if you will. That's a 2×4 never measures more than 1½×3½ as a dressed 2×4.

drip—A projection of the roof so rain water won't run down the outside walls.

drip cap—A thin board or strip of metal over the top of the window to keep water from running down walls and coming inside.

dry wall—Plasterboard used as an indoor wall covering. Comes in sheets. Has replaced the old lathe-and-plaster routine.

dry well—A hole in the ground usually filled with gravel for draining water from gutters.

duct—A shaft, usually metal, used to transmit heating or cooling.

easement—The right held by a person or company or government for the use of land belonging to someone else for a single, specific purpose—like setting telephone poles.

eaves—That part of the roof that overhangs the wall.

edge pull—A door pull set flush on the edge of a sliding door.

elbow—Not the thing that gets sore in tennis. A pipe or drain fitting with a 90 degree angle.

elevation—A straight-on view of an object. Usually exterior or interior walls of a house drawn to scale and represented in that manner.

end cap—A metal cap that goes at one end of a gutter.

end grain—The grain at the ends of boards.

entourage—An indication of plants on a floor plan, elevation, or perspective drawing.

escutcheon—The piece of metal, usually fancied up a bit, that you see around faucets and pipes, or on both sides of a door lock set, or other such.

excavation—Hole in the ground for your foundation, walls, or footings.

excavation lies—Usually dotted lines shown on building plans that indicated the outside and inside edges of footings or foundation walls.

expansion joint—An asphalt impregnated strip of fiber put in grooves made in concrete to prevent the concrete surface from cracking.

exterior finish—Finishing materials such as siding, clapboard shingles, and so forth.

face of rafter—The top side of same indicated by a bevel cut at the end.

face shells—The outer part of a concrete block.

fascia—Finish board covering the ends of roof rafters.

fascia bracket holder—It is a hanger attached to the fascia and holds gutters in place.

felt—Tarpaper used under floors, siding, and roofing materials.

ferrule—A sleeve, usually metal, placed around a tool handle to keep it from splitting.

fieldstone—Natural stone used in construction of foundation and retaining walls. Also used for paths and stepping stones in yards.

field tile—Short lengths of drain with ¼-inch gaps between them.

filler box—A box form of wood the size of the proposed window or door used in building finished concrete foundation walls.

finish—In painting, the final coat applied of paint, varnish or wax. In carpentry, putting up the exterior trim, interior trim, countersinking nail holes, or final sanding.

finish hardware—The hardware such as knobs, locks and hinges.

finishing nail—A small-headed nail used in wood when countersinking is planned.

firebrick—Brick made from fireclay that is used to line fireplaces.

fireclay—Refractory clay used for bricks and for the mortar that holds bricks together. Refractory refers resistant to heat.

fireplace unit—A prefabricated metal box that lines the inside of your fireplace opening.

fire-stop—Fire-resistant insulation used to prevent the spread of fire.

five-quarter—A board cut to 1¼ inches thick and dressed to 1⅛ inches.

flagstone—Flat stones used for floors, pathways and sidewalks.

flashing—Strips of nonrusting metals put into both sides of a joint to prevent water from seeping in.

float—A small, flat tool used by concrete finishers.

floating—Smoothing the surface of freshly poured concrete to a rough finish.

flue—A space in the chimney for the passage of smoke and fumes.

flush joint—To be exact; a joint flush with a masonry surface.

fly rafter—The end rafter of a gabled roof that overhangs the main wall and is supported by lookouts and roof sheathing.

footing—The base on which the foundation of a building rests. Usually twice the width of the thickness of the foundation wall. Can also support pier and beams and other types of pillars or posts.

footing pads—Single footings that provide bases for bearing pillars.

forms—Wooden structures used in pouring concrete to hold it in place until it has hardened.

foundation—A concrete or block wall, sitting on the footings, that supports the plates and floor joists for the first floor.

four-way switch—Used with two three-way switches so that a light or an appliance can be turned on or off from three different locations.

framing—Balloon framing in which wall studs extend from foundation sill to roof line and to which the floor joists are attached. Not used much in these days. Platform framing in which each floor is built separately and serves as a foundation for the walls. That's what we use most today in wood-frame buildings.

framing square—A measuring and leveling tool.

frieze board—A finish board at the top of the wall directly underneath the eaves.

frost line—The depth to which the ground freezes in the winter. The footing must go below the frost line to prevent heaving and movement during freezing and thawing.

furring—A thin wooden framework used to thicken a wall or ceiling or, most commonly, to provide a nailing surface for paneling or tiles.

furring strips—Wood or metal strips fastened to wall, ceiling or other surface to serve as nailers or to provide an air space.

gable—The vertical triangle end of a wall from the eaves to the roof ridge.

gable roof—A roof line at the end of a double sloped roof. Forms a triangle from the peak of the roof to the bottom of each rafter.

gang box—Two or more electric outlet boxes mounted side by side.

girder—Horizontal beam carrying one or more intermediate beams. Heavy member, either single, built-up, or iron I beam, used to support heavy loads such as joists or walls over an opening.

grade—The slope of the ground in regard to a specific reference point, usually the top of the foundation or the ground-floor elevation.

grain—Direction of fibers running in wood.

grout—A kind of mortar, with or without sand, that is used to fill in between wall tiles. Floor tiles are sometimes set directly into a grout bed and then the spaces in between the tiles are filled in with more grout.

gutter—A metal trough that carries rain water from the roof to the downspouts.

gypsum board—Also called Sheetrock or plasterboard.

gypsum board sheathing—Panels with a core of

gypsum between two covers of water-repellent paper that are used as sheathing.

hardboard—A man-made material made from wood and similar in most aspects to wood. Comes in sheets or panels, usually 4×8 feet and in thicknesses of ¼ of an inch.

header—A wooden beam in a floor or roof that is between two long beams and is supporting the ends of one or more intermediate beams. A beam placed as a lintel over a door or window opening. A beam placed at right angles to joists to form openings—such as skylights, stairwells.

header joist—A floor joist connecting the ends of regular floor joists and forming part of the edge of the floor framing (the opposite of a stringer joist).

hearth—The floor of the fireplace that extends into the room.

hip—The sloping ridge formed when two sloping sides of a roof meet.

hip roof—A roof that is sloped up from four sides, one slope to a wall of the house, that has a short ridge.

hollow-core door—A door that has an air space and some filler between the two outside surfaces.

hub—The end of a soil pipe.

I-beam—Steel beam used to support joists running long distances or also used as an extra long header over windows or doors.

insulation—Sound material made mostly of fiberglass that reduces the transmission of sound through walls, floors, and ceilings. Thermal: material made from fiberglass, mineral wool urethane, or styrene or other similar material that prevents heat loss when placed between exterior and interior walls, in attics, between roof rafters, and under floors.

intersecting roof—One roof passes through another roof seemingly as a gable roof intersecting a hip roof.

interior finish—Materials used to finish interior walls: plasterboard, paneling, wallpaper and wallcloth.

joint compound—A plaster-like material, that has glue in it, used to fill in the spaces between plasterboard panels and also the nail head on the panels.

joint gauge—A board with uniform markings to help in laying bricks or concrete blocks with equal-size joints.

joist—One of a number of parallel beams that are supported by girders or bearing walls.

joist hangers—Metal fasteners to secure joist ends directly to a girder or another joist.

keyway—A V-shaped groove cut into the center of the basement wall footing to provide a way of bonding the wall to the footing.

lally column—A concrete-filled pipe column.

landing—A platform that divides a flight of stairs into two sections. This can be a straight stairway or one that makes a right-angle turn.

lap joint—A joint in which two pieces of wood overlap so that they form a single surface on both sides.

lath—Wood, metal, or plasterboard used as a base for plaster.

lath stripping—Thin, narrow strips that hold edges of building paper temporarily in place on the roof decking.

lattice—Framework with crossed wooden or metal strips and air spaces in between.

layout—The arrangement of rooms, the plan of a house, a story or wing of a house.

ledger—A strip of wood nailed to a girder or joist on which other joists are set.

ledger board—Board on a wall that is to receive one end of the lookouts.

level—A tool to test if a surface is even.

line length—The distance between the center of a ridge and the end of a rafter.

line voltage—The number of volts supplied by the service wires that come from the utility company's power supply. For instance 115 volts to have current for the lights in the house.

lintel—A horizontal support over a door or window opening.

lookouts—Short pieces of 2×4s set between the lower end of rafters and the ledger board on the side of the wall, set in horizontally.

louver—An opening, usually with a screen, that has slats allowing air passage in and out. Used for ventilation in attics, basements, crawl spaces, and pantry closets.

mantel—The shelf above the fireplace. Often includes the trim (wooden or tile, around the fireplace opening.

matched lumber—Tongue-and-groove boards.

millwork—Trim and components of doors and windows.

miter box—The gadget used to make miter cuts without tears.

miter joint—A joint made of two pieces of wood each cut to a 45-degree angle that forms a regular right-angle corner.

modern—In architects' jargon, a building erected with current skills and materials. Usually synonymous with contemporary, but can stand for a modern reproduction of, for example, a salt box.

modernistic—Architectese meaning imitation contemporary.

modular concrete blocks—Concrete blocks of one standard size.

molding—Decorative strips of wood used in trim and detail work inside and outside.

mortise—A hole cut into a piece of wood into which another piece of wood is placed for an exact fit.

mullion—A post frame or double jamb that vertically divides two windows or large panes of fixed glass.

muntin—The horizontal strips dividing windowpanes.

nosing—Projecting molding. Especially the projecting part of the tread over the riser on stairs.

on center—Used in the spacing of studs and joists. Means measuring from center of stud or joist to the center of next of the same. Standard is 16 inches, but 24 inches is sometimes used.

orthographic view—A single-plane view of an object such as a floor plan or an elevation.

panel—A thin piece of wood fitted into grooves as in door panels. Thin wood used to finish walls.

particle board—A sheet made by gluing wood chips or particles together under pressure. This comes in various thicknesses and sizes. Once only used for underlay. With the escalating prices of wood, it has become a paneling material as well as a regular building component for shelves and such.

partition—An inner wall that subdivides space.

partition junction stud—A triple stud that forms an inside corner on both sides of a partition frame.

pegboard—Hardboard with holes. Good when you need ventilation or want to hang up things.

penny—A measurement of nails that formerly indicated price per hundred. Now used as part of a designation for size of nail.

pier—A column of masonry, usually heavy, that is used to support a structure.

pier and beam—A type of foundation consisting of a number of piers to which beams are attached. On the beams is built the floor for the first floor.

The beams raise the structure for 2 to 4 feet above ground level and the space is left open and only skirted at the walls with siding or trellises.

pilaster—An upright column that's rectangular and is part of a wall.

pitch—A drawing or diagram, usually to scale, that shows the arrangements of the rooms of a house. Also, a drawing of a building seen from above without the roof.

plaster—A lime, sand and gypsum mixture troweled onto lath in several layers to be used as a finished wall.

plasterboard—A type of board used as a substitute for plaster.

plate—A floor plate or sole plate is the bottom horizontal member of a stud wall that is attached to the slab or the subfloor. A top plate is the top horizontal member that supports the roof rafters or the second floor joists.

plenum—A main air duct that either carries cool air from the blower coil of the air-conditioning unit to the cold-air ducts or carries warm air from the branch warm-air duct to the blower coil.

plumb—Level in the upright position.

plywood—Wood made by laminating thin sheets together with the grain running in opposite directions. Comes in various sizes, thicknesses and grades.

polyethylene—Plastic sheeting used as a vapor barrier. Also used to cover building materials to protect them from the weather during construction of a building.

preservative—A copper- or pentachlorophenol-base liquid that when painted on wood, will keep wood from rotting, at least for a while.

primer—First coat of paint job.

quarter-round—A three-sided molding with a curved face used around the bottom of baseboards. A molding one-quarter of a dowel.

rabbet—A groove at the end of a board going across the grain cut to receive a second piece of wood.

rafter—A beam, usually about 2 inches thick, that helps support the roof.

rafter tail—A section of a rafter between the plate and the lower end of the rafter.

rail—Horizontal frame piece of a window or paneled door. Also the upper and lower pieces of a balustrade or railing.

rake—Sloped edge of a gable roof.

ready-mix concrete—Concrete mixed by the experts in special trucks and brought to the site.

reinforcement—Steel rods or mesh placed in concrete to give it added strength.

rendering—A pictorial representation or perspective of a building or some part of one.

resin nail—A nail that is coated to give it greater holding power.

ridge board—A board between the uppermost ends of common rafters spiked together from opposite sides.

ripping—Sawing lumber with the grain.

rise—On stairs, the vertical height of the flight or also the height of one step. The number of inches a roof rises for every foot of run.

roof decking—Boards or sheets of plywood that covers the rafters and serve as a nailing surface for shingles or other roof cover.

roofing felt—Asphalt paper fastened to the roof sheathing before applying the shingles.

rough fascia—A board nailed to the bottom ends of rafters.

rough—Bare framing.

rough-in measurements—Measurements showing the size and locations of plumbing fixtures and other built-in fixtures.

rough opening—Opening in a frame wall for a door or window, in a floor for stairs or chimney, or in a roof for a skylight.

rubbing brick—A brick especially made to give concrete surfaces a finish.

run—The horizontal dimension of a stair.

saddle—The threshold of a door. A metal, wood, or marble tread running the full width of the opening about ⅝ of an inch high.

sash—The framework that holds the glass in a window frames. A single unit of the frame containing one or more lights of glass.

scaffold—A temporary structure with a top platform that is used by the workers during building.

scale—A reference standard in measurement. Proportions relating a representation to actual size. Also, a calibrated line that shows such a relationship.

scale drawing—A rendering of a building or parts thereof in precisely reduced proportions. For instance, a scale of ¼ inch could represent 1 foot.

screed—A guide used in smoothing freshly poured concrete.

scribe—Marking with a pointed instrument as a guide for sawing.

sealer—A liquid that seals the wood as a base for paint, varnish, or other finish.

sealing stain—A handy sealer/stain that makes a one-step operation out of two.

shake—A thick, wood shingle you can either use on exterior walls or the roof.

sheathing—The exterior covering of a wall. It will be covered by siding in most cases.

shed roof—A flat roof with a slight, single slope.

shims—A strip of wood or metal, or a wedge of same, that will fill in a small space. Shingles are often used for that job around windows, doors, and the finished job.

shingles—Roofing material made of tapered wood, metal, slate, or asbestos. They come in bundles or in strips and are applied in an overlapping fashion.

siding—The exterior finish of a wall. Such things as clapboard, shingle, board and batten, aluminum, and vinyl.

silicone sealer—A liquid that will waterproof masonry above the ground level.

sill—The bottom of a window or door.

sill plate—That part of the side wall that sits flat on the foundation.

slab—A concrete section often used as a foundation for a house.

sleeper—A board 2 inches thick that is fastened to a concrete floor as the base for the wood floor above it.

soffit—Usually the horizontal surface between the end of the rafters and the outside wall of the house. The underside of a cornice or boxed eaves. The meaning has been extended to include that space between your top cabinets and the ceiling in your kitchen which is usually boxed in.

soil stack—Usually abbreviated to stack. A vertical pipe that extends through the roof and vents sewer gases to the outside.

soil tests—Very important sampling of the soil at different depths to see what kind of footings are necessary for a building.

sole plate—The horizontal timber in a frame to which the outside wall studs and partition studs are attached and on which they rest.

solid-core door—A door that has softwood blocks that fill up all the spaces between the two surfaces of the door.

span—The distance between the supports of a beam, arch, or truss.

specifications—Also known as specs. A document usually prepared by the architect, but can be done by the person who designed the building, the owner, or the contractor. Details about the proposed building that can not be included in the working drawings. Examples are hardware for cabinets, style of trim, light fixtures of a specific kind, and so forth.

splash guard—Material placed under the down-spout to keep the topsoil from washing away.

starter strip—A metal strip that is used to fasten the bottom edge of roof sheathing. A narrow strip of rolled roofing that is fastened to the lower end of roof sheathing before putting down roof shingles.

stool—The ledge under a window frame.

stop—A molding on a window sash or sliding door frame that stops the window or door from going any further.

storm sash—Insulating windows made of wood or aluminum (wood is preferred) fitted over the outside of the windows of a house. Sometimes applied inside.

straightedge—A board with true edges to draw straight lines.

stringers—The side pieces that form the frame for stairs.

stucco—A siding material, made with cement as a base, that is applied to the outside walls over a metal lath.

studding—Upright framing in walls.

studs—Upright timber, usually 2×4s used in framing. Sometimes metal studs are used.

subfloor—Rough floor made out of planks or plywood nailed to the floor joist. The base for the finished flooring.

suspended ceiling—A ceiling that hangs from the joists by brackets or wires.

tail beam—A short joist supported by a wall on one side and a header on the other, usually around fireplaces.

template—A pattern usually made out of thin wood or metal. It can be cut out of cardboard or heavy paper. Used as a guide for cutting.

termite shields—A series of metal plates formed over the foundation walls to prevent termites from getting in.

threshold—The bottom part or sill of a doorway.

tie rods—Special steel rods that hold the concrete forms together.

toenail—A technique for fastening lumber by nailing it at an angle. The nail goes in at an angle.

tongue-and-groove—A very special joint in which one board has a groove along a long edge and the other has the edge of one long side so trimmed that it fits into the groove.

top plate—The horizontal member of a house frame at the top of the studs.

trim—Finishing material. Also called millwork or woodwork.

truss—A set of rafters with a collar beam and other connecting lumber in place. They are prebuilt and ready to install to connect opposite walls.

underlayment—Plywood, particleboard, or hardboard installed over the subfloor as a base for floor tile or sheet flooring.

unit rise—The rise, in inches, that the common rafter extends in a vertical direction for every foot of unit run.

valley—The angle formed where two sloping roof sides meet.

vapor barrier—Material used to keep out moisture.

veneer—Thin sheets of wood, applied over cheaper, coarser wood for a finished panel or in furniture.

vent pipe—A pipe used to release sewer gas above the roof line and to prevent back pressure and siphonage.

walers—Timbers that help hold concrete forms true and straight.

wall plate—The covering that hides the inside of your switch or electrical outlet.

weather strip—A narrow piece of wood, plastic, or some other material placed between a door or window and its frame to act as insulation.

window unit—Window jambs, outside casings, trim, and window mounted into sash as a unit ready to put into your rough window opening.

wiring diagram—A drawing or plan that explains a wiring system such as the one for your electric stove or your air-conditioning system.

working drawings—Those all-important drawings that show exactly how a building shall be put together.

wrecking bar—A tool that one uses if the workmen do not follow working drawings.

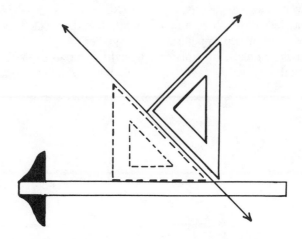

Bibliography

Armstrong, Leslie *The Little House*. New York: Macmillan Publishing Co., Inc., 1979.

Baker, John M. *How to Build a House without an Architect*. New York: J. B. Lippincott Company, 1977.

D'Amelio, Joseph *Perspective Drawing Handbook*. New York: Tudor Publishing Co. 1964.

Dazell, J. Ralph *Plan Reading for Home Builders*. New York: McGraw Hill Book Co., 1972.

DiDonno, Lupe and Sperling, Phyllis *How to Design and Build Your Own House*. New York: Alfred A. Knopf, 1978.

Doblin, Hay *Perspective—A new System for Designers*. New York: Whitney Publications, Inc., 1956

Glegg, Gordon L. *Making and Interpreting Mechanical Drawings*. Cambridge: Cambridge University Press, 1971.

Goodban, Wm. and Haysett, Jack J. *Architectural Drawing and Planning*. New York: McGraw Hill Book Co., 1971.

Hornung, Wm. J. *Architectural Drafting*. Englewood Cliffs, New Jersey: Prentice-Hall, 1971.

Myller, Rolf *From Idea into House*. New York: Atheneum Publishing Co., 1974.

Roberts, Rex *Your Engineered Home*. New York: M. Evans & Co., Inc., 1964.

Tatum, Rita *The Alternative Home*. Los Angeles: Reed Books, 1978.

Wade, Alex and Ewenstein *30 Energy Efficient Houses You Can Build*. Emmanus Pennsylvania: Rodale Press, 1977.

Waschek, Carmen *Your Guide to Good Shelter*. Reston, Virginia: Reston Publishing Co., Inc., 1978.

Wilson, Roy L. *Build Your Own Energy Saver Home or Upgrade Your Existing Home*. Austin, Texas: Energy Saver Home Co., 1978.

Index

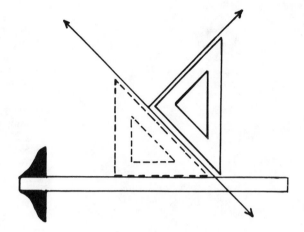

Index

324

Other Bestsellers From TAB

☐ **THE BUILDING PLAN BOOK: Complete Plans for 21 Affordable Homes—Bryant**

Here, in one impressive, well-illustrated volume, are complete building plans for a total of 21 custom-designed homes offering a full range of styles and features—efficiency dwellings, ranches, capes, two-story homes, split-levels, even duplexes. It's a collection of practical, good looking home designs that not only offer comfort, convenience, and charm but that can be built at a reasonable cost. 352 pp., 316 illus., 8 1/2″ × 11″.

Paper $14.95   **Hard $24.95**
Book No. 2714

☐ **ILLUSTRATED DICTIONARY OF BUILDING MATERIALS AND TECHNIQUES**

Here's a one-stop reference for do-it-yourselfers and professionals that gives you clear, straightforward definitions for all of the tools, terms, materials, and techniques used by builders, contractors, architects, and other building professionals. It includes almost 4,000 terms and abbreviations from the simple to the complex, from slang to the latest technical information. 272 pp., 172 illus., 7″ × 10″.

Paper $14.95   **Hard $22.95**
Book No. 2681

☐ **TILE FLOORS—INSTALLING, MAINTAINING AND REPAIRING—Ramsey**

Now you can easily install resilient or traditional hard tiles on both walls and floors. Find out how to buy quality resilient floor products at reasonable cost . . . and discover the types and sizes of hard tiles available. Get step-by-step instructions for laying out the floor, selecting needed tools and adhesives, cutting tile, applying adhesives, and more. 192 pp., 200 illus., 4 pages in full color. 7″ × 10″.

Paper $12.95   **Hard $22.95**
Book No. 1998

☐ **HARDWOOD FLOORS—INSTALLING, MAINTAINING AND REPAIRING—Ramsey**

Do-it-yourself expert Dan Ramsey gives you all the guidance you need to install, restore, maintain, or repair all types of hardwood flooring at costs far below those charged by professional builders and maintenance services. From details on how to select the type of wood floors best suited to your home, to time- and money-saving ways to keep your floors in tip-top condition . . . nothing has been left out. 160 pp., 230 illus., 4 pages in full color. 7″ × 10″.

Paper $10.95   **Hard $18.95**
Book No. 1928

☐ **THE COMPLETE BOOK OF BATHROOMS—Ramsey and Self**

Simple redecorating tricks . . . remodeling advice . . . plumbing techniques . . . it's all here. Find literally hundreds of photographs, drawings, and floorplans to help you decide exactly what kind of remodeling project you'd like to undertake; plus, step-by-step directions for accomplishing your remodeling goals. It's all designed to save you time and money on your bathroom renovations! 368 pp., 474 illus., 7″ × 10″.

Paper $15.95   **Hard $24.95**
Book No. 2708

☐ **101 PROJECTS, PLANS AND IDEAS FOR THE HIGH-TECH HOUSEHOLD**

If you're looking for decorative effects, you'll be impressed with the number of projects that have been included. And electronics hobbyists will be amazed at the array of projects—all of them with clear building instructions, schematics, and construction drawings. You'll also find exciting ways to use your microcomputer as a key decorative element in your high-tech atmosphere. 352 pp., 176 illus., 7″ × 10″.

Paper $16.95   **Hard $24.95**
Book No. 2642

☐ **CABINETS AND VANITIES—A BUILDER'S HANDBOOK—Godley**

Here in easy-to-follow, step-by-step detail is everything you need to know to design, build, and install your own customized kitchen cabinets and bathroom vanities and cabinets for a fraction of the price charged by professional cabinetmakers or kitchen remodelers . . . and for less than a third of what you'd spend for the most cheaply made ready-made cabinets and vanities! 142 pp., 126 illus., 7″ × 10″.

Paper $12.95   **Hard $19.95**
Book No. 1982

☐ **DO YOUR OWN DRYWALL—AN ILLUSTRATED GUIDE**

Proper installation of interior plaster board or drywall is a must-have skill for successful home building or remodeling. Now, there's a new time- and money-saving alternative: this excellent step-by-step guide to achieving professional-quality drywalling results, the first time and every time! Even joint finishing, the drywalling step most dreaded by do-it-yourselfers, is a snap when you know what you're doing. 160 pp., 161 illus.

Paper $10.95   **Hard $17.95**
Book No. 1838

Other Bestsellers From TAB

☐ **HOW TO BE YOUR OWN ARCHITECT—2nd Edition—Goddard and Wolverton**

The completely revised version of a long-time bestseller gives you all the expert assistance needed to design your own dream house like a professional. You'll save the money that most custom-home builders put out in architect's fees—an estimated 12% to 15% of the total construction costs—to pay for more of those "extras" you'd like. 288 pp., 369 illus., 7" × 10".

Paper $14.95   **Hard $22.95**
Book No. 1790

☐ **SUPERINSULATED, TRUSS-FRAME HOUSE CONSTRUCTION**

A revolutionary home building technique that's faster and easier to construct . . . and far less expensive than traditional methods! If you're planning to build or buy a new home . . . or wish you could . . . this book will show you how superinsulated, truss-frame construction can mean having the high-quality, energy-efficient home you want at a fraction of the price you'd expect! 240 pp., 244 illus., 7" × 10".

Paper $14.95   **Hard $21.95**
Book No. 1674

☐ **CONSTRUCTING AND MAINTAINING YOUR WELL AND SEPTIC SYSTEM—Max & Charlotte Alth**

A practical, money-saving guide for do-it-yourself homebuilders, homesteaders, and non-urban homeowners! Here, in step-by-step format, is all the information you need to plan, construct, and maintain water and septic units that will stand up to your needs for many years to come. Even if you're not interested in doing all or part of the work yourself, this guide will prove invaluable! 240 pp., 206 illus., 7" × 10".

Paper $12.95   **Hard $19.95**
Book No. 1654

☐ **WHAT'S IT WORTH? A Home Inspection and Appraisal Manual—Scaduto**

Here's a guide that can save home buyers and home owners thousands of dollars in unexpected maintenance and repair costs! You'll find out what types of structural problems occur in older and in new homes, even condominiums . . . cover everything from foundations and crawl spaces to attics and roofs . . . learn simple "tricks of the trade" for spotting problems and discover how professional appraisal techniques can be applied to any home! 256 pp., 281 illus., 7" × 10".

Paper $12.95   **Hard $21.95**
Book No. 1761

☐ **THE COMPLETE PASSIVE SOLAR HOME BOOK —Schepp and Hastie**

You'll get down-to-earth pointers on basic energy conservation . . . a clear picture of the passive solar home design options—underground homes, superinsulated homes, double envelope houses, and manufactured housing. Plus, you'll get expert how-to's for choosing a passive solar design . . . how to deal with architects, designers, and contractors . . . and more. 320 pp., 252 illus., 7" × 10".

Paper $16.95   **Hard $24.95**
Book No. 1657

☐ **STEEL HOMES—Giles**

Here's the handbook that provides you with step-by-step instructions for everything from laying foundations to installing gutters, nearly everything you need to know is included. You'll learn how to assemble the frames, install the steel sidewall panels, do the roof sheeting, install insulation, attach a sun deck, and that's just the beginning. You'll find loads of cost-cutting ideas on paneling, layouts, decorating and more! 320 pp., 350 illus.

Paper $16.95   **Hard $21.95**
Book No. 1641

*Prices subject to change without notice.

Look for these and other TAB books at your local bookstore.

TAB BOOKS Inc.
P.O. Box 40
Blue Ridge Summit, PA 17214

Send for FREE TAB catalog describing over 1200 current titles in print.

OR ORDER TOLL-FREE TODAY: **800-233-1128**